RACE & RESTORATION

MAKING THE MODERN SOUTH
David Goldfield, Series Editor

RACE & RESTORATION

Churches of Christ and
the Black Freedom Struggle

BARCLAY KEY

Louisiana State University Press
Baton Rouge

Published by Louisiana State University Press
Copyright © 2020 by Louisiana State University Press
All rights reserved
First printing

DESIGNER: Michelle A. Neustrom
TYPEFACES: Whitman, text; Gotham, display

Cataloging-in-Publication Data are available from the Library of Congress.

ISBN 978-0-8071-7274-2 (cloth: alk. paper) — ISBN 978-0-8071-7308-4 (pdf)
— ISBN 978-0-8071-7309-1 (epub)

The paper in this book meets the guidelines for permanence and durability
of the Committee on Production Guidelines for Book Longevity of the
Council on Library Resources. ∞

For my parents,
DeWayne and Donna Key

Contents

Acknowledgments

Family members are conventionally mentioned last, but I feel compelled to start with the people who have endured with me from the beginning of this project. Sonya and I have pursued many adventures together and, while she has never been inclined to read every word I write, her experiences and perspectives have always been helpful. She also loves books as much as I do and reads them more quickly. People inevitably tell their stories, I'm told, and to some degree this book contains a small part of our story. We make a good team, and I am grateful for the many sacrifices that she has made to make this book possible.

The parenting adventure began for us in 2004 and shows no signs of slowing. Our son Langston arrived during the initial stages of research, and our daughter Zora made our family complete a few years later. Who knew that trips to playgrounds and various elementary and middle-school activities were not conducive to reading and writing?! I hope that we have done them justice and that the stories herein seem foreign to them.

My parents, DeWayne and Donna, asked the obligatory question when I was an undergraduate history student: what will you do with a history degree? Sometimes I'm still uncertain of the answer. Nevertheless, they've remained a reliable source of good humor, home cooking, storytelling, board-game competition, financial assistance, and occasional childcare. I definitely won the parent lottery. I'm also proud to have Logan, Leslie, Mabrey, and Annie, and countless friends and family members in Moulton, Alabama, who have influenced me. John Hardin, now at the Alabama Department of Archives and History, deserves some of the blame for my interests in history and theology and my career choices.

Several professors at the University of North Alabama sparked my desire to study history, none more than Larry Nelson. I learned a lot about the Bible and myself at David Lipscomb University. Mentors at the University of Florida were especially patient. With good cheer and reassurance, Brian Ward set me on a path to completing the doctoral program. Jack Davis made me a better writer. Jon Sensbach helped me think more creatively, and Sheryl Kroen offered timely encouragement. Sonya and I were both inspired by Gwendolyn Zoharah Simmons. Bertram Wyatt-Brown ensured that an initial research trip was funded. Numerous classmates were amiable and tolerant of my eccentricities, especially Mike Bowen, Craig Dosher, and Ben Houston. Eric Brown and Kevin Bird kept me grounded. The Florida Gators men's basketball teams were phenomenal.

Colleagues at Iowa State University and Western Illinois University provided important opportunities and meaningful support, especially Larry Balsamo, Ginny Boynton, Peter Cole, Febe Pamonag, and Tim Roberts. Contrary to what one might guess, distractions became more plentiful in little Macomb, Illinois, but they were well worth the time and trouble. Teaching American History grants provided a chance to study southern history with junior and senior high school teachers in west central Illinois, and two tours took us through Alabama, Georgia, Louisiana, Mississippi, and Tennessee. A Fulbright award landed the family and me in Kielce, Poland, for a semester, where we encountered a statue of Miles Davis and fell in love with Kraków. A second Fulbright award in 2017 took us to beautiful Xalapa, Mexico, and a much richer appreciation for our neighbors to the south.

John Kirk urged me to join the history faculty at the University of Arkansas at Little Rock, where I've discovered a camaraderie like no other. If we must have a chair, Jess Porter is a great one. Kristin Mann is the best teacher and always eager to help. Jim Ross and I thought that we might help the Little Rock School District, but we were soon disabused of that notion by the principalities and powers. We fought the law, and the law won.

The archivists and librarians at several institutions deserve more credit than these lines would suggest, but I must mention a few by name. Not long after I first embarked on this endeavor, I connected with Don Haymes. He not only helped me write and think more carefully, but he also provided a seemingly endless supply of additional essays that warranted my attention. Don helped arrange access to some crucial sources, provided an oral history for the ages one evening in Temple Terrace, and made the trek to New Orleans for a panel.

Carisse Berryhill at Abilene Christian University could not have been more helpful or hospitable. Although we correspond infrequently, I did not hesitate to contact her when it was time to tie up loose ends. Of course she was eager to help. Her colleague Mac Ice also accommodated some last-minute requests.

Several historians have asked helpful questions and offered insights on my research, including Dan Williams, Calvin White, and Ed Robinson, whose numerous books have made significant actors in Churches of Christ more accessible. Readers for LSU Press provided many valuable suggestions, and Rand Dotson has been exceedingly patient. I accept responsibility for the shortcomings that remain, of course, while hoping that readers will be as gracious as all of these thoughtful colleagues.

Abbreviations Used in Text

Abilene Christian College	**ACC**
Abilene Christian University	**ACU**
American Standard Version	**ASV**
David Lipscomb College	**DLC**
King James Version	**KJV**
National Association for the Advancement of Colored People	**NAACP**
National Council of Churches	**NCC**
Nashville Christian Institute	**NCI**
New King James Version	**NKJV**
Southwestern Christian College	**SWCC**

RACE & RESTORATION

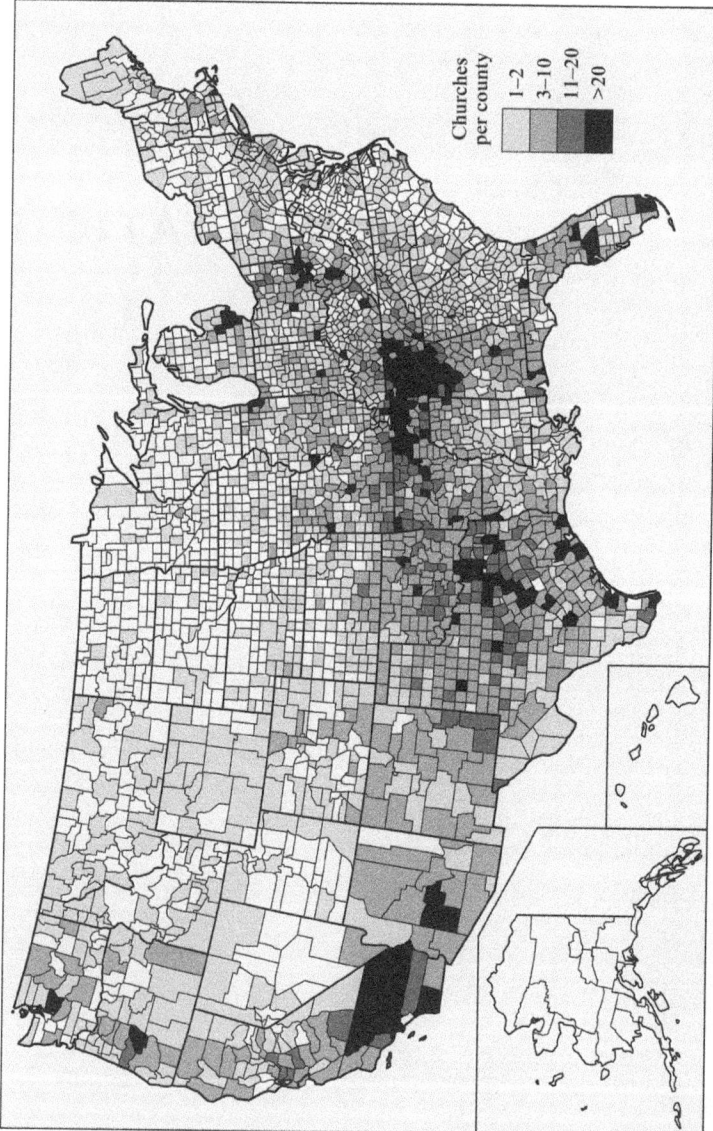

Geographic density of Churches of Christ by county or parish in the United States in 1960.
Map by Mary Lee Eggart.

Churches
per county

1–2
3–10
11–20
>20

INTRODUCTION

Churches of Christ are peculiar. Visitors are often struck by the simplicity of their worship and facilities. There is no common liturgy, and one would be hard-pressed to find anything more decorative than flora or landscape art inside their houses of worship. Men, usually wearing their "Sunday best," lead congregations in a cappella singing and voice unscripted prayers. The preacher's sermon will not follow any set calendar but will instead reflect his (and never her) or the church's current concerns or choice for study. The Eucharist, or "Lord's Supper," is observed every Sunday. Icons, statues, and kneelers are absent. Apses consist of nothing more than a stage, a pulpit, an altar, and perhaps a bench or two. Baptisteries allowing for full immersion can usually be found behind the stage, and modern churches may have a projection screen. Outside of robust singing or an occasional "Amen!" during a sermon or after a prayer, emotions are held in check.

Another notable distinction is more subtle. Churches of Christ have no governing hierarchy beyond a local church. An individual church is governed by a select group of elders, an indeterminate number of local men chosen by the local church to govern it. Individual churches also choose their own ministers. No ordination, training, or particular level of education is required, although a Bible degree from a Church of Christ college serves as a preferred qualification. While popular periodicals, colleges, or regular lectureships have helped establish and maintain normative practices within Churches of Christ, the denomination does not even have a regular convention to which local churches might send delegates or vote on significant issues.

While certainly not unique within Christianity, these idiosyncrasies helped cultivate and perpetuate an exclusivist disposition among church members that dates back to restorationist movements of the nineteenth century. Churches of Christ evolved out of restorationist groups that were variously known as Disciples of Christ, Christian Churches, and Churches of Christ, and they attracted adherents with two competing aims. One sought to establish unity among Christians, a sharp rebuke to the proliferation of denominations unfolding across the North American landscape. The second aim shared the critique of denominationalism while advocating a return to, or "restoration" of, Christianity as it was practiced in the first century.

Divisions eventually developed in this movement, based largely on sociological and regional differences between northern and southern followers. With no hierarchy or convention, a formal division never occurred, but churches identifying themselves as Churches of Christ came to dominate this restoration movement in the South. Even today, Churches of Christ are concentrated in eastern Texas and Oklahoma, Arkansas, Tennessee, and northern Alabama. Over time, they largely abandoned the quest for unity that characterized some of their predecessors and came to perceive themselves as "the New Testament Church." Historian Richard Hughes frankly observed how "these people have argued that they have restored the primitive church of the apostolic age and are therefore nothing more or less than the true, original church described in the New Testament." Other churches were pale imitations of "the Lord's church" at best and certainly remained outside of God's favor. Churches of Christ commonly used the term "denominations" to refer to other branches in Christendom but never in reference to themselves. As their Baptist or Methodist detractors often observed, Churches of Christ "believe they're the only ones going to heaven."[1]

Apart from their simplicity and sectarianism, the characteristic that distinguished Churches of Christ in the twentieth century more than any other was the significant presence of black members within a predominantly white denomination in the Jim Crow South.[2] At first glance, a church composed of blacks and whites in the segregated South seems highly unlikely, if not impossible. No less an observer than Martin Luther King Jr. helped popularize the cliché that "eleven o'clock on Sunday morning is one of the most segregated hours."[3] But customs of racial segregation were more complicated for people who understood themselves as "the true church," an identity that made them "susceptible to the illusion that they have escaped the influence of history and culture altogether."[4]

Of course, Churches of Christ escaped neither history nor culture. They practiced racial segregation but often with fascinating caveats that challenged conventional notions of a strictly segregated South. Blacks periodically attended white churches for a time, while cooperating in efforts to build separate churches. Revivals, or "gospel meetings" as they were more commonly called in Churches of Christ, were coordinated, led, and attended by both blacks and whites whose primary goal of winning souls sometimes supplanted racial etiquette. This black presence within Churches of Christ belies the monolithic terms (such as "the black church") that we often use to assess race and religion. Indeed, the racial dynamics of Churches of Christ show the need for historians to more carefully evaluate the construction of two competing identities, one racial and one religious, as they evolved during the twentieth century.[5]

This book follows several studies that examined more populous denominations, such as the Baptists, Methodists, and Presbyterians. These studies primarily focused on the perspectives of whites who sought to negotiate the ambiguities between their faiths and their acceptance of racial discrimination. For example, in books about the Southern Baptist Convention and Presbyterian Church, U.S., historians Mark Newman and Joel Alvis Jr. organized whites into categories that reflected levels of commitment to the preservation of Jim Crow practices. Newman labeled his groups as militant segregationists, moderate segregationists, and progressives, while Alvis opted for the formulaic conservative and liberal distinction. Alvis examined some relationships between black and white Presbyterians, especially as they related to the Negro Work Program, an agency by which the denomination made concerted, if paternalistic, efforts to foster education and evangelism for blacks, who composed only a slight percentage of that church's membership. Historian Peter Murray explored similar dynamics by examining how the Central Jurisdiction of the Methodist Church, a segregated district that defied geographic bounds, functioned within the hierarchy of the predominantly white Methodist Church. Meanwhile, Newman devoted almost exclusive attention to whites, noting that black Baptists formed a separate denomination.[6]

I am indebted to these historians, and readers who want to learn about denominations more populous than Churches of Christ will find ample sources for further study. But with two million members concentrated largely in the South at mid-century, Churches of Christ, with their unique polity and profound self-perceptions, provide crucial nuance that is not readily apparent in other denominational studies. Other denominations experienced formal divisions during the sectional crises over slavery in the mid-nineteenth century and eventually spawned separate black denominations during and after Reconstruction. Even blacks who remained in the predominantly white Methodist Church were organized separately. Believing themselves to be the one, true church circumscribed the ways in which Churches of Christ might navigate the vagaries of racial etiquette. Although the denomination had its influential leaders, the absence of a formal church hierarchy, with its policies and edicts, provides historians with fascinating sources for understanding how black and white laity understood and experienced race and faith.[7]

Several themes punctuate my effort to explain the racial dimensions and religious identities of Churches of Christ. First, Churches of Christ show that faith commitments sometimes trumped racial identities. The intense desire to "restore New Testament Christianity" facilitated interracial cooperation and interaction among Churches of Christ. When racial identities were subordinated under the guise of Christian unity, blacks and whites interacted with surprising frequency in the segregated South, based on their perception of Churches of Christ as the "true church" that stood in opposition to "the denominations." While other Protestant churches formed what amounted to racially exclusive denominations or administrative districts, Churches of Christ did not because they understood themselves as the only authentic expression of Christianity. Within this context and with few exceptions, white supremacy remained largely unchallenged. Whites even preached against racial prejudice and offered support to black churches, preachers, and schools, yet whites also maintained segregated colleges in the South until the 1960s and generally ignored the pervasive racial discrimination that characterized life in the United States.

The second theme involves the ways in which the denomination's exclusivist disposition and insularity cultivated hesitancy toward civic activism among both blacks and whites. Church members were generally unwilling to associate with other denominations in a common cause, so by the time that the civil rights movement was assigned religious significance by some leading activists, including many devout Christians, Churches of Christ were predisposed to reject their endeavors. This antipathy seemed natural alongside the church's longstanding aversion to civic engagement, best illustrated by the strong strain of pacifism in the denomination's history that included the Civil War. Even as this pacifism waned in the twentieth century, whites had no trouble invoking the principle when civil rights were at stake, and many blacks ironically did the same. The urgency and earnestness by which Churches of Christ pursued evangelistic endeavors also undermined whatever sympathy may have existed for civil rights. Many blacks and whites simply believed that securing eternal salvation warranted greater attention than correcting contemporary social injustices. From this perspective, denominational preachers, who gave so much time and energy to the civil rights movement and seemed to neglect their pastoral duties, provided firm evidence that they were not "members of *the* church."

In addition to examining the interplay between the church's curious self-perception and its racial dynamics in the twentieth century, this book highlights the Bible as a significant battleground in debates over racial equality, the meanings of Christian fellowship, interracial marriage, and the civil rights movement. The Bible obviously played a pivotal role in shaping the self-perception of Churches of Christ, but this study proves broadly applicable to the faith commitments of many southerners. Church of Christ members prided themselves on their extensive knowledge of the "Word of God," employed the scientific method to interpret the scriptures, and thus expected reasonable people to agree on "the essentials" for Christian faith and practice.[8] Just as Christians prior to the Civil War debated what the Bible said about slavery, the black freedom struggle of the twentieth century provoked comparable discussions.[9] Devotees whose vision of Christian fellowship included all people, irrespective of color, as well as people who believed that racial segregation was divinely ordained, found biblical support for their positions. Disparate opinions about activism and integration were buttressed with scriptural references amid debates over the church's and a Christian's role in fostering racial harmony. Incongruent definitions of "racial prejudice," which was sinful by all accounts, plagued these debates.

The fourth theme, also broadly relevant among Protestant denominations, emphasizes the generational fissures that developed within Churches of Christ as the civil rights movement unfolded in the 1950s and 1960s. For different reasons, black and white youth ran afoul of church leaders. As black college students joined organizations such as the Student Nonviolent Coordinating Committee, black youth from Churches of Christ could not easily understand why they were prohibited from such associations, even as black leaders were increasingly strident in their calls for racial equality within the denomination. Meanwhile, white youth, particularly students at Church of Christ colleges, grew weary of excuses proffered to maintain segregation. Both black and white youth largely accepted the restorationist impulse and rhetoric of Churches of Christ, but their interpretation and application of the scriptures called into question the church's acquiescence to racial segregation. These generational tensions complemented broader, more popular conflicts from the era over the burgeoning youth culture.

Finally, the exclusivist disposition among both blacks and whites meant that

Churches of Christ were uniquely positioned to facilitate interracial dialogue and seek racial reconciliation, once these pursuits became publicly acceptable. As de jure segregation began a slow, uneven decline, the dynamics of race relations and segregation evolved. Following the passage of civil rights legislation, blacks had equal access to public facilities, could vote, or might be seated anywhere in a restaurant as far as the law was concerned. In practice, however, implementation of such legal changes involved more than congressional approval and the president's signature. In this context, several Churches of Christ provided public forums in which blacks and whites could air their concerns and grievances and perhaps bridge racial divides. These occasions illustrate grassroots efforts by churches to accept, understand, and, to a lesser extent, implement government decrees, but they also reveal the limits of private efforts to support the dramatic changes wrought by civil rights legislation.

This study ultimately confirms how "racial interchanges" that occurred in Churches of Christ defy the categorizations about race and religion often employed by historians.[10] The discovery of gradations of racial attitudes and multifaceted practices of segregation demanded that I largely avoid dichotomous labels, such as segregationist and integrationist or conservative and liberal. While helpful in some circumstances, these labels can easily distort as much as they illuminate. Readers will discover, in their place, compelling narratives that illustrate the fluidity of race and religion among people of faith.

The following chapters are organized both thematically and chronologically. The first two separately examine black and white members in the first half of the twentieth century, addressing why blacks joined Churches of Christ, the challenges that they faced from their white brothers and sisters, white racial attitudes, and how both groups formulated ideas about race and theology. Chapter 3 focuses exclusively on the desegregation of Church of Christ colleges and the periodic conflicts between white students and administrators over desegregation. Some white students became advocates for desegregation in the 1940s but, even if they accepted the admission of black students, many white students rejected their full inclusion into the college's dormitories or social clubs. The fourth chapter more broadly shows how Churches of Christ reacted to the civil rights movement of the 1960s, especially in the South where so many notorious confrontations occurred. Although these events transpired outside of the immediate concerns of the church, they often awakened black members and emboldened them to speak out against the injustices and slights they experienced in Churches of Christ. Chapter 5 summarizes the often painful reckoning process that occurred between blacks and whites in Churches of Christ in the 1960s, when racial justice was no longer dismissed so easily, while the final chapter explores the ways in which Churches of Christ sought, but often failed to achieve, racial reconciliation.

1

DEFINITIONS OF
RACIAL PREJUDICE

Recent studies of the black freedom struggle in the first half of the twentieth century are haunted by champions of white supremacy who committed heinous crimes. People and events serve as signposts in history classes on their semester-long march through the past: lynching and other racial violence, *The Birth of a Nation*, the reconstitution of the Ku Klux Klan, or even the racial disparities of the Great Depression, New Deal, and World War II. The racial attitudes of whites appear self-evident in these stories, but Churches of Christ complicate any monolithic depictions. One could hardly overstate the physical, emotional, and psychological terror that blacks endured, but at the same time, Churches of Christ show how whites were not summarily bent on violence and terror. Religion in this case ameliorated the most violent aspects of white supremacy while catering to its social and psychological demands.

A cacophony of voices within white Churches of Christ struggled to find an acceptable range of practices for engaging blacks under the strictures of Jim Crow. Competing racial attitudes emerged, even as notorious events unfolded across the country and across the South in particular. These attitudes appeared in a variety of contexts. Some whites might not object to having black students attend the denomination's colleges but would be appalled at the prospect of interracial romance. Others might favor the abolition of legal segregation, while opposing organized resistance to Jim Crow laws. At the level of individuals, common categorizations often failed to capture the warring ideas about race and religion that jostled for ascendancy in the minds of many white church members.

To be clear, some whites simply wanted nothing to do with blacks. However, most whites favored the maintenance of cordial relationships, even as they subscribed to common notions of white supremacy and paternalism. Spiritual equality, in the opinions of most whites, did not necessitate social, political, and economic equality, but this assertion did not preempt discussions of race relations within churches. Churches of Christ sometimes contemplated the meanings of racial harmony in Bible classes. Worship assemblies that included blacks and whites were typically segregated with designated seating, even though there were occasional exceptions to this practice. Black and white churches cooperated in evangelism, while collaborating in the creation of separate churches within the same communities. Whites generally seemed unaware, or perhaps willfully ignorant, of the racial disparities that existed in the form of educational, political, and economic inequalities. Those whites who were aware might support minimal endeavors to help local families, particularly "members of the church," but they were unprepared and unwilling to become vocal over social or political affairs because such matters fell outside the bounds of spiritual concerns.

Churches of Christ fully embraced the idea that primitive Christianity was an end unto itself, and the denomination's identity was shaped accordingly. The restorationist impulse was so strong that many members came to believe that New Testament Christianity was not just something to be restored; it had been restored in the form of Churches of Christ, who regularly used a lowercase "c"—churches of Christ—to emphasize that this was not just another denomination. It was the church, the one mentioned in the Bible, the one commonly known in the United States in the twentieth century as the Church of Christ. For obvious reasons, such a disposition did not endear Churches of Christ to other denominations, but the alienation that developed only served to affirm their self-perception and partly explained the exceptional attendance rates for Churches of Christ that persisted to the twenty-first century.[1] Since denominational identity was so important, whites were more likely to welcome like-minded blacks into the fold. Whites who might otherwise show condescension toward blacks recognized all members as spiritual brothers and sisters, even as whites abided by and often reinforced Jim Crow laws and customs. If some whites empathized with the black freedom struggle, advocacy of racial equality in the present was never a priority. As Isabel Wilkerson recently observed about whites of this era who were appalled at the mistreatment of blacks, "What few people seem to realize or perhaps dared admit was that the thick walls of the caste system kept everyone in prison. The rules that defined a group's supremacy were so tightly wound as to put pressure on everyone trying to stay within the narrow confines of acceptability."[2]

David Lipscomb, a white stalwart among Churches of Christ at the dawn of the twentieth century, sometimes challenged these confines by advocating unity among blacks and whites. His position as editor of the *Gospel Advocate*, the most influential periodical among Churches of Christ, and his role in founding the Nashville Bible School (now David Lipscomb University) elevated his influence among Churches of Christ. In several instances, Lipscomb opposed the creation of racially segregated churches, even as his advice went largely unheeded. When he learned that a white Texas church had refused to admit a black member in 1878, he unequivocally denounced the decision in the pages of the *Gospel Advocate*. "We believe it is sinful to have two congregations in the same community for persons of separate and distinct races," he pointedly observed. "For our part," he continued, "we would much prefer membership with an humble and despised band of ignorant negroes, than with a congregation of the [most] aristocratic and refined whites in the land, cherishing such a spirit of defiance of God and his law, and all the principles of his holy religion." Lipscomb did not waiver from this position. In 1901 he wrote that "white men need not fear the curse of God because of the presence of the Negro. We are suffering it [already]. This terrible crime and the constant dread of it is the penalty we are paying for keeping the Negro in our midst ignorant and depraved, and using them for selfish ends." Six years later, when the Bellwood Church of Christ in Nashville bickered over the attendance of a black girl who had been adopted by a white couple from the church, Lipscomb again berated those people who wanted to maintain segregated churches. "To object to any child of God participating in the services on account of his race, social or civil state, his color or race, is to object to Jesus Christ and to cast him from our association. It is a fearful thing to do." Lipscomb's 1878 remarks still seemed applicable in 1962, when he was quoted by no less a figure than Rev. Will Campbell, another white southerner who wrestled with the tensions between faith and praxis in race relations.[3]

Lipscomb's words were likely read and debated, much like the Sunday school literature that the Gospel Advocate Company produced for Churches of Christ. Sunday school lessons suggest fascinating possibilities for the ways in which white Churches of Christ discussed race relations. Classes were typically divided between children and adults, and the latter often used curriculum such as *Elam's Notes on Bible School Lessons* to guide them through a careful study of the scriptures. These lessons were helpful in several respects. No rigorous preparation was required of the teacher since a general outline was already prescribed, complete with brief commentaries about relevant biblical passages. Churches also trusted the Gospel Advocate Publishing Company to prepare lessons that were "biblically sound" and affordable. To that end, the company developed lesson booklets that were designed to have wide appeal, and they provide valuable insights into what many churches were reading and discussing with regard to race and faith, topics that were undoubtedly approached in ways amenable to the company's customers.[4]

Elam's Notes contained a lesson for every Sunday in the calendar year, and church members could prepare for Sunday school in advance by studiously following the daily Bible readings that accompanied every lesson. The most diligent students might set aside time each day to read their Bibles, while many must have done their best to catch up on Saturday night and Sunday morning, if they followed the readings at all. Such was the case in the week preceding Sunday, November 17, 1929, when the scheduled readings included three sections from the Acts of the Apostles, two Pauline passages, and brief narratives from the Gospel of John and Book of Ruth. "Living with People of Other Races" was the title of that Sunday's lesson.[5]

Many Churches of Christ assembled that morning and undoubtedly invoked divine blessing upon the nation's economic woes. The infamous stock market crash had occurred less than three weeks prior, and the Great Depression would soon define the subsequent decade. Church members may have also turned their thoughts to the recent popularity of the Ku Klux Klan, as they read the scriptures for that day's lesson, Galatians 3:28–29 and excerpts from Acts 10, that served as the focal point of the lesson. "Of a truth I perceive that God is no respecter of persons: but in every nation he that feareth him, and worketh righteousness, is acceptable to him," Acts 10:34 explained (ASV). The lesson's expository notes included several statements, supplemented by other scriptures, that taught "how to live without friction or trouble among people who are of different nationalities." The lesson couched its antidiscrimination sentiments in spiritual language, noting that the apostle Peter struggled "to understand that he should go to another race and preach the gospel; it was difficult for him to lay aside racial prejudices." Notwithstanding the apostle's shortcomings, the lesson reiterated that "God is 'no respecter or persons,' [so] God's people should not be. As the gospel is for all . . . then we should carry the gospel to all." This evangelistic emphasis extended to an understanding that "there can be no distinction between members of different races or nationalities in the church . . . we should not let any nationality, race, or color separate us as the children of God."[6]

These statements appeared unequivocal, but they were qualified in ways that revealed the tensions between denominational identity and an acceptance of white supremacy and the practices that sustained it. Although the lesson highlighted some of the Bible's most egalitarian passages, the authors concluded that the lesson "does not mean that we are to associate with those of another race in such a way as to break down customs and make common with them socially. We can treat all as the children of God; we can be kind and courteous and helpful to all with whom we have to do. This we must do if we are faithful to the Lord." A list of practical suggestions that followed the lesson again insisted that the church should have "no racial or national distinctions. . . . All are admitted into the church on the same conditions and receive the same blessings." The lesson acknowledged with dismay how "Some have even taught that the negro is a beast—that the negro has no soul," before proclaiming "Christianity will destroy this racial prejudice and will make the servant of God a minister of righteousness to all." This mention of "the negro" is the only such reference in the entire lesson, and the authors apparently perceived no glaring contradiction between spiritual equality and the political and economic subjugation of blacks in the South. Sunday school classes closed that day with a list of discussion questions. "To what extent may we associate with other races?" one asked. "Does the negro have a right to the gospel?" asked another. While the first likely precipitated some interesting debate, the second was rhetorical. Most classes closed their study with prayers seeking divine guidance in countering racial prejudice within themselves and among their peers, though how such prejudice was defined must have differed markedly among blacks and whites.[7]

Lessons about race relations were irregular in Sunday school classes, but the lesson from 1929 was hardly unique. The same series included a similar lesson with the same title but a different author in 1932. The topics for daily scripture readings were suggested by headlines: "The Unity of the Nations" and "All Belong to God." The 1932 lesson also contended that the "ignoring of racial distinctions to enjoy common blessings in Christ . . . was plainly stated by the Lord . . . [and] was actually realized in the apostolic church." The firm reference to "the apostolic church" left no doubt about what Churches of Christ should believe and practice with regard to racial inclusion. Another section further described how Jesus associated with a Samaritan, a person of "mixed race with a mixed religion." Modern race relations were never explicitly addressed, but "mixed race" carried strong connotations that must have brought to mind local people whose lineage included blacks and whites. Even so, the lesson also qualified interracial contact by flatly asserting, "God expected the races to remain within their bounds—preserve their own existence."[8]

While Sunday school teachers benefited from the guided literature, periodicals such as the *Gospel Advocate* supplemented biblical studies and often provided a forum for questions from subscribers and answers from the *Gospel Advocate*'s esteemed editors or contributors. The *Gospel Advocate* generally ignored race relations, although it provided news regarding black churches and preachers in a regular column, "Among the Colored Brethren," which existed until 1964, when it was already anachronistic. News about the number of conversions at gospel meetings, an evangelist's travels, or the creation of new churches dominated the column's content. In this manner, the *Gospel Advocate* fashioned itself as friendly to blacks, interested in their salvation and the success of their churches. But there were a few notable exceptions to the general silence about race relations. These exceptions were significant because the *Gospel Advocate* served a normative function within Churches of Christ, especially with its publication of questions and answers. "Difficult queries arise as churches and individuals search for a 'thus saith the Lord' and do not find it, or find it ambiguous, or find it distasteful," historian Don Haymes once observed about the *Gospel Advocate*'s "Query Department." While the journal certainly had no binding authority, its editorial positions wielded tremendous influence.[9]

This general silence was breached in 1927 when a reader asked if one could be a member of the Ku Klux Klan and a follower of Christ. "I have my doubts that it is possible," the reader intoned, but he wanted to hear the *Gospel Advocate*'s position. The inquiry was timely. The Ku Klux Klan enjoyed tremendous popularity across the country during the 1920s, and historian Nancy MacLean later found that Churches of Christ were among the Protestant groups particularly attracted to the Ku Klux Klan. H. Leo Boles responded to the query with an answer that was circumspect in its denunciation of the Ku Klux Klan but clear in stating that a Christian should not associate with the hooded order. His reasons, however, were partly due to the fact that "no one can claim Scriptural authority for being a member of it" and that the Ku Klux Klan had been outlawed in parts of the country. These legalistic answers ignored any moral assessment of membership in the Ku Klux Klan, although Boles described it as "a menace to our civilization" and suggested that "what good it may have can be enjoyed by the child of God as a Christian in the church of Christ." He admitted knowing "gospel preachers who were led into the Klan, but they have seen the error of their way and turned from it." Boles urged his readers to do the same.[10]

During and after World War II, the tenor of such lessons changed slightly. In 1944, "The Christian and the Race Problem" expounded on familiar Bible stories to stress that in "preaching the gospel and extending the kingdom of God, there should be no race problem—the gospel is for all men." But subsequent lessons included language that foreshadowed the rhetoric of white resistance to the civil rights movement. While acknowledging that civil governments "do not always function as God intended," the lessons employed strong language that urged readers to obey and respect their government, a message that resonated amid wartime concerns. Disobedience to "the laws of the land" equated to disobedience to "the law of God, unless the laws of the land are contrary to the laws of God." This assertion contained the essence of future theological debates regarding the leadership of clergy in the civil rights movement. The author concluded that a "Christian should be the most law-abiding citizen of his community. He must not become a law unto himself and disobey a law because he thinks it interferes with some of his natural rights." This lesson illuminates the setting of the postwar civil rights movement, as Christians from a variety of denominations wrestled with the competing demands of scripture and the state. Blacks and whites lent religious significance to the fight against fascism and communism during and after World War II. As these international disputes strengthened the resolve of blacks to fight for equality in the United States, whites concurrently developed a renewed sense of patriotism and national loyalty that affirmed American exceptionalism.[11]

This renewed emphasis on obedience to the state found expression in another lesson that examined "A Christian and His Government." Echoing earlier sentiments, the author stated, "Sometimes a member of the church will disobey a law because he thinks it is useless, or because he thinks it interferes with some of his fancied natural rights. He becomes therefore a law unto himself; that attitude toward his government is the essence of anarchy. . . . Sometimes certain laws do seem to be useless, but so long as such laws are in existence they should be obeyed." Although these lessons acknowledged that Christianity could flourish under a variety of governments, these affirmations of civil authorities fit their context. Loyalty was important, and the language here established a precedent for future skepticism and critique of the civil rights movement from both blacks and whites. When some people expressed a preference for "law and order" during the civil rights movement, it was not always a convenient excuse to maintain segregation. Yet from this perspective, black protestors were easily characterized and discounted as "lawless." The point here is not to suggest that "law and order" rhetoric was free of segregationist motives, but the rhetoric had a history of its own, a lineage that predated the most momentous events of the postwar civil rights movement.[12]

This movement took shape as President Harry Truman grappled with his conscience and strategy for the 1948 election. In 1947 the president's Civil Rights Commission published *To Secure These Rights*, thereby documenting the myriad ways that blacks faced discrimination, and Truman subsequently issued an executive order to desegregate the military in 1948. Despite formidable challenges, Truman prevailed in the election, but the competition for black votes among the major political parties caught the attention of whites. A 1949 Sunday school lesson by Roy Lanier Sr. about "Jesus and Other Races" assessed the current state of affairs:

> And we have a race problem today which is gradually coming to a head. Our national leaders are using it to get votes. Each party wants the negro vote, and to get it they are offering advantages to the negro which violate customs and distinctions of long standing. All races are entitled to every blessing to be had in Christ. (Gal 3:28, 29.) Furthermore all races are entitled to an education, to take a part in their government as their ability will permit, and they are entitled to an opportunity to improved living conditions. But this is far from saying that the races should intermarry, or even that their children should be thrown together in the schoolroom and on the playground. There are differences in ideas and moral standards which cannot be disregarded without injury to those who are holding the standards as high as possible. (1 Cor. 15:33)

This biblical citation includes the phrase, "Evil companionships corrupt good morals" (ASV). Lanier tried to balance a professed belief in the universality of the gospel with his white supremacist assumptions about the immorality of blacks and the necessity of racial segregation. Until this lesson, both blacks and whites could have largely agreed on the expository content from the Gospel Advocate Company, but Lanier clearly crossed a line.[13]

Black Churches of Christ often used the same Sunday school curriculum, but blacks also utilized the *Christian Echo*, a monthly periodical, to establish networks among themselves and report on their evangelistic endeavors. Race relations among Churches of Christ in the first half of the twentieth century seemed amicable based on reports in the *Christian Echo*, but a sharp critique of Lanier's lesson published there pointed toward a closer scrutiny of whites by blacks. A New Yorker named M. C. Smithers quoted the lesson before noting "that some of our leading brethren are violating the basic principles of Christianity by encouraging bigotry and discrimination. . . . Segregation as we know it in the South and other sections is unscriptural and un-Christ like, and any person who upholds this practice is walking contrary to the teaching of Christ." Smithers cited some of the same biblical passages from past Sunday school lessons, but a reader could not mistake his application of these verses: "some of our white brethren feel that they are superior to their colored brethren."[14]

Two years later, in 1951, Lanier published another such lesson, "The Christian and Other Races," that refocused readers on spiritual applications, urging them to "recognize every human being as our brother or sister, and do our best to carry the gospel of salvation to every nation and every individual in every nation. It is not our duty to live with nor like them," he added, "but it is our duty to preach Christ to them." In light of his previous remarks, one can easily imagine what Lanier meant, but what was most ironic about this lesson was his use of a story from the apostle Paul's epistle to the Galatians. Paul described a hostile encounter between himself and the apostle Peter. According to the narrative, Peter shared meals with Gentile Christians, but when some Jewish Christians came to see him, he "drew back and separated himself" from the Gentiles for fear of upsetting his Jewish brothers. Paul took exception to Peter's actions and "resisted him to the face." The sharing of a meal, an intimate form of fellowship in ancient Palestine and the American South, was the heart of the story. In Peter's unwillingness to openly associate with Gentiles, Lanier observed "race prejudice, race distinction, and race pressure brought by a man who knew better. We need to exercise care today lest we be guilty of the same thing." No comments about loose morals followed, but a discussion question asked, "Does racial equality in Christ demand free and unlimited social intercourse between any two races such as whites and negroes? Can we practice racial equality in Christ as taught by Jesus and his apostles, and still maintain our practice of segregation as it is known in the South? These questions should be discussed calmly and intelligently. They are live issues." Indeed they were. One can only speculate as to how these questions were answered inside Churches of Christ across the South, but the fact that these were questions instead of strict instructions suggested they were open to a variety of answers. Over the next twenty years, such questions would haunt many members of Churches of Christ who sought to strictly adhere to the New Testament.[15]

In addition to the ways in which race was discussed in Sunday school literature, weekly church bulletins provide more localized evidence for discerning racial attitudes among whites. Larger churches typically published newsletters to facilitate communication among members, but even smaller churches often produced weekly or monthly bulletins that served several purposes. They kept members informed of the latest news regarding upcoming events, sick members, or people who requested prayers. Preachers were often responsible for the publication of these bulletins, so they frequently included brief stories or sermonettes that were intended to encourage members throughout their workweek. Likewise, humorous stories might bring a smile or bit of joy to members who were struggling with the grind of daily life. Some churches even used bulletins as evangelistic tools by placing any interested party on their mailing list. While discussions of race were not a primary function of church bulletins, whites sometimes mentioned blacks in ways that betrayed how they imagined them as subordinate and subject to disdain or ridicule.

Bulletins from the Center Street Church of Christ in Fayetteville, Arkansas, offered several examples. Between an announcement about a gospel radio program and a list of "Ten Commandments for a Lively Church" in a 1952 bulletin, the following quip appeared: "An old colored preacher said that his favorite verse was where they loafs and fishes." The statement referred to a story from the Gospels about Jesus feeding thousands with just a few loaves of bread and some fish, but its intended humor relied on the stereotype of blacks as lazy. Such items were not regular features, but they appear to have been fairly common. A few years later, the same church printed a prayer supposedly spoken by an "old Negro preacher of the deep south, who never had to worry about empty pews." The prayer was written in dialect: "Oh, Lawd, give they servant dis mowin' de eye of de eagle and de wisdom of de owl: connect his soul wid de gospel-telfome in de central skies . . . turpentime his 'magination; grease his lips wid possum oil . . . 'noint him all over wid de kerosene oil of salvation and set him on fire all over! amen!!!" In these ways, white Churches of Christ exhibited the same whimsical condescension about blacks that was widely popular, christening their humor with religious jargon to make it appear harmless.[16]

As the civil rights movement pricked many white consciences and gained momentum in the early 1960s, whites struggled to both condemn overt racial prejudice and maintain their established traditions. In the spring of 1961, the Center Street church printed a story about an "old colored man" who entered "a Nashville church and sat unobtrusively in the back row." The reader must assume that this was a white church because at the conclusion of the service, the preacher approached the man and said, "Tom, I suppose you know that you caused all sorts of commotion when you came in here." According to the story, Tom did not realize that he had caused a stir, and the preacher suggested that he "go and talk this over with God and see if he wants you to come back here next Sunday." The two met later in the week, and the preacher asked Tom if he had prayed about the matter. "Yessuh," Tom replied. "I done talked de matter ovah wid de Lord . . . an' he told me, 'Tom, doan yo' worry about dat at all. Ah've been trying to get in dat church myself, evah since . . . it was built.'" Although it relied partly on racial stereotypes, the parable was clearly designed to challenge any strict segregation of churches. Its readers would have readily associated the parable with the recent 1960 sit-ins, so its timing invited a broader application than just the church. While it included a black man who sat in the back and answered "Yessuh," the inclusion of the story communicated this church's openness to desegregation.[17]

Despite the sentiments of that story, Churches of Christ generally sustained segregated churches, just as other denominations did, even as many members considered themselves the only manifestation of authentic Christianity. Some blacks might occasionally worship with whites, but both blacks and whites sought to create and maintain their own churches. In the early 1950s, when white members of the Hatcher Street Church of Christ in Dallas grew wary of the influx of blacks moving into the community, they decided to follow the white flight out of the city and move to a location more suitable for their socioeconomic and demographic preferences. But in the process of relocating, the church hired Alvertice Bowdre Sr., "a colored minister who has had good success among his people." On Sundays, white members gathered for worship and a sermon from their white preacher, before Bowdre led a service for black members. The *Dallas Morning News* spoke favorably of the arrangement that would "continue for perhaps a year or until Brother Browdre can assemble about him a flock to carry on a church of their own. Then the present white congregation will go over to [another community] and build themselves a new church house." It was a vivid example of white flight, but these events also coincided with the growing furor over the Supreme Court's instructions in the case of *Brown v. Board of Education of Topeka, Kansas*. In 1955, one year after issuing its decision, the court instructed public school systems to desegregate "with all deliberate speed." What would normally have been a private affair among church members was made public because an explanation was now needed about why these black and white members might be occasionally sharing a relatively public space.[18]

Efforts to secure separate churches were not confined to the South. In the summer of 1948, seven white members in Racine, Wisconsin, decided to form a new church. Until that time, they had been meeting with the local black

Church of Christ or driving to a white Church of Christ in Milwaukee. The new church grew quickly. A building was purchased in 1952 but, six years later, they wanted to relocate. They explained the circumstances in a letter that sought financial assistance for their move. "The neighborhood is almost completely filled with colored people, or with people who are of some sort of foreign extraction. We have been unable to reach them at all with the gospel. For our own membership, they do not hurt the environment, but many people will not attend services in the neighborhood, thinking we are all colored, Mexican, etc. That is true even here in the north in very many instances." The letter suggested that they tried to become a racially inclusive church, but their desire to grow and assuage discontent over community demographics precipitated the move. At the same time, the church's original seven members had met with a black church for at least a year before creating a separate church. This interaction was common among Churches of Christ, especially with evangelistic endeavors.[19]

Revivals, or gospel meetings as they were usually called, were a popular mode of evangelism that would include both blacks and whites. If a black preacher visited a community at the invitation of a white church in the South, then a rope strung down the middle aisle of the auditorium or tent usually segregated the black side from the white. But even this arrangement was occasionally altered. Photographs from a gospel meeting in Abilene, Texas, in 1950 shows blacks seated at the front of the audience, surrounded by whites (fig. 1). Blacks and whites are clearly seated separately, but no specific sign or rope appeared to demarcate the arrangement. One person who attended such assemblies later recalled an occasion when a close white acquaintance removed a rope and sat in the black section at a gospel meeting in Carlsbad, New Mexico, in the 1950s. This navigation of public space reflected the competing thoughts that blacks and whites had regarding their faith and the broader social expectations of racial segregation.[20]

At the same time, white members were less likely to attend functions sponsored and led exclusively by black churches, yet cooperation between black and white churches was common. Black preachers received invitations to speak to predominantly white audiences and, conversely, white preachers sometimes spoke in the pulpits of black churches. Richard Nathaniel (R. N.) Hogan, a black preacher and longtime editor of the *Christian Echo*, was well acquainted with both black and white audiences. On numerous occasions, he received invitations to speak from white churches like the Center Street church in Fay-

FIGURE 1. A 1950 gospel meeting with Marshall Keeble in Abilene, Texas, drew an audience of black and white believers.

Jack Beard Collection, 1950, Center for Restoration Studies MS #207, Abilene Christian University Special Collections and Archives.

etteville which sought his services for a gospel meeting that was conducted in concert with a youth camp in 1953. A black man named Marshall Keeble was arguably the most popular preacher among blacks or whites in Churches of Christ. Indeed many white churches invited Keeble to preach as part of the process of establishing a new black church in their city. Keeble's general unwillingness to broach the subject of race relations made him safe for white churches who sought his services. Keeble and other black preachers were typically welcome to attend college lectureships, even if they were not invited to speak. A 1945 copy of the student newspaper at David Lipscomb College (DLC) pictured black and white men at a lectureship there.[21]

Anecdotal evidence indicates other ways that the restrictions of segregation were breached. A 1941 issue of the *Bible Banner,* a periodical established by a white Texan named Foy Wallace Jr., captured one of the most intriguing exchanges concerning the interaction of blacks and whites in Churches of Christ. Historian Richard Hughes described Wallace as a "major transitional figure in the history of Churches of Christ" and "perhaps the most pivotal and influential figure in the Churches of Christ throughout the 1930s and 1940s." Thus Wallace's observations in an essay titled "Negro Meetings for White People" reveal much, both about his disposition on race relations and the activities of some people within the church who seemed to ignore racial customs. The essay was a harangue aimed at several individuals, both black and white, as well as some churches. "The manner in which the brethren in some quarters are going in for the negro meetings leads one to wonder whether they are trying to make white folks out of the negroes or negroes out of the white folks," he lamented. Wallace specifically mentioned reports that he had received of "white women, members of the church, becoming so animated over a certain colored preacher as to go up to him after a sermon and shake hands with him *holding his hand in both of theirs*" (emphasis in original). This behavior was "pitiable" according to Wallace, who was astounded over the thought of a white woman who would "forget her dignity" and "lower herself" in this manner. He went on to complain about a black husband and wife who operated a home for orphans and espoused "social equality," and about the whites who were "apparently encouraging them." Wallace told of visiting a predominantly white church where the black janitor, who was also a preacher, would frequently attend services and shake hands with members as they exited the building. "When I insisted that it be discontinued some of the white brethren were offended," Wallace wrote. "Such as this proves that the white brethren are ruining the negroes and defeating the very work that they should be sent to do, that is, preach to the negroes, their own people."[22]

Wallace was also appalled that a young white preacher and journal editor named Ira Rice Jr. had recently boarded for two nights with R. N. Hogan, the prominent black evangelist. Wallace somehow learned that the circumstances had even required them to share a bed, a situation that Wallace described as "an infringement on the Jim Crow law . . . a violation of Christianity itself, and of all common decency." His disgust was directed toward both men, but he was especially disturbed by Hogan, who "has been too much inclined to mix with the white people and to favor, in attitude, a social equality." Much to Wallace's chagrin, Hogan was also known to preach gospel meetings for white churches and not exclusively as an effort to evangelize among blacks.[23]

Wallace's essay yields two important insights. First, some black and white church members clearly violated segregation customs, if not laws, by interacting so freely. One cannot estimate how widespread such practices were. Wallace undoubtedly uncovered exceptional circumstances, but these activities were common or well known to such a degree that a person of his caliber felt inclined to address them in print. Whether it was simply shaking a black preacher's hand, sharing a place to sleep, or participating in a worship assembly, some whites traversed the color line because of a shared faith, particularly a common restorationist vision, that served as the impetus for such interactions. These examples do not mark Churches of Christ as bastions for social progressives, but they do suggest a measure of flexibility when eternal matters were at stake.

Second, Wallace's essay simultaneously revealed both his own prejudices and those of some whites in the denomination. While the *Bible Banner* never rivaled the *Gospel Advocate's* influence, Wallace was a former editor of the *Gospel Advocate,* and his popularity as a writer and combative preacher left an indelible mark on Churches of Christ. People within the church who had misgivings about racial segregation may well have retreated in the face of Wallace's vitriol and, conversely, if one was already overtly racist or inclined to support racial segregation, then Wallace's perspectives vindicated those beliefs. "I am very much in favor of negro meetings for the negroes, but I am just as much opposed to negro meetings for white people, and I am against white brethren taking the meetings away from the negroes and the general mixing that has become entirely too much of a practice in these negro meetings," Wallace concluded. "Such a thing not only lowers the church in the eyes of the world but it is definitely against the interest of the negroes." Whites habitually speculated about what was in the best "interest of the negroes," typically with little, if any, candid input from blacks, and evangelistic motives could easily mingle with dreams of tighter social control of blacks. In 1931, ten years before Wallace's diatribe, David Lipscomb's nephew marveled at the worthwhile investment that whites made in Marshall Keeble, whose success meant "that we now have better farm hands, better porters, better cooks, better housemaids than ever before." The *Gospel Advocate* began that same year with a column that advocated equal pay for black and white evangelists because the author did not believe there was "any real danger of our colored evangelists receiving enough from one year to the next to turn their heads."[24]

Wallace's tirade did not go unnoticed, but Keeble wrote the only response from a black preacher that was published in the *Bible Banner.* In a manner that came to characterize his public deference to whites, Keeble complimented Wallace's essay as "instructive and encouraging" and expressed hope that his conduct would not bring regret to Wallace or any of Keeble's friends. Keeble's note lends itself to a variety of readings. Wallace called it "characteristic of the humility of M. Keeble." Given the fact that Keeble was in his early sixties, almost twenty years older than Wallace, and had been interacting with whites for decades, one may also detect in Keeble's language a parental patience, a wisdom that realized the futility of arguing with a man like Wallace. While this published response from Keeble became part of the lore regarding his ambiguous relationships with whites, Wallace's interpretation of Keeble certainly became the standard. "[This letter] is the reason why he is the greatest colored preacher that has ever lived," Wallace proclaimed. He described Keeble and another black preacher as men "who know their work and do it. They know their place and stay in it, even when some white brethren try to take them out of it."[25]

Keeble's peaceful overture to placate Wallace disclosed that he, too, was concerned first and foremost with evangelism. Though private and less cordial, R. N. Hogan's correspondence with a white patron likely communicated more clearly what black preachers felt about Wallace, who was clearly jealous of some black preachers' popularity. Hogan was not surprised to be the target of Wallace's attack "because he sent an appointment to the churches in the Valley during my [gospel] meeting in Weslaco [Texas] and because the white people wouldn't stop attending my meeting to come and hear him he was provoked to the extent that he decided to give them a raking over through the columns of his paper." Hogan continued his letter by defending himself against Wallace's charges. "He is the first person . . . who has accused me of conducting myself in a way that shows that I am interested in 'mixing with the white people' or 'social equality.' Such has NEVER intered [sic] my mind and is no part of the truth" (emphasis in original). These comments are particularly revealing in light of Hogan's past and future essays on segregation, but like Keeble he seemed resigned to focus his attention on evangelism. Indeed most of Hogan's letter shared church and ministry news, and his final paragraph about Wallace was written in response to a direct inquiry from his white friend. "I trust that God will forgive brother Wallace and the like of him," Hogan concluded, "but I know that before God will forgive him he MUST repent. Your letter was an encouragement to me and you may rest sssured [sic] that I'll press on. A number of the white people who saw that article have informed me that his paper shall enter their home no more" (emphasis in original).[26]

Other instances of interracial exchanges occurred outside the purview of Wallace and others who so vehemently opposed them. Another example involved piano recitals at Harding College in Searcy, Arkansas, unlikely moments of interracial activity that fell outside the bounds of official college business. A Harding music teacher and part-time piano instructor named Ann Sewell accepted two black teenage girls into her private classes in the early 1950s. They studied alongside Sewell's white pupils and participated in recitals on campus. Sewell once recalled a recital when the girls invited family and friends. Upon arrival, the pupil's guests asked where they should be seated, and Sewell told them to "Sit just anywhere you would like to." She later moved practices and recitals to her home, where the girls continued their lessons and recitals. "We all had refreshments together, and enjoyed the association," Sewell remembered. She considered these experiences examples of "quiet, peaceful integration in Searcy among Christians." On another occasion, when a choir from a historically black college could not find lodging, Sewell and her husband contacted members of the Harding faculty about opening their homes. "[W]ithout exception," she later explained, "the answer was a quick unequivicable [sic] 'Yes.'" Reflecting on these stories more than a decade later, she guessed that they were probably the first of their kind around Searcy, so "it was remarkable then that it all happened so easily and naturally." These relationships were not necessarily based on shared visions of racial equality. Sewell also noted how she enjoyed black students because they "were more polite, more appreciative, and in many cases had a better sense of rhythm than white students." At the same time, her inclusion of these students illustrates the occasional fluidity of the color line.[27]

Abilene Christian College in Abilene, Texas, also witnessed activity that challenged strict racial segregation. Its board of trustees did not formally decree its desegregation until 1961, but a Bermudan student of African descent was accepted in the late 1950s. Carl Spain, a preacher and professor there, explained in correspondence to a colleague how the young lady "was negro by her own admission. She stayed in the girls' dormitory with white girls who knew she was negro." The student also attended Spain's church and taught a children's Bible class. She was "graciously received by faculty, administration, and student body. Some said she was not a 'negro.' But her ancestral lineage was identical with other negros [sic] who were imported during the days of slavery. Some tried to cover the matter over by calling her 'Burmudan' [sic]." Based on these remarks, some whites in the college community were uncomfortable with her presence, but those who simply did not mind apparently outnumbered them. Spain concluded his account by noting that, when the young lady left Abilene, she married "one of her own people" in an African Methodist Episcopal church in Bermuda.[28]

More strident critiques of racial segregation began to appear sporadically in white Church of Christ media during the 1950s, spurred in part by developments in the broader black freedom struggle. Woodrow Whitten wrote a two-part series on Christianity and race relationships that was published in early issues of the *California Christian* in 1953. The first part explained how the "concept of a 'pure' race is a pure myth," while the second part wrestled more directly with the ways in which normative cultural and legal practices conflicted with his conception of Christianity. Whitten recognized that a person could take a theoretical position much more readily "than to take a forthright stand against race covenants or Jim Crow segregation in his own community!" He did not advocate social activism, however, opting for the more idyllic notion that love was needed to "triumph over the disruptive forces of racial prejudice." He concluded by citing the lyrics of an ageless song that children regularly sang in their Sunday school classes: "The Christian cannot forget that 'red and yellow, black and white'—all are precious in his sight." Whitten neither made an explicit call for integration on any level, nor did he propose immediate actions for correcting racial injustices. But he clearly associated common practices of racial discrimination with sin, even if that association was easier to make in California than in the South where most Churches of Christ were located. Writers such as Whitten represented a clear alternative to Foy Wallace, even as their restorationist theologies differed little. On the same page of the first part of Whitten's series, a letter from a Presbyterian minister in West Virginia complimented the *California Christian* and ordered a subscription. Below the letter, the editor wrote, "I would be unworthy as a Christian if I failed in this very first issue to say that I believe you are in error and that the Presbyterian Church is not the church of the Bible."[29]

Less than two months after the Supreme Court issued its 1954 *Brown* decision, the *Christian Chronicle*, a periodical devoted to church news more than doctrine, addressed the issue of segregation in an editorial pointedly titled "Segregation—Or Christianity." The editor lambasted anyone who might oppose integration and asked a series of rhetorical questions to emphasize the point: "Where are the Negro names upon the lists of students in the Christian schools? Where are their names in our church directories? . . . Christ, 2000 years ago, opened the door for the Negro into the church along with everyone else. Why can not we, mere mortals, have the strength to open our class-rooms, dormitories and church pews to them?" The editorial also acknowledged the usual excuses proffered against integration: tradition or pressure from local citizens. "What childishness!" the editor exclaimed. "Why don't we open the school doors? When will we fully fellowship [with] them in our worship?" While these calls for integration were generally ignored, they were significant in illustrating the presence of urgent, white voices that lamented racial discrimination within Churches of Christ.[30]

Others were just as firm, if less strident or specific. James Willeford, a founder and preacher for the *Herald of Truth* radio program, expressed similar thoughts in a sermon broadcast on January 29, 1956, "Call No Man Common." By the close of the 1960s, the *Herald of Truth* enjoyed widespread popularity across the nation but, even by 1956, the program was carried by more than thirty American Broadcast Company (ABC) network stations. While the program's preachers wrote their own material, each sermon had to be approved by the elders of the Highland Church of Christ in Abilene, Texas, the congregation responsible for creating and sustaining the program. "Call No Man Common" exemplified the stock approach that preachers commonly used to voice opposition to racial discrimination. Willeford stressed that racial problems were both historically and culturally common and widespread, and he cited examples of what he considered racial prejudice from ancient Egypt and Palestine to modern nations such as South Africa and Nazi Germany, the ultimate example. By emphasizing the existence of ethnic strife across the ages, preachers deflected direct criticism that, in this instance and many others, were aimed primarily at an audience largely composed of white southerners. This homiletic technique almost invariably included "the North" in its critique, too. Willeford's sermon referred to people who claimed that their customs forbade "inviting the colored man into our houses of worship. I have heard this excuse offered in both the North and the South," he explained.[31]

Otherwise, Willeford's sermon contained the familiar exposition of biblical texts that by command or example opposed racial prejudice. Like Whitten, he addressed common misconceptions about racial differences by noting that the "evidence shows that with equal opportunities any two racial groups would be equal in intelligence" and by citing biologists from Abilene Christian College who wrote an article about superficial physical differences among humans. Willeford also employed a string of rhetorical questions to reiterate his main points. "Do we have a right to demand that because we are white we must have a white God? . . . Can you imagine the Lord Jesus dying for a man and then discriminating against him? Or allowing His disciples to either? . . . When we shun others, and make light of them because they belong to another race, are we obeying the golden rule of the Bible? . . . did the Lord mean that we should preach the gospel to the Indian, baptize him into Christ, and then shun him by 'putting him in his place'?" he asked. Using "Indian" instead of "Negro" might have diffused reactions from white listeners who felt threatened by sermons directed toward their prejudices against blacks, and Willeford, like Whitten, offered little by way of practical advice for overcoming racial prejudice. However, without using the term, he mentioned "integration" of churches. Near the conclusion of his sermon, he observed, "We are all glad for [whites] to take a front seat in our church buildings, but some of us bar the colored man. We will visit his services when we please. . . . We send our white preachers to Africa, and there the whites and blacks worship together. What hinders our having such fellowship in America? Most of us will let negroes cook our food, take care of our babies, and play ball with our sons, but some of us bar them from worshiping God with us!" Willeford recognized that many of his listeners justified their segregated assemblies because of custom, but he reminded them of a question that Jesus once posed to the Pharisees: "Why do ye transgress the commandment of God by your tradition?" Such traditions, in Willeford's estimation, "lead us into open rebellion against God."[32]

Few members of Churches of Christ would have disagreed with Willeford's exegesis, but many whites likely winced at the notion that churches and schools should be integrated. In their minds, racial segregation was not necessarily related to discrimination but was rather a political question without biblical or moral ramifications. This perspective was apparent in the spring of 1956 when another Church of Christ periodical, the *Firm Foundation*, published a column that asked, "What Does the Church of Christ Teach on Segregation?" According to author Ross Dye, the question arose as "several religious bodies," or other Christian denominations, made official pronouncements regarding "the issue of segregation of the races in the publicly owned institutions." Despite his essay's title, Dye completely dodged the question because the inquiry implied "that the church is a body invested with the authority to legislate and impose its will upon all dissenters." In his view, "The church has no authority to teach anything except what the Bible teaches," and since the Bible obviously remained silent on the integration of public institutions in the United States during the twentieth century, the church should, too. The "policies with respect to publicly owned institutions and other functions of government are political issues, and therefore outside the scope of the New Testament. The church had just as well take a position for or against flexible price supports or the highway bill as to take a position on segregation of the races in public schools," Dye asserted. At the same time Dye avoided the question, he concluded his column by citing several of the same verses and interpreting them in the same way as Willeford and others. "Men of every race, tribe, kindred and tongue are in Christ, and are therefore our beloved brethren. Let us 'love the brotherhood.'" Such remarks opened the door for individuals to affirm their love for everyone and accept or even defend segregation because it was a political issue, not a moral one.[33]

These sources illustrate the divergent experiences and perspectives among white Churches of Christ in the years preceding the 1960s. Admonitions against racial prejudice could serve as the basis for a Sunday school lesson, but jokes that depended on crude racial stereotypes might appear in church bulletins or sermon outlines. Black preachers could preach to predominantly white audiences, and white preachers could speak in black churches. But most communities, in the South and elsewhere, maintained separate facilities for blacks and whites. Even in these paradoxical contexts, personal and interracial relationships were sometimes established. And all along, most white members of Churches of Christ would affirm without equivocation that all people were equal in Christ and that God was "no respecter of persons." The primary objective, however, for both black and white Churches of Christ was practicing their conception of New Testament Christianity. Maintaining their identity as restorers of the primitive church took precedence above all temporal concerns, including race relations.

As civil rights battles unfolded in courtrooms and the streets, this perspective largely remained. Church members gradually refrained from unseemly racial humor. White churches patronized black churches in the name of evangelism, and black churches typically accepted whatever was offered, even as they established greater independence from whites.[34] Both blacks and whites still forged their identities based largely on their fixation with being "the first century church." Personal correspondence from members and preachers reflected this restorationist priority.

James Bales may have personified white attitudes among Churches of Christ better than anyone else. Bales was a prolific writer, preacher, and popular professor at Harding College. His vast correspondence exhibited the ambiguities and tensions that characterized many whites. As racial tensions mounted at mid-century, he fondly recalled how his first sermon and later first revival were conducted in black churches. In a 1943 letter published "To My Colored Brother," Bales assured his "colored brother in Christ that the love which binds us together as members of the same body . . . will not be disturbed by the hate and conflict which those of the world manifest toward men of another race or color." His poignant note warned that "the racial prejudices which are abroad in our land today are un-Christian. . . . Thus I do not share or contribute to the animosities which are growing today in many hearts." Bales likely wrote in response to the Detroit race riot that took the lives of twenty-five blacks and nine whites and demarcated in a very public way the country's simmering racial tensions during World War II. Over the next two decades, as the civil rights movement raised significant questions about equality and political rights, Bales became increasingly defensive, even offended, when complaints were lodged against the United States or its governance. Bales persistently affirmed that Christian principles should guide how people treat others, regardless of race, but his inability to recognize and respond to the pervasive effects of structural racism upon black opportunity left him indifferent to the social hardships faced by blacks and alienated him from racially progressive whites and civil rights activists who were advocates of substantial reform. This myopia, coupled with perceived threats posed by communism at the height of the Cold War, accentuated in Bales a desire for order and stability and a commitment to only the most gradual changes in racial customs.[35]

In the late 1950s, Bales privately wrestled with whether Harding College should admit black students. A cryptic, typewritten page among his voluminous papers asked, "When is it time [to desegregate]? I do not know. I think we should be happy that our brethren of various races, except the Negro, have been welcomed here and without disturbance from Community or parents. I doubt now is the time with all the excitement about Little Rock." These thoughts, likely composed in the latter months of 1957, displayed more of a concern for peace than any contempt for integration. Bales ultimately deferred to the people who were charged with making such decisions by concluding, "I leave it with board." At the same time, Bales conveyed misgivings over the blatant mistreatment of blacks. He penned a letter in October 1957 to Essin Essin, a native African and church member who was attending Southwestern Christian College (SWC) in Terrell, Texas, the historically black college affiliated with Churches of Christ. Essin was assaulted by a police officer in Henderson, Texas, when he refused to move to the back of a Trailways bus. Bales expressed "deep sorrow" and conveyed his hope that the incident would not summarily taint Essin's view of the United States. "It is too bad that there are prejudices and customs in various parts of the world which lead to unfortunate incidents," Bales continued. "No country, of course, is free from such prejudices. Although great changes do not come overnight I am confident that the record will show that a great deal of progress has been made in the past half century in the question of race relationships in this country." After this defensive disclaimer, Bales again apologized for what transpired, but a postscript revealed his homage to local custom. "All of us, of course, should take into consideration the customs and prejudices of a community, state or nation and try to avoid unnecessarily arousing antagonism." At the conclusion of an otherwise polite letter, Bales could not resist sharing this unsolicited advice, demeaning the person whose feelings he was attempting to assuage and failing to appreciate the gravity and danger of such an assault in east Texas.[36]

Nevertheless, Bales consistently lamented outbreaks of violence against blacks. After a riot erupted at the University of Mississippi in 1962 when James Meredith enrolled, Bales deplored "the mess in Mississippi" in a letter to a colleague. In another privately drafted paper, Bales wrote about a Christian's obligation "to manifest good will toward people of all races," the type of affirmation that was reflected in Sunday school literature. During his travels, Bales would sometimes stay with blacks whom he counted as friends, a courtesy that he returned when visitors came to his home in Searcy, Arkansas. Although he always deflected the harshest criticism against the United States' social record at the height of the Cold War, Bales observed how racism plagued all societies, but "the fact that racial prejudice is universal has not been pointed out in order to justify it, or to imply that Christians ought to share the prejudices of the world." On one occasion, he mused over the possibility of starting and maintaining integrated churches. He claimed that his primary interest was the feasibility of evangelism when so many people expected churches to be either black or white. Like David Lipscomb, Bales surmised that blacks "should be welcomed in the assembly," but unlike Lipscomb, he doubted that "the best way to evangelize the colored race would be by eliminating colored congregations."[37]

Bales's ambiguity contrasted sharply with a speech given by Carl Spain at the 1960 Abilene Christian College lectureship, but the occasion provided insights into their perspectives. "God forbid," Spain exclaimed, "that churches of Christ, and schools operated by Christians, shall be the last stronghold of refuge for socially sick people who have Nazi illusions about the Master Race. . . . A Methodist college will admit our own Negro preacher brethren and give them credit for their work. Baptist colleges in Texas will do as much. Our state universities will admit them. There is no law of our state or nation that will censor us. The Bible does not rule against it. Why are we afraid?" Spain went on to describe a fascinating incident that illustrates the dynamic environment in which Churches of Christ functioned. Blacks from a Church of Christ in

Spain's hometown wanted to use the baptistery at the white Church of Christ. He sarcastically opined, "The Blue-blooded members of the Royal Order of the Master Race, including many members of the church of Christ, the Baptists, the Methodists, and Presbyterians, protested loudly. . . . Before the baptismal service was over, police came to put a stop to it, just like the Communists broke up services in Warsaw, Poland, last year." To reinforce his position, Spain associated those people who opposed sharing the baptistery with denominations and totalitarianism, but he also noted that the baptism occurred as planned. "Police patrolled the area around the church building. The Lord's church was branded as a Communist front organization where whites and Negroes socialized as brothers. The community systematically boycotted the business establishments of some of the Christians for months, nearly causing them to go bankrupt." In the process of lamenting the persistence of segregation in Churches of Christ, Spain showed how the interracial nature of the denomination, such as it was, could still become a target for rabid segregationists.[38]

One of the most opportune times for Bales to share his thoughts on integration came shortly after Spain's speech, when Spain composed a cordial letter to Bales that reiterated his main points and addressed percolating rumors about a debate between the two men over the issue, arranged by an editor of a Church of Christ periodical. The editor indicated that Bales was prepared to defend segregation, and the student newspaper at Abilene had already reported on the coming debate. Spain refused to accept the editor's proposition because "I felt that you and I were agreed on the aspects of the problem which I had emphasized in my lecture." Spain's letter asked Bales to reply with his point of view.[39]

Bales greeted Spain as an "Old friend" and delicately articulated a position that illustrates the sentiments that were weighing on the minds of many whites. He claimed that he was "neither for nor against segregation" and insisted "that one without prejudice can, and should, take into consideration the attitude, customs and laws in the surrounding community." Yet in the very next sentence, he commented how there was a "definite lack of spiritual growth of any Christian who would refuse [communion] with another Christian." Bales sought to ground his opinion on the basis of what might prove most expedient to evangelism. Thus, an integrated church "in many, many places is [not] the way to reach either the white or the black race." He went on to claim "that the integrationist who maintains that we must integrate 'regardless' . . . [and] the extremist who maintains that segregation is *the* Biblical position" were both wrong. Toward the end of his letter, Bales reemphasized the need to "teach and practice good will toward all people," but he insisted that churches should not "become centers of agitation for or against segregation." Bales's final paragraph disclosed feelings pertaining to his own situation and his habitual deference to the college president. "Although I shall be glad to have qualified negro students in my classes, I am willing to abide by the decision of the administration. In time undoubtedly they will be admitted; as to the time I leave it to the judgment of the administration."[40]

Bales's reply foreshadowed his subsequent positions on the civil rights movement, as well as the conflicted nature of many whites' opinions on race relations in 1960. Bales affirmed a basic unity among all Christians but one that did not require integrating churches and schools. His preeminent concern with social order can be observed in his recommendation that churches refrain from political activism and his deference to college administrators. Once again, evangelism was a significant priority. This otherworldly perspective and the fact that he enjoyed the benefits of white supremacy gave him little reason to advocate social reforms and every reason to mold his opinions of desegregation around the urgency with which he viewed spreading the gospel. He was not alone.

The opinion page of the *Christian Chronicle* contained an editorial and letters from readers that typified positions taken by whites in the wake of Spain's speech. The editorial was relatively bland compared to the newspaper's more forceful rhetoric after the *Brown* decision. It referred to Spain as "one of the most respected preachers and teachers in the church today," whose lecture "has caused considerable thought in an area which we have tended to minimize and overlook." Yet the editorial completely ignored the issue of segregation itself, noting only that "other brethren have long been guiding lights in pointing up the fact that God can use a black man as an efficient and effective tool in spreading his kingdom." Serious discussion of race relations was subsumed by a preoccupation with evangelism. The piece also mentioned Marshall Keeble, who "has been quietly sowing the seeds that will eventually break down the barriers that cause mistrust among Negro and White." Once an adamant proponent for integration, the *Christian Chronicle* now softened its position by highlighting Keeble's work, contrasting it with civil rights activism. Keeble worked "quietly," in a manner that would "eventually" result in better race relations. His style differed starkly with recent boycotts, marches, and especially sit-ins, the latest method of defiance and protest that was becoming more widespread as Churches of Christ were processing Spain's remarks. The final portion of the editorial quoted extensively from an Iowa newspaper that had covered one of

Keeble's revivals. The newspaper observed, and the *Christian Chronicle* affirmed, that Keeble had "no racial agitation nor hate in his path. He is typical of those Negro Moderates who understand and sympathize with the error and sins of the whites. His message is so much more inspiring than that of such Negro leaders as the Rev. [Martin] Luther King, the Alabama boycott expert, who has spoken in Iowa." The *Christian Chronicle* indirectly acknowledged that racial problems existed, that whites were largely to blame, and that racial barriers should be broken down, but the preferred method for dismantling segregation was to emulate Keeble, who converted thousands but never publicly chastised whites for racial discrimination.[41]

Two letters to the editor appeared alongside the editorial. One lauded Spain's speech and expressed outrage over the continued segregation of the Church of Christ colleges in the South. The second letter, written by a reader from Searcy, Arkansas, was far more reserved in its assessment of Spain but was considerably perturbed that the *Christian Chronicle* was giving the speech so much attention. "I was certainly very disappointed when I picked up the last issue to see your feature article consist of different type of material," the writer complained. "Regardless of the merit or demerit of Brother Spain's lecture, it would seem far better to me for you to continue with your original purpose rather than take part in items of this nature. . . . Why not . . . leave other areas to other publishers." The "original purpose" of the *Christian Chronicle*, according to this subscriber, did not include coverage of events pertaining to race relations. Subsequent letters to the editor that mentioned Spain's speech commended the *Christian Chronicle* for its coverage, but there was a strong undercurrent within Churches of Christ of people who insisted that racial problems involved political questions and were therefore secondary to the work of the church.[42]

At the moment when the integrationist agenda of civil rights activists was gaining traction across the country, Churches of Christ, who could have easily positioned themselves to lead integration efforts in the South, doubled down on sectarian evangelism. By January 1963, the Center Street Church of Christ in Fayetteville targeted local blacks for evangelism through a new church which they helped create, the Combs Street Church of Christ, rather than make concerted efforts to include blacks in a church that already existed. "Isn't it thrilling to see this new work among our Negro brethren doing so well?" a church bulletin asked. "Let us strive to *give more* that we might be able to *do more!*" (emphasis in original). Of the many paths that led away from the overt racism of the past, white Churches of Christ often chose the easiest route, one that included the practice of investing money in black churches and paying their ministers instead of integrating churches. This practice was customary for many years before the modern civil rights movement but, given the momentous changes that were unfolding, approaches that may have once appeared benefi-cent now seemed anachronistic, if not hostile, to black aspirations and notions of full equality. On the one hand, churches criticized the apostle Peter for his inconsistency in associating with Gentile Christians and taught that worship assemblies should be open to all people but, on the other hand, white churches attempted to keep their black brothers and sisters out of sight, segregated in churches that struggled to maintain facilities and clergy, during an era when segregation was under sustained attack. In an informational booklet published by the Center Street church in 1966, the ministry of the Combs Street church is mentioned alongside efforts to minister to college students at the University of Arkansas: "A part of our work in spreading the borders of the kingdom is the support of Riley West as he work [sic] among his people in our city." The brief account continued by noting that "the brethren at Combs Street are assuming more and more of the support of the work. . . . [They] work with us . . . at all times and they are grateful for the support of this church." The ties of faith that once bound black and white Churches of Christ grew increasingly tenu-ous as the broader civil rights movement unfolded. Whites grappled with best approaches to evangelism, a parochial concern, and the desegregation of its colleges, which related more broadly to events outside of the denomination.[43]

When Harding College finally accepted a few black students in 1963, Rena Chaney of Vicksburg, Mississippi, contacted James Bales to learn about the de-tails and express her objections. Her five-page, handwritten letter exemplified extreme racism, while Bales only mustered a cool, detached response. Among other outrageous statements, Chaney suggested that a black man who wanted to marry a white woman should be sterilized "so that he'd not be passing the stigma of negro blood on to untold generations who would resent it, and yet were powerless in the matter." Drawing on a perverse combination of current events and theology, she argued against "integration on any social level." At the close of her letter, she warned, "If the white race is destroyed, civilization, and Christianity with it are lost to the world." Bales did not address these wild assertions. He recited the basic facts regarding the admission of the first black students, emphasizing that the "students are all members of the church and they live in town. . . . They want an education. They are not agitators." His response encapsulated the importance of faith, education, and social order in his approach to racial matters, but he appeared indifferent regarding Chaney's white supremacist vitriol. Bales mentioned that the students lived in town to mollify any fears that the newcomers would be housed with white students, and the fact that they were "members of the church" was emphasized to establish some connection and familiarity, however perfunctory.[44]

As the tumultuous 1960s unfolded, many whites felt bombarded by challenges to their most fundamental assumptions about government, power, and religion. With the civil rights movement launching unprecedented protests against oppressive institutions within American society, Bales grew increasingly alarmed by the constant turmoil and unrest and came to associate civil rights activism with provocation and chaos. Without giving careful attention to who or what instigated violence, rioting, or other breakdowns in civil society, Bales perceived all forms of protest as threats to domestic tranquility. He became increasingly defensive about the opportunities allotted to all Americans regardless of race, especially in comparison to other nations. Legitimate grievances held no sense of urgency for Bales amid the fervent patriotism of the Cold War in the 1960s. As a prolific writer and speaker among white Churches of Christ, Bales typified the "law and order" perspective that emerged within the denomination. Never one to withhold his opinion, Bales wrote countless letters to newspaper and journal editors during his career and, after 1964, these letters expressed a new urgency against "mob pressure" while demonstrating his inability to distinguish the variety of demands made by civil rights activists or the range of methods by which different groups sought change.

Shortly after the Harlem riots in July 1964, Bales wrote to the *Atlanta Constitution* and derided those people who "don't associate extremism with those who have for several years advocated the violation of certain laws which they did not want to obey." In the *Arkansas Gazette,* he criticized "Civil Rights agitators" who used religion to push for reforms, while acknowledging that "Christians should be interested in reforms and in a thoughtful consideration of the means which bring about true reforms." Unlike many activists, Bales believed that society's faults could be attributed to people rather than institutions. In the same letter to the *Arkansas Gazette,* Bales reverted to his restorationist heritage to criticize civil rights activists. "The first Christian missionaries did not make it their goal in life to free the slaves, although through freeing men from slavery to sin the spiritual values preached by Christianity did undermine slavery ultimately." This assertion carried with it the implication that people should emulate the first Christian missionaries. He acknowledged that Christianity might stand in opposition to social evils, but Bales insisted that the church should not take upon itself the responsibility of addressing institutional racism. "So many today do not give emphasis to the development of character," he lamented, "but think that the fault lies in social institutions and not in persons. They think that by changing social institutions, without changing people, that people will thereby be changed." Bales personified the gradualism that had long been associated with white opinions of the black freedom struggle.[45]

The ambiguity and paradoxes in Bales's thinking were evident in a 1964 article that he published in the *Gospel Advocate*. "Neither Race, Rank Nor Sex" revisited the ongoing discussion of how Galatians 3:28 received a wide array of interpretations. In the King James Version of the Bible the verse states, "There is neither Jew nor Greek, there is neither bond nor free, there is neither male nor female: for ye are all one in Christ Jesus." His most perplexing comment stated how there was a sense in which "a Christian should be color blind, but there are other senses in which the Bible does not require that he be color blind." The apparent contradiction may be partially explained by other private writings that note the continuance of slave-master relationships in the Pauline epistles or the existence of Jewish and Gentile churches during Christianity's formative years. Bales further contended that adhering to Christian faith "does not mean that one therefore has the duty to ignore all of the laws and customs of society which he does not like. . . . He may not feel that others are practicing the Golden Rule as they ought, but does that give him the right to ignore all of the attitudes, customs and even prejudices of others?" Bales likely represented many whites when he displayed a propensity for acknowledging Christian unity while diminishing the injustices that the civil rights movement hoped to address. In other words, Bales believed that Christian unity did not necessitate erasure of social distinctions within society, even those distinctions that reflected or perpetuated inequalities.[46]

The heightened Cold War tensions of the 1960s provided the context in which Bales assessed race relations and maintained a critical disposition toward the civil rights movement while not wholly dismissing some black grievances. The first sentence in *Communism and Race in America*, a book that he published with renowned spy Herbert Philbrick, confessed that "America has problems which are not due to communism and this is true with reference to racial problems." The authors admitted "that improvements, by lawful means and in accordance with the basic principles on which this country was founded, need to be made in our society." However, such improvements must be pursued with an understanding that communists would try to prey on the nation's social ills. The bulk of *Communism and Race in America* warned of communist infiltration into reform movements, government institutions, and churches, while the authors insisted that they "do not in any way oppose or protest lawful struggle for Civil Rights." Bales reiterated, however, that society's problems would be solved "when a person is changed within himself." Segregationists had long claimed that communists plagued the entire civil rights movement, but the book's tone indicated that these authors were not completely oblivious to racial injustices.[47]

Bales was not alone in his attempt to forge such a middle ground. A couple from Gulfport, Mississippi, complained to Bales that the state was "literally crawling with communists" and that the efforts of the Mississippi Freedom Democratic Party to hold parallel elections in 1964 were "a farce" because blacks voted in this couple's precinct "and were treated most cordially." They ignored the fact that most Mississippi blacks were not even allowed to register but obsessed over the perception that communists were invading their state: "Anyone who is against God is wrong, and we believe that Mississippi will lead the fight." In a similar way, Bales criticized Martin Luther King Jr. for importing "lawlessness" to Selma, Alabama, in March 1965, but he also reprimanded the state and local governments. "The parallel is that both of them believe that they have the right to violate the law of the land if they do not like the law. . . . Thus there is imported lawlessness in Alabama, as well as home grown lawlessness." A subsequent letter surmised that "a prayer circle" should be formed around civil rights demonstrators in Selma in hopes that their frustrations might be allayed, another indication that Bales believed a "proper" Christian disposition would restrain civil rights activities.[48]

Bales did not appear to have serious misgivings about the passage of civil rights legislation, but he remained skeptical about government's capacity to bring meaningful, long-term changes. Urban rioting and President Lyndon Johnson's War on Poverty provided the context for a wider critique of the liberal state. Bales, who had no qualms about boarding with blacks, wrote an essay suggesting that white policymakers and activists who blamed segregation for the nation's urban woes move into black neighborhoods to ameliorate segregation's negative effects. He rhetorically asked, "Do these leaders accept a vicious type of racism which says that the Negro when he lives with other Negroes will become vicious; that the Negro needs the presence of white man in order to enable him to be civilized?" Urban rioting, he suggested, was a "matter of character not of color" and, in his estimation, poverty and discrimination were never adequate explanations. Bales's naivete showed most clearly when his proposed solutions emphasized evangelism in black communities throughout the country.[49]

A white acquaintance commended Bales, surmising that his own life experiences were comparable to the discrimination and poverty faced by blacks. If he could make something of himself, so could they. This monolithic assessment frequently plagued white observers. The "one who has least will [always] consider himself bitterly deprived, no matter how much he has. He will do so . . . until he learns the lesson of 1 Timothy 6:6–11, which brings us back to your plea for evangelism." The first verse in this citation states that "godliness with contentment is great gain." This cold assessment demonstrates the ignorance of many whites in confronting injustices that had been perpetuated for centuries against blacks. Poor whites certainly faced hardships attributable to an unjust economic system or lack of educational opportunities, but Bales and others failed to comprehend the persistent effects of racial discrimination, much less the economic and political legacies of slavery and segregation. This stubborn unwillingness to empathize prevented whites from cultivating any semblance of working-class solidarity or identifying black allies who might have welcomed their support.[50]

Subscribing to the assumption that the preponderance of civil strife simply could not be a result of systemic injustices, Bales found it easy to associate social protests of all kinds with communist influences. The early years of the postwar civil rights movement elicited little response from Bales. He understood the need for some changes to be made, especially in people's hearts, and his attitude about racial prejudices was clearly expressed in his 1943 letter "To My Colored Brother." Over the next two decades, however, Bales spent much of his time researching and combating communism through speeches and publications, working alongside an archetypical anticommunist and segregationist in George Benson, Harding College's longtime president, whose National Education Program garnered national attention for its right-wing propaganda. As civil rights activism persisted after the 1964 Civil Rights Act and 1965 Voting Rights Act, Bales believed that communist influences were partly responsible, a paranoia that characterized many whites across the nation, including government officials.[51]

White Churches of Christ revealed a diversity of perspectives about race, defying the historian's impulse to classify. Categories commonly affixed to complex, nuanced opinions fail to describe the gradations of racial attitudes that permeated white perceptions. A variety of issues confronted whites who wrestled with the tensions between Christian ethics and pronounced racial injustices, but the restorationist impulse weighed most heavily on the minds of whites in Churches of Christ. This identity as the New Testament church may have blunted some of the more violent or blatant expressions of racism. For the most part, white Churches of Christ recognized their black brothers and sisters as spiritual equals. This recognition, though often paternalistic in nature, did not translate into social equality in most circumstances, as members did their best to distinguish spiritual concerns from temporal ones. While they may have passively accepted the desegregation championed by the federal government or the extension of the franchise, white church members were unwilling to actively and publicly advance any sort of civil rights agenda. Whether from conviction or convenience, some whites believed that social activism fell outside the bounds of Christian duty. Many of their black counterparts in Churches of Christ felt the same way.

2

MADE OF ONE BLOOD

While many blacks established institutional independence by forming separate denominations from whites in the closing decades of the nineteenth century, blacks in Churches of Christ faced a theological dilemma that prevented them from formally separating from whites. While several predominantly white denominations included some black members, the concentration of Churches of Christ in the South and the relatively high number of blacks in the church made their situation unusual. With no denominational administrators determining the boundaries between blacks and whites, relationships between churches and individual members sometimes operated apart from conventional racial customs both within and outside the South, thereby raising numerous questions about racial and religious identities as conflicts over civil rights and the meanings of equality unfolded during the twentieth century. Black ministers who, in diverse ways and with varying degrees of success, built alliances with whites in order to sustain their ministries largely precipitated the expansion of Churches of Christ into black communities. Letters from across the nation to the *Christian Echo,* the periodical within Churches of Christ owned and operated by blacks, offer compelling details about how racial and spiritual relationships worked among regular churchgoers. Both the preachers and the *Christian Echo* illuminate how blacks and whites interacted as members of the "true church" and how blacks constructed their spiritual identities alongside whites who advocated Christian primitivism and accepted prevailing norms of white supremacy.

Blacks and whites in Churches of Christ generally shared the same theological convictions, particularly with regard to their mission and religious identities. Sermons and writings indicate a common resolve to restore New Testament Christianity. However, faced with the indignities and discrimination of racial segregation, the daily lives of black members could differ markedly from their white counterparts. Tentative biracial relationships that formed prior to

World War II began to dissolve as the civil rights movement focused the nation's conscience on racial injustices. By the 1960s, blacks in Churches of Christ became increasingly strident in their insistence that the church's institutions reflect the racial equality and justice that the scriptures seemed to demand. Meanwhile, the postwar economic boom presented blacks with new opportunities to establish their independence from white churches and the paternalism that often accompanied them. They no longer needed the benevolence of whites to construct churches, sponsor revivals, or hire preachers. Although they shared much by way of theology, black and white churches gradually drifted apart, ironically, as the civil rights movement—with its integrationist agenda—peaked in the middle of the 1960s. The fissures that developed within Churches of Christ show the limitations of their interracialism. Interracial cooperation waned at the moment when contentious debates about racial equality in the general public empowered blacks to challenge various forms of oppression, leaving well-meaning whites struggling to explain how they were neither prejudiced nor responsible for institutional racism.

The early leaders of the nineteenth-century Stone-Campbell movement from which Churches of Christ evolved were white but, from the outset, numerous churches associated with the movement included blacks. Their inclusion derived in part from the disdain for slavery among some influential leaders, even though some early leaders also owned slaves. Strong antislavery sentiments developed in the movement shortly after the Second Great Awakening, such that a contemporary observer noted "that the christians [sic] of these parts abhor the idea of slavery, and some of them have almost tho't that they who hold to slavery cannot be christian [sic]." As church historians David Edwin Harrell and Richard Hughes have noted, abolitionist sentiment within this movement may be attributed to the humanitarian zeal that sprang from the Second Great Awakening and the apocalyptic worldview that came to characterize the perspectives of some leaders. Whatever the motives, blacks were listed as members of churches in Kentucky and Virginia as early as the 1820s. Whites typically limited the roles that blacks could have within a given church, but some blacks preached or served as deacons.[1]

While David Lipscomb served as a crucial white voice in Churches of Christ after the Civil War, Samuel Robert Cassius became one of the most important black voices and certainly the most prolific. He personified several themes relative to Churches of Christ and the broader challenges faced by blacks in that era. His Christian primitivism echoed many of his white counterparts, and the self-improvement strategies that he championed reflected his admiration of Booker T. Washington and the limited options for blacks during the nadir of race relations. Cassius was born into slavery in 1853 and sold in 1860. He received a public school education after the war in Washington, DC. By the middle of the 1870s, he was a committed member of Churches of Christ who had dedicated himself to a career in ministry. These decisions eventually took him to Oklahoma, where he established a church and an industrial school. Inspired by Booker T. Washington, Cassius sent his son, Amos Lincoln (A. L.), to Tuskegee Institute. The elder Cassius was an outspoken critic of racism, especially within Churches of Christ, and he eventually determined that segregation, though immoral, provided the most promise for solving "the race problem" in the United States. He frequently published articles in Church of Christ periodicals, but his most fascinating commentary on race relations appeared in his 1920 book, *The Third Birth of a Nation.* As the title suggested, Cassius wrote partly in response to D. W. Griffith's 1915 cinematic breakthrough, *The Birth of a Nation,* but Cassius must have also been mindful of the growing popularity of the Ku Klux Klan. The book included the familiar tirades of many preachers of the day against new social habits and values. He criticized soft drinks, for example, because "there is only one step from the soft drink parlor to the opium den, and just one more step to the place of prostitution."[2]

Cassius's primitivist disposition was evident throughout *The Third Birth of a Nation,* but the work was more significant for its advocacy of black separatism, critique of white supremacy, and explanations of racial origins. Churches of Christ believed that the Bible was the inerrant Word of God, so Cassius related scriptures to each of his assertions. Blacks and whites alike sought clarification from the Bible regarding their essentialist conceptions of race, often constructed from a literal understanding of the Flood, Noah, and his three sons: Shem, Ham, and Japheth. Cassius believed that people with "burnt faces" could trace their origins back to Mitzraim, a son of Ham who settled in the land that eventually became known as Egypt. ("Mitzraim" is the ancient Hebrew word for Egypt.) Whites often asserted the same, but Cassius and other black theologians aimed to correct the theological racism that often accompanied whites' exegesis. "Even when diverging on specific points," historian Paul Harvey noted, "these race writers collectively disputed the racist notions of inferiority inherent in the Western idea of blackness." Cassius contended that the term "Egypt" could literally be translated as "burnt faces," so he emphasized the magnificence of ancient Egyptian civilization because it was constructed by nominally black people. Both blacks and whites speculated on possible theological significance to racial differences. Cassius repeatedly noted that "God made of one blood all nations of men," a direct quotation from the Acts of the Apostles, but like many whites he also stressed that God did not intend for these "nations" to mix.[3]

The *Christian Echo* shared similar thoughts on racial origins. The periodical often included a section of inquiries from readers and, in a 1945 issue, someone asked, "What caused Colored people, where did they start from? Does the word niger [sic] in the Bible mean Negro or colored people[?]" The *Christian Echo* provided a response that was common to blacks and whites who interpreted the biblical narratives in Genesis as literal events. "All races come from the three sons of Noah," the *Christian Echo* explained. "The Hammites settled in what is now known as Africa and is father of the Negro race. The white people came from Shem. The Chinese, Japanese and Indians from Japeth." The reader's second question referred to a passage from the Acts of the Apostles that mentioned a person named Simeon who was called "Niger," and the *Christian Echo* suggested that the term "simply means black, [and] this has no reference to the Negro as a race." A previous essay in the *Christian Echo* had also stated "Ham was the father of Canaan. He is the father of all the black race," while another writer proclaimed, "Miscegenation means to mix nations or races. Do I believe in it? No! I could not believe in it and believe in God at the same time." This author even attributed the demise of ancient Egyptian civilization to "the mixing of the Hebrew blood with the Egyptian blood."[4]

Such sentiments were previously explored in *The Third Birth of a Nation*. The book briefly outlined world history beginning with the story of Adam and Eve. Cassius hoped "to show that there is not now, nor ever has been, any superiority in race, or any difference in color; that God made man out of the earth and took woman out of the man, thus making them the same flesh, bones and blood." In his overview of biblical history, Cassius found comfort in scriptures that offered parallels to black struggles in the United States. He recounted the story of God preserving Noah and his family during the Flood and surmised, "So will God deliver the American Negro out from under the stigma of his present condition, if he will trust God and do His will." Like other black commentators, Cassius emphasized the significant role of "the people that the American nation has dubbed as Negroes" in world history, particularly the ancient civilizations of Egypt and Ethiopia, whose demise, according to Cassius, could be attributed to miscegenation and religious liberty, respectively. Cassius ironically utilized the language of white segregationists when he observed that American history was about a "mongrel nation" where "every kind of religious propaganda is allowed to flourish."[5]

In stark contrast to the era's hypernationalism, Cassius offered a scathing narrative of United States history. Unlike many whites who acknowledged that biblical narratives accepted, if not sanctioned, slavery, Cassius contended that Americans "broke the law of God by introducing slavery." With considerable detail, he outlined how Africans were brought to America as slaves and how freed slaves largely had to fend for themselves after the Civil War. In spite of numerous obstacles, Cassius took pride in the strides that blacks had made since emancipation and suggested that the "real cause" for white racism could be found in the "fears that the black man will supplant [the white man] in the matters of trade, business and profession."[6]

While many of his criticisms were aimed at whites with political and economic clout in American history, Cassius also expressed dismay at blacks who seemed content to support white oppression and discrimination. For example, he was deeply disturbed that black-owned newspapers sometimes publicized minstrel shows. "While these mirth producing pictures draw crowds," he wrote, "they at the same time lower the standard of the race in the eyes of the people who pay to see them make fools of themselves." Although many preachers extolled their churches to stay away from the cinema, Cassius chastised blacks for visiting the "white moving picture shows" and allowing themselves to be "'Jim Crowed' to a dirty, unsanitary part of the theatre." Abiding by the customs of segregation, he believed, was "an admission on the part of those who attend . . . that they do not consider themselves as good as the white people and are not worthy to sit even in the same part of the house with them."[7]

Like many commentators, religious and otherwise, Cassius wrestled with the "great race question" and determined that six options loomed: amalgamation, miscegenation, assimilation, Christianization, separation, or extermination. Although he addressed each one, the first three were dismissed as forbidden by God. Cassius equated the concept of nations with the concept of race and read the Bible accordingly. Thus, a passage that urged the ancient Israelites not to intermarry with surrounding nations was interpreted as a prohibition against interracial marriage. White segregationists sometimes employed the same reasoning. Cassius retold the biblical story of the Tower of Babel, asserted that the ancient Egyptians faltered because of their intermarriage with Hebrews, and quoted a verse from the Acts of the Apostles: "And [God] hath made of one blood all nations of men for to dwell on all the face of the earth, and hath determined the times before appointed, and the bounds of their habitation" (KJV). Cassius neither equivocated nor left room for alternative interpretations. "I could not believe in [miscegenation] and believe in God at the same time," he wrote.[8]

Left with Christianization, extermination, and separation, Cassius thought the latter was the best option. Extermination was "barbarous," of course, although Cassius reminded readers that the Bible included instances when God commanded the extermination of certain nations, a fact that reiterated his choice of separation. There was a sense in which Cassius agreed with David Lipscomb and future integrationists who would utilize Christianity in favor of desegregation. He described Christianity as "the only force that can possibly bridge the chasm that separates man from man, because Christianity is the only means that so changes our minds that one man will not think himself better than another." The catch was that the United States was decidedly unchristian so, for this reason, he did not conceive of racial equality as a viable option. The "lack of a pure Bible religion in America," Cassius asserted, "is the cause of the race problem." He conceded that race problems would be solved "if the so-called Christian people of America would take the word of god as the man [sic] of their counsel and its teachings as their rule of faith and practice," but he did not foresee such an occurrence. Cassius had personal experiences that bore on his assessment, including an instance at a revival with a white preacher. The sermon compelled Cassius to come forward, or visit the "mourner's bench," where people could confess their sins, ask for prayer, or request baptism. A white man visited the mourner's bench at the same time as Cassius but immediately reconsidered. As Cassius recalled the incident, "it made him so mad to think that a 'nigger' was mourning at the same bench with him that he quit mourning and 'wouldn't get religion.'" Cassius subsequently searched for the man, "hoping to catch him out and fight him, because he did not want to mourn with me." He could only conclude that "the majority of the white people of this nation would rather spend an eternity in hell than worship in the same house with a negro."[9]

Even though Cassius resented how white supremacy infiltrated Churches of Christ just as it did American society, his theological commitments and resolve would not permit him to simply choose another denomination. Just like whites in Churches of Christ, Cassius believed that, if people simply accepted the Bible as the word of God, and presumably interpreted it just as he did, then

there "would be no such thing as Baptist, Methodist, Presbyterian, Congrega-
tionalist, and the many other brands of religion; we would all speak the same
thing, do the same thing, hope the same thing and expect the same reward."
He even implied that these denominations were partly to blame for the persistence of white supremacy in American society and that Churches of Christ
held the possibility for redeeming the nation. The section of *The Third Birth of a
Nation* that dealt with Christianity concluded, "Therefore it is up to the *Church
of Christ* [italicized in original] to make good its boast that they are serving
God just as God has ordered his servants in his word." Cassius did not insist on
the integration of churches or society per se, but he suggested that whites had
some role to play in fostering racial harmony and spreading the gospel among
blacks. Integration was something for which to strive, even if it was not an
explicit demand.[10]

His acceptance of segregation was rooted in practical concerns, although
he also proffered a biblical justification, reminding readers that God required
the ancient Israelites to permanently leave their old captors. Since the United
States would not allow blacks to exercise the same civil rights as whites, Cassius
proposed that the federal government purchase property owned by whites in
Oklahoma, Arizona, and New Mexico, while simultaneously compelling blacks
throughout the country to sell their property to the government and move to
these states. Cassius represented another voice in a long line of observers who
suggested some form of colonization or relocation for black Americans. Like
those predecessors, Cassius appeared to have garnered little support. Nevertheless, Cassius was exceptional as a black voice within Churches of Christ who
spoke so boldly and publicly against racial discrimination. His strong primitivist faith did not prevent him from openly expressing righteous indignation.
Most other black preachers within Churches of Christ, however, made their
reputations by focusing primarily on advancing the restorationist agenda of
the church.[11]

Many of these preachers traced their intellectual and spiritual heritage to
Nashville, Tennessee, and the Jackson Street Church of Christ. This church
began as the result of theological disputes involving "innovations" in the Stone-
Campbell movement, such as instrumental music in worship and missionary
societies. A black preacher named Alexander Campbell, whose namesake
helped initiate the Stone-Campbell movement in the nineteenth century, with-
drew from a Nashville church and convinced Samuel Womack, a black member
of a local Christian Church, to join him in organizing the Jackson Street Church

of Christ in 1900. Both Campbell and Womack had backgrounds in the Stone-Campbell movement. Womack recalled "the grand privilege that the white church of Christ [in Lynchburg, Tennessee] . . . gave the colored people during their first protracted meeting just after the Civil War. . . . A short time after that, in the fall of 1866, I was baptized by a white preacher." Womack became a noted preacher and church organizer among Christian Churches throughout Tennessee, experiences that served him well as a member of the Church of Christ in the early twentieth century.[12]

The new church initially met inside Campbell's home, until a facility was acquired on Jackson Street. They were joined by George Phillip (G. P.) Bowser and Marshall Keeble. Bowser was a convert from the Methodist Church who was rebaptized into the Christian Church in 1897 at the age of twenty-three, while Keeble grew up in a home beside Womack, was baptized in 1892 at age fourteen, and married Womack's daughter. Campbell and Womack served as mentors to Bowser and Keeble. Through their evangelism, journalistic endeavors, and efforts to secure education for blacks, Bowser and Keeble became two of the most influential figures within Churches of Christ and were indispensable to the growth of the denomination among blacks.[13]

Campbell and Womack quickly established relationships with local white Churches of Christ. Womack regularly visited David Lipscomb, who invited him to publish articles in the *Gospel Advocate*. In the process of becoming acquainted with their white brothers and sisters in the faith, black preachers affirmed the exclusivism that became so distinctive among Churches of Christ. "Instead of seeing black Baptists and Methodists as fellow Christians," historian Edward Robinson wrote, "African American preachers in Churches of Christ viewed them as enemies of God, who needed to be converted, corrected, or restored." Black members matched the restorationist zeal of whites, thereby securing their position within Churches of Christ and developing a measure of camaraderie that relied on the denomination's sectarianism.[14]

Although a full array of women's voices is difficult to discern from extant sources, women also subscribed to these perspectives. Annie Tuggle, the most influential black woman in the denomination in the twentieth century, remembered her conversion to Churches of Christ and her mother's disappointment that Annie did not seek her father's permission or a letter from the Methodist Church. Tuggle explained to her mother, "No, I didn't tell papa I was going to accept the invitation that Christ offers to everyone who wishes to be saved. Christ says in his word that whosoever loveth father or mother or sister or brother more than me is not worthy of me. And as for the Methodist Church, it's the devil's work and I don't have to get permission from the devil to obey Christ!" In addition to her dim view of Methodism, Tuggle's conversion to Churches of Christ was a moment of liberation from her father's control, especially ironic given her new denomination's narrow view of women's roles in church and society.[15]

Blacks' affirmation of and commitment to the particular theological nuances of Churches of Christ cultivated trust among blacks and whites within the church and established a foundation upon which evangelistic and other cooperative endeavors would build. In this respect, Womack and Campbell sought white patrons who could help sustain black ministers and churches. In the face of economic and educational discrimination, black churches pursued financial assistance from whites, whose generosity assuaged whatever concerns they might have had about the plight of blacks, especially in the South where the vast majority of blacks lived and where Churches of Christ proliferated. While white assistance was often tainted by paternalism, black preachers expressed appreciation for this patronage in the pages of the *Gospel Advocate* and *Christian Echo*. Reports to the *Gospel Advocate* often mentioned whites who helped purchase a revival tent or who attended revivals to show support or solidarity with the evangelistic mission. These reports confirmed to whites that their financial contributions were well received and wisely spent, but blacks were not simply trying to placate sponsors. White patronage served as a means to a specific end, one with eternal ramifications. Blacks wanted their churches to grow, their friends and families to convert to Churches of Christ, and their children to read and write. They found whites who concurred with those goals and who could help piece together the financial means of obtaining them. No one personified this relationship better than Marshall Keeble, and he became the most popular preacher, black or white, in Churches of Christ during the first half of the twentieth century.[16]

Occupational options were severely restricted for blacks when Keeble entered adulthood. He was certainly driven to preach by a strong personal faith, but menial labor in two factories undoubtedly helped him see the light. Campbell and Womack, "two old heroes" he called them, gave Keeble opportunities to preach and the responsibility of serving as church treasurer. Keeble learned a lot about preaching from them, but he also developed a knack for interacting with whites in advantageous ways. His congeniality, coupled with his impeccable integrity, served Keeble well. Later in his life, Keeble also noted the influence of Booker T. Washington on his thinking. One Keeble biographer described Washington as a boyhood idol from whom Keeble learned how "to respect his race, to hold a high opinion of himself, and especially how to get along with white people." To these ends, Keeble focused his ministry on growing and edifying black churches, goals that allowed him to receive white patronage but largely prohibited him from publicly criticizing racial discrimination.[17]

Keeble was an enigmatic figure who can best be understood in the context of the restorationism espoused by Churches of Christ. While he wanted to emulate Washington's pride and resourcefulness, he altogether exemplified the exclusivism of Churches of Christ. "He was my idol," Keeble once said of Washington, "all he lacked was being a Christian." After 1914, when Keeble decided to focus solely on a career in ministry, he became one of the most successful preachers of his era by navigating racial customs and prejudices and using them to affect his desired result: growth of "the New Testament church" among blacks throughout the country. His popularity and success did not come easy. During his early years as an evangelist, Keeble traveled from town to town conducting revivals, while his wife continued to operate a small grocery store to sustain an income. Keeble accepted whatever payments his listeners could afford, including farm animals or food. On some Saturdays, when towns would fill with people from the surrounding countryside, he would find a platform and begin preaching, accepting whatever change that passersby could spare. Keeble also accompanied Campbell during some of his evangelistic forays throughout middle Tennessee, and on these occasions he sometimes received opportunities to speak. Keeble later adopted this same practice with young black men, "boy preachers" they were often called, whose parents wanted something more than what fledgling black schools or cotton fields could offer. By 1916 Keeble was submitting reports to the *Gospel Advocate* and steadily gaining popularity for his oratorical skills. In that year alone, he traveled over seven thousand miles, delivered over three hundred sermons, and baptized more than one hundred people.[18]

By the 1920s, Keeble caught the attention of some wealthier whites in Churches of Christ who wanted to support him. In particular, A. M. Burton, who made a fortune with his Life and Casualty Insurance Company in Nashville, began financing some of Keeble's activities. Burton relished some of the prestige that came with the association. "I certainly would like for you to know him," Burton once wrote to a friend. "He is one of the most wonderful characters, white or black, that I have ever known." To this same friend, Burton bragged that Keeble had "baptized over fifteen thousand people," an exaggeration, perhaps, but a claim in which Burton felt some responsibility. For whites like Burton, Keeble was a sound investment in their paternal hopes of improving the general well-being of blacks while also advancing their evangelistic goals of recruiting more people into the church. He was their contribution to domestic missions and their absolution for racial discrimination. At the same time, Keeble occasionally served as a source of entertainment in an era when such distractions were not readily available to most people. His disarming style and penchant for down-home parables were amusing in ways that could invite ridicule, especially from whites. While many people certainly learned something about the Bible and Christian primitivism or found comfort in his sermons—he did convert thousands of blacks *and* whites over the course of his ministry—others viewed him with condescension, as a black man of slight stature who could amuse people with his biblical knowledge, wit, and folk wisdom.[19]

Yet Keeble's popularity among whites in Churches of Christ contained subtle, if unintentional, challenges to Jim Crow. A sizable number of blacks and whites attended Keeble's revivals, although the expressed purpose for his visits was usually to start or grow a black church (fig. 2). Assemblies were usually segregated but, from the perspective of an outsider who was unfamiliar with Churches of Christ or Keeble, a gathering of blacks and whites to hear a black preacher could easily give the appearance of "race mixing," a potentially dangerous taboo. The resurgence of the Ku Klux Klan coincided with Keeble's rising popularity within Churches of Christ in the 1920s, and the Klan threatened Keeble's revivals on several occasions. Klansmen interrupted one of his sermons during a 1926 revival in rural Georgia and forced him to read a note that stated, "The Ku Klux Klan stands for white supremacy. Be governed accordingly." In Jacksonville, Florida, the Klan appeared at one of Keeble's revivals and forced all of the whites in the audience to leave. He received written threats of physical violence during a trek through Alabama. During the altar call at a 1939 revival in northwestern Tennessee, a white man pretended to respond to the sermon before attacking Keeble with brass knuckles. Keeble exhibited tremendous resolve in the face of such adversity and, on this occasion, observers described how he literally turned the other cheek before his assailant was stopped. Keeble refused to press charges, despite attempts by local whites to persuade him otherwise. Conflicts with the Klan appeared to have no effect on Keeble. He continued to preach each night until the revival's scheduled conclusion, and he returned to locales where he had previously been threatened. At the very least,

FIGURE 2. Marshall Keeble frequently preached to predominantly white audiences, like this one in Abilene, Texas, in 1950.
Jack Beard Collection, 1950, Center for Restoration Studies MS #207, Abilene Christian University Special Collections and Archives.

these instances showed that Keeble's activities threatened the values that the Klan cherished during the interwar period. While he did not openly espouse an end to segregation, Keeble's stoicism in the face of white intimidation and violence revealed his faith, determination, and discipline, traits that also characterized later civil rights activists who practiced nonviolent direct action. Had he belonged to another denomination, Keeble would have been an ideal soldier in a nonviolent army, but his affiliation with Churches of Christ largely prohibited such activism.[20]

Thus Keeble's interactions with whites spanned a wide range of experiences. His resolute focus on preaching and converting people to the primitivism of Churches of Christ best explains most of his interactions with whites, although financial considerations inevitably affected these relationships. Keeble was comfortable working alongside whites, as he often did during revivals when he preached and a white song leader directed attendees in a cappella hymns. He was often invited into communities by white churches who wanted to help the local black Church of Christ or establish a Church of Christ for blacks in their cities. Keeble accepted these invitations because of the shared mission and notwithstanding any humiliation or discrimination he anticipated or endured. In some instances, Keeble even baptized whites, although shared spaces by blacks and whites in water, namely "mixed swimming," provoked riots in some parts of the country. In a 1931 letter written from Florida to Benton Cordell (B. C.) Goodpasture, the editor of the *Gospel Advocate*, Keeble stated, "I haven't kept count of how many white people I have converted, but I am sure it would be around 800 or more, and some have demanded that I baptize them. . . . I would always ask the white brethren should I do it, and they have always said go ahead, if they want you to." Keeble clearly deferred to "the white brethren" when confronted with the possibility of baptizing whites, but his deference did not diminish the profound implications of what transpired. Churches of Christ believed that a person is saved at the moment of a baptism that always occurred by full immersion. A person's baptism was a new beginning that marked a transformation in a person's life. White converts asking Keeble to conduct their baptisms indicated their high regard for him and the profound influence of his message upon them. Keeble issued similar reports about locations throughout the South where his revivals attracted thousands of people, and whites in Churches of Christ issued effusive praise. One white minister from Birmingham proclaimed, "Those who come into the church under the preaching of Brother Keeble do not come in thinking that they are just swapping denominations, but they come in knowing and believing that the church of Christ is the only church that offers salvation to the world."[21]

Keeble's witty, plainspoken, and combative style of addressing preachers from other denominations who came to hear him both charmed his audiences and won more people to his way of thinking. About one revival, Keeble wrote, "I intended to close here last night, but twenty-one came forward, and the white brethren begged me to remain. . . . The brethren both white and colored are rejoicing, saying they [have] never seen it on this order. . . . before the invitation was given a Methodist Presiding Elder attacked the Doctrine, and in five minutes I had him fixed. this [sic] great number came almost running over each other. God's Kingdom is spreading, and he is being Glorified." This disposition toward other denominations was characteristic of black and white Churches of Christ, as they were generally convinced that their biblical interpretations and worship practices were not just correct, but that the denominations were often wrong and therefore sinful and outside of God's favor. This attitude sometimes loosened inhibitions that black preachers might otherwise have had toward whites from other denominations. For example, some black members reported to the *Christian Echo* that, during a 1939 revival in Kansas City, Missouri, a "white Pentecostal preacher raised up and rared [sic] a little, but we soon had him tied with the Word of God." This perspective also precipitated cooperation between black and white preachers who felt that they were fighting the same battles. They believed part of their calling as preachers was to defeat leaders from other denominations in debates. When a black Church of Christ preacher in Texas reported on his pneumatology debate with two Church of God in Christ pastors, he noted that the hostile audience included "two church of Christ brethren[,] . . . one colored and one white."[22]

As Keeble gained fame for his homiletic prowess and hundreds of converts, G. P. Bowser worked primarily as a journalist and educator. His personal background fueled his drive to educate black preachers and congregants. Bowser was born in 1874 and, while growing up in Nashville, Tennessee, he attended Walden University, a Freedmen's Aid school originally founded by the Methodist Church. In the course of his education, Bowser studied Greek, Hebrew, French, German, and Latin, in addition to Methodist doctrine. At eighteen years old, he was licensed to preach and, three years later, Bowser was appointed as pastor of a church in Cleveland, Tennessee. The burdens of pastoral duties and a meager income were overwhelming, however, and he soon returned to Nashville, where he met Alexander Campbell and Samuel Womack. Under their tutelage, Bowser underwent a spiritual transformation that concluded with his eager embrace of Churches of Christ and their devotion to restorationist ideals. Bowser now dedicated himself to evangelism, only to discover that he was sometimes the only person at a revival or church meeting who could read. In stark contrast to Methodists, Churches of Christ had no abundance of teaching materials, so he decided to create the *Christian Echo* and establish a new school.[23]

Work on the latter proceeded unevenly during the first half of the twentieth century, in part because Bowser's relationships with whites within Churches of Christ were sometimes contentious. He did not curry favor as Keeble did, but he sometimes accepted white patronage. "I don't like to complain to anyone concerning my condition," Bowser once explained. "I always like to do all I can to help myself and then if I see that I can't make it, I believe I would be justified in asking someone else to help me." Bowser's fierce independence was also evident in his rejection of southern racial mores. In 1920 he was invited to teach Bible and serve as principal of a new school in Nashville for blacks. The white superintendent wanted to enforce the custom of having blacks enter the back door of the school. According to one Bowser biographer, the superintendent "insisted that the support of whites demanded the practice, and he would be ashamed if his friends came and saw it otherwise. Bowser said it was a black school and he would not subject the pupils to such indignity in their own school." Bowser left within a week and, six weeks into its first term, the school was forced to close because students shared, or were perhaps inspired by, his disgust. They chose to quit rather than follow this degrading custom. One of the students who left was sixteen-year-old Richard Nathaniel (R. N.) Hogan, a Bowser protégé who would later become an outspoken critic of racism within Churches of Christ, particularly the refusal of church colleges to grant admission to blacks.[24]

Although Bowser and Keeble exhibited different degrees of tolerance for Jim Crow, they shared the theological outlook of Churches of Christ. Their popularity showed that the zeal for restorationism and the exclusive disposition toward other denominations characterized black Churches of Christ like their white counterparts. Keeble spared no one in his attacks on other Christian denominations, but he most often blasted the Baptists and Methodists that dominated the religious landscape across the South. Keeble additionally expressed disdain for overly demonstrative preachers from any church, particularly those who reinforced the stereotype of black churches as emotionally charged but intellectually stunted. In a sermon aptly titled "Been to Worship, But Wrong," Keeble emphasized how well-meaning people might attend church every Sunday, but their actions might not be acceptable to God. "You have been taught to believe that you have got to go through some great excitement and emotionalism in order to become a child of God," he warned his listeners during a 1931 revival in Valdosta, Georgia. "I am of the opinion and belief that the more of the word of God you get in you, the less emotionalism, and the more of the word of God you get in you, the less excitement." During an era when the charismatic activities of Pentecostal churches were becoming more widespread, he urged everyone to "think of the person who claims to be in possession of the Holy Ghost such that it takes two or three members to hold him. . . . Has God got a wild Holy Ghost?"[25]

The same sermon also singled out Baptists and Methodists. Keeble employed a favorite rhetorical strategy of inserting modern figures into biblical narratives. After recounting the story of the conversion and baptism of an Ethiopian eunuch by the apostle Philip, Keeble said, "I know Philip wasn't a Methodist preacher. If he had been, he would have asked the eunuch how he wanted to be baptized. He would have said 'Yes Sir, Now we have got three kinds, what kind do you want?' . . . Jesus never authorized three modes of baptism and the baptism my Bible talks about is found in Romans 6:4." Listeners might have turned their Bibles to this verse to see baptism compared to a burial, as Keeble was insisting that full immersion was the only proper method of baptism.[26] Keeble then turned to the Baptists for criticism. "Brother Baptist has been buried, but he is worse off than Brother Methodist because, after he got buried and wringing wet with water, he doesn't know what it's for. Went off and got wringing wet and don't know what it was for. There is not a Baptist in this town, from the preachers on down, can tell you what he was baptized for, scripturally." Churches of Christ taught that baptism was the final, necessary step to a person's salvation, while Baptists generally taught that salvation occurred when a person believed and confessed that Jesus was the son of God and savior of the world. Like all other Church of Christ preachers, Keeble insisted that baptism was the culminating moment when a person was actually saved. He told his audience that the apostle Philip was not Baptist either because otherwise, he would have had "to carry the man to the church, hear his testimony and let him be voted on."[27]

Bowser's theological credentials among Churches of Christ matched Keeble. In a sermon titled "Which Way?" for example, Bowser described various Christian denominations as forks in the road that a traveler must avoid. Catholics, Episcopalians, Methodists, Baptists, Presbyterians, and Adventists were all named, alongside one or two of their doctrines that Bowser found erroneous. Other denominations were listed, too, but Bowser noted that none "can prove their identity with the apostolic times." In answer to the question in his sermon's title, Bowser concluded that there was only one way, "only one safe course." He suggested, "Take the guide Book, the New Testament. Find out from it what Church the Lord built; How to become a member of it; How to worship acceptably therein." Where some preachers left implications, Bowser was explicit: "Honestly, the Church of Christ is that True Church. If you will Repent and be baptized, God will forgive your sins and add you to that Church." Like Keeble, the themes of primitivism and exclusivism pervaded many of Bowser's sermons. On another occasion, he exhorted his audience to understand that the "church of Christ is the only sanctified church, as we are the only people that have the whole truth, nothing but the Truth, so help me God." In another homily, "The Evils of Denominations," Bowser asked, "Does it not look reasonable that had God wanted all, or any of these denominations, He would have mentioned them in the book divine[?]" Another sermon, "The Way That Is Right and Cannot Be Wrong," detailed how Churches of Christ were the only church that followed the New Testament pattern for faith and practice. Perhaps an amateur poet best captured the aura of a Bowser sermon when he wrote,

One night in his hand the Bible he took
And to all he did tell
If you don't obey this book! book! book!
You will die and go to hell.[28]

This exclusivism and the rhetoric of restorationism functioned as the glue that held many black and white relationships together within Churches of Christ, relationships that would have been otherwise inconceivable, especially in the South. While Keeble was exceedingly popular among whites as well as blacks, he was neither the only black preacher whom whites wanted to hear, nor was he the only one who sought their beneficence. The *Christian Echo* included numerous vignettes that mentioned regular interactions between blacks and whites across the United States and further evidence of a shared religious outlook. Discussions of political equality or social justice were largely absent, but authors occasionally condemned racism more forcefully and persuasively than their white counterparts in Sunday school literature, for example. Like other prominent periodicals within Churches of Christ, the *Christian Echo* was primarily occupied with indoctrinating its readers, not dismantling segregation.

Almost every issue included a section titled "The Outlook" in which reporters at Churches of Christ across the United States were given space to share news from their local churches. Numerous reports relayed how whites attended the revivals of black churches or religious debates between black preachers. These accounts often described how whites assisted black churches in their efforts to evangelize their communities. Even in Deep South cities such as Montgomery, Alabama, a debate between a black Church of Christ preacher and a black Church of God preacher would be "well attended by both colored and white," according to the *Christian Echo.* Black women frequently served as reporters to the *Christian Echo,* and they also shared in this tenuous interracial dynamic, such as a women's Bible class in Dallas, Texas, that was taught by both black and white women. Serving as amateur journalists or teaching a women's class were two of the few ways that women could actively engage a larger audience in a denomination that strictly prohibited them from serving as preachers or holding formal titles like deacon or elder.[29]

Samuel Robert Cassius's son, A. L. Cassius, became a popular evangelist in Texas, where his revivals were often hosted by white churches. Bowser's protégé, R. N. Hogan, received widespread support from whites. In 1938 a white law student at Pepperdine College in Los Angeles, California, was converted by Hogan and decided to become a preacher. In the following year, black churches in Los Angeles invited Hogan to hold a two-week revival, at which time three people, two black and one white, were converted or restored to fellowship. A black preacher named F. A. Livingston conducted several revivals throughout Texas in 1939, including one in Vernon where he was specifically invited by a white church. Livingston's report to the *Christian Echo* offered extensive praise for the assistance from whites in Abilene, who provided a meeting place for the revival and helped lead the singing. While he preached in Lubbock, thirteen people were converted, eleven black and two white. "We thank God for the great work that is being done throughout the state by the white disciples to help my race in this great work," Livingston wrote. His venture into New Mexico yielded six baptisms, five of whom were white. Seventy-eight people, nearly half of them white, responded to Hogan's preaching in a 1940 revival in Bakersfield, California. A white man "walked out and obeyed the gospel" during a 1942 revival at a black church in Montgomery, Alabama. In fact the *Christian Echo* includes reports of revivals with numerous black preachers in Alabama, Arkansas, Florida, Mississippi, Tennessee, Texas, and a host of locations outside of the South that were well attended by blacks and whites.[30]

Discerning the scope of these relationships requires a bit of imagination, but clues exist in a number of these reports. Relationships between black and white churches sometimes included certain caveats, instances when paternalism outweighed shared theological visions, particularly when a white church provided financial assistance to a black church. For example, white churches in Oklahoma City sponsored a 1938 revival that featured R. N. Hogan and J. S. Winston, another popular black preacher and former student of G. P. Bowser. The purpose of the revival was the creation of a new church and, within two years, a vibrant congregation of over one hundred blacks met regularly on the 1400 block of Seventh Street in Oklahoma City. However, the white churches who initiated this evangelistic effort chose the new preacher, a black man named Walter Weathers, and they convinced a local white church leader to work with Weathers. Although he would later become one of the fiercest critics of racism within Churches of Christ, Hogan accepted this arrangement and expressed only praise for these white churches. "The white churches did not stop there," Hogan wrote of Weathers's hiring. "The Capitol Hill congregation (white) therefore, sacrificed one of their best Elders to help with the Colored work. . . . This is one of the finest Christian couples that I ever had the privilege of meeting. . . . [They] told me, and I quote: 'We wouldn't take anything for our work among the colored people here, they are a fine group of people.'" Hogan continued to support this church by holding revivals there in subsequent years and, according to one member there, "The white disciples manifested great interest by attending in large numbers."[31]

Of course Weathers may well have been an excellent choice and may have had previous connections to the white church. The new black church may have approved the final decision and may have requested the presence of a white leader to assist them as they stabilized and grew. The sources simply do not say. But the strict congregational autonomy that was so characteristic of Churches of Christ was sometimes supplanted by a paternalistic impulse, such as this arrangement suggests. A more direct example unfolded in the summer of 1943, when doubts arose concerning the reputation of a black preacher in Fayetteville, Arkansas, the elders of the Center Street Church of Christ—the local white church that helped support his congregation—met and discussed the situation. Some had alleged that the preacher, known only in church minutes as Brother Hall or H. Hall, drank alcoholic beverages, incurred heavy debts, and spoke disparagingly of the white church. The Center Street church elders then invited him to their next meeting, at which time they questioned him about these accusations. According to the meeting minutes, Hall summarily denied the drinking charge but acknowledged some personal debts and negative statements about the white church. The white elders agreed "to notify Hall that he must satisfy the officers of this congregation relative to the accusations circulated against him and make some amends for the past. Otherwise the elders felt it just to notify the congregations in surrounding communities as to their attitude concerning him." By the end of the summer, the elders followed through with their threat. "Thought we should go ahead with the charges of drinking, bad debts, and false reports against the Fayetteville congregation by H. Hall, colored preacher," the minutes explained. "This letter [is] to be written and signed by the elders of the congregation." Available evidence does not reveal the veracity of their claims against Hall but, by simply monitoring his personal behavior, these white elders asserted control over his church and their investment. By circulating a letter that warned other churches about him, they practically commanded the authority to determine his employment as a preacher in that region.[32]

Paternalistic relationships were pervasive among black and white Churches of Christ. Contrary to what David Lipscomb proffered, before the mid-1960s little or no thought seems to have been given, at least not consistently, to maintaining one, integrated church in any given community, despite an ardent belief that only members of Churches of Christ were counted among the saved. Therefore, whites who wanted to evangelize among blacks in their communities invariably sought to create a separate church. To some extent, black churches complied with this arrangement because it benefited everyone. Both blacks and whites understood this strategy as a way to save the most souls. One could not waste time bickering over the particulars of segregation or church polity when so many people, including Baptists and Methodists, were in eternal jeopardy! Meanwhile, as a relative upstart, Churches of Christ rarely had the wealth that may have been available to older, more established denominations. Blacks and whites built and relied on networks of churches to organize gospel meetings, construct new buildings, or print and disseminate religious literature. Black southerners, in particular, often needed financial assistance to build their own churches. They accepted assistance from whites to meet their own goals, even as they often had to endure the meddling that might be attached to white beneficence. At the same time, black churches certainly did not rely solely on whites for financial support. Their members gave what they could and, when that amount was not enough, they looked for other readily available sources. Therefore both theology and economics, along with racial stereotypes, explained why blacks and whites frequently interacted but still maintained segregated churches. Racial and religious identities and ideologies remained dynamic in this context.

Skeptics might reasonably argue that theology and economics merely served as a cover for whites who simply did not want to associate with blacks. This argument undoubtedly held true in many instances, but letters to the *Christian Echo* from the 1940s suggest that relationships between black and white churches sometimes defied this pattern. A black preacher named R. E. Holt described his experiences in Springfield, Illinois, "a hard field" made easier by the support of a local white church. "The white brethren help us some," he wrote. On one occasion, the "white minister came over with his congregation and we had a grand time." A similar sentiment was expressed by a woman named Berthina Martin from Oakland, California, when she wrote, "We enjoyed immensely the presence of our white disciples. . . . It is always encouraging to have our white disciples because it shows a step toward friendly racial relationship." Martin also eulogized an elderly white woman with remarks that complicated notions of white paternalism. "Our hearts are heavy because of the loss of our white Sister Larimore. She did much to make it possible for us to have this building in Oakland, in order that we might worship God. I trust that she will be one in that number we read about in Matt. 25:34," a quotation from Jesus that says, "Then shall the King say unto them on his right hand, Come, ye blessed of my Father, inherit the kingdom prepared for you from the foundation of the world" (KJV). A black man from Nashville, Tennessee, thanked blacks and whites from area churches who "assisted me in the expense of my wife's operation." A black soldier stationed in tiny Walnut Ridge, Arkansas, explained how there were few blacks in the area and not "any colored members within thirty miles of here. But there is a very nice white congregation here though. I attend their services frequently." This latter example is particularly significant because it illustrates that a critical mass of blacks was usually necessary before an evangelistic effort would be made to establish a separate black church. Otherwise a few black members might be found in white churches.[33]

Smaller black churches sometimes sought the camaraderie of larger white churches, too. A black church forty miles north of Abilene, Texas, reported to the Christian Echo, "We are doing fine, have no regular minister but the whites are so nice to us; some of them meet with us each Lord's day. Their minister preaches for us. They seem to be willing to do all they can for us." G. P. Bowser, whose fierce independence from whites had been made abundantly clear through the years, heaped similar praise upon a white church and its minister in Jonesboro, Arkansas, where he was invited to preach a revival in 1943. "I seldom meet a body of white disciples to cooperate more freely. Brother Gussie Lambert, their minister is a genuine Christian worker. Through him a piece of property was bought for the colored worship." Bowser was so enamored with Lambert that he subsequently invited him to write articles for the Christian Echo. One of Lambert's essays, "Baptist Doctrine in the Light of Truth," illustrated how Christian primitivism and sectarianism were such binding forces among blacks and whites in Churches of Christ. Members found common ground in their restorationist theologies and their drive to expose the shortcomings of other denominations.[34]

While whites initiated evangelistic endeavors that would create black churches, they were not exclusively responsible for their creation. For a variety of reasons, blacks sometimes wanted to establish their own churches, and more effective evangelism usually figured prominently in that decision. In 1940 the black members of a predominantly white church in Manhattan,

New York, broke away to form a new church in Harlem. Paul English, who wanted to preach and saw Harlem as a significant mission field, first proposed the idea. He was a diligent worker who "walked the streets of New York by day and night finding members of the church who had moved there from other parts of the country. Every time he found one he heard of two or three others." While the stated purpose was evangelism, this account suggests that simply finding and organizing black members of Churches of Christ was a high priority. Many were recent migrants from the South. The black members who already belonged to the Manhattan church had joined within the last six years. The idea of a separate church apparently won consensus, and whites identified a person who "would keep in touch with the mission and help Brother English in any way he might need help." Whites from the Manhattan church shared their weekly financial collections with the new Harlem church, and two white churches helped pay English's salary. But the account in the *Christian Echo* also emphasized how the new church enjoyed a measure of independence in that the "Harlem congregation handles its own money affairs." They paid the rent and incidental costs while the white churches paid English. In this instance, the presence and mission of a new church outweighed any theological significance that one fully integrated church might represent.[35]

More typical was a story recounted by G. P. Bowser in 1947 about his visit to Benton Harbor on the eastern shore of Lake Michigan. Bowser was invited "by the white Church of Christ for a tent meeting among my people." The church had one black member, but Bowser reported, "Four others were soon found and lined up with the work. Indications are that there will be a regular worship among the colored . . . after this meeting." A woman from Springfield, Ohio, spoke of a similar situation. "My husband is not a member of the body, but I believe he would be if there was a colored congregation here. There is a small white congregation," she continued. "I attend with them each Lord's day, and also Bible study each Wednesday evening." Perhaps most remarkable, if exceptional, was the creation of the Smyrna Church of Christ in Germantown, Tennessee, just outside of Memphis. The church was composed exclusively of black women. Without the presence of a man, an elder from a nearby church granted Annie Tuggle "permission to conduct our services since our congregation was composed of women only. . . . I made friends with several white Christians in Memphis . . . and they helped wonderfully in every way they could. We advanced to the point that through the help of others we had a gospel meeting and one of the white preachers from Memphis did the preaching." This complicated vignette also showed how Tuggle challenged normative gender roles by conducting services but succumbed to them by gaining permission and having a man preach the revival.[36]

A similar scenario transpired in Tuscaloosa, Alabama, where an elderly black woman named Joanna Shackelford moved from Montgomery in 1948. Shackelford's health was failing, so she moved in order to live closer to her daughter but quickly discovered that "there was not a Church of Christ for the colored people there." With no other option, Shackelford attended the white church where the people "always made her feel welcome." Nevertheless, she eventually approached the church's elders about starting another church for blacks. Shackelford's eulogy in the *Christian Echo* said, "Her plea to them was to establish a congregation for her people because they needed to be saved, too." The white church followed her suggestion. They invited a black preacher to conduct a revival where fifteen people were baptized. Along with Shackelford, they formed the nucleus of a new black church, and "white people aided them in building a very nice meeting house." Upon her death nine years later, both blacks and whites attended Shackelford's funeral and fondly remembered her. Several preachers spoke, including the local white preacher, who "concluded by saying that all the colored people that have been saved and that may be saved in the vicinity is a result of the effort and faithful work of this dear sister." While one might expect whites to praise a black woman for initiating a process that eventually created a separate church "for her people," this story and the white preacher's remarks were printed in the *Christian Echo*. The eulogy was written by a black woman, about a black woman.[37]

These examples show a strong degree of amiability among black and white Churches of Christ, but one could not possibly measure how characteristic these relationships were. Theological conformity among black and white Churches of Christ appears more certain, however, and this shared worldview undoubtedly eased whatever racial tensions might have otherwise arisen. The same literature was often used to instill the primitivist faith in black and white churches. Many black churches utilized the quarterly series of lessons published by the Gospel Advocate Company, and the *Christian Echo* frequently ran advertisements for books about church doctrine that were authored by prominent white preachers. Subscribers could order collections of sermons by black and white preachers or transcripts of religious debates. The *Christian Echo* occasionally included advertisements for other periodicals, including the *Christian Chronicle*, the primary news source within the denomination. In 1959 the *Christian Echo* urged churches to develop their own libraries and recommended books by several authors, including such disparate figures as David Lipscomb and Foy Wallace, the latter known in part for his staunch belief in racial segregation. Through these various formats, both black and white Churches of Christ participated in the same studies, imbibed the same ideas about restorationism, and largely reached the same conclusions about their own sectarian faith.[38]

Like Bowser and Keeble, the *Christian Echo* left little to implication. A 1949 issue included an illustration of how denominations originated with Satan (fig. 3). Below the bold title "'SECTS OF PERDITION' 2 PET. 2:1," a drawing of a

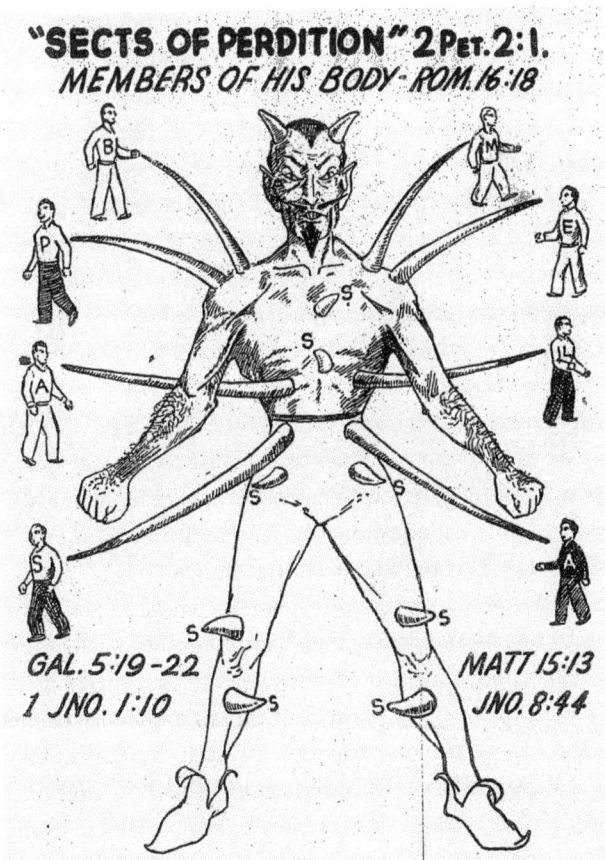

"SECTS OF PERDITION" 2 PET. 2:1.
MEMBERS OF HIS BODY- ROM. 16:18

GAL. 5:19-22
1 JNO. 1:10

MATT 15:13
JNO. 8:44

FIGURE 3. Churches of Christ suggested that denominational divisions, or sects (S), originated with the devil, including Baptists (B), Methodists (M), Presbyterians (P), Episcopalians (E), atheists (A), Lutherans (L), and agnostics (A).
Christian Echo, *1949.*

devil appears, complete with two horns and a goatee. Tentacles extend from the devil's body, and each one represents a different "sect," or denomination, such as Baptists or Methodists. Second Peter 2:1 speaks of "false prophets" and "false teachers among you, who privily shall bring in damnable heresies, even denying the Lord that bought them, and bring upon themselves swift destruction" (KJV). Other biblical citations were just as inflammatory, including one from the Gospel of John: "Ye are of your father the devil, and the lusts of your father ye will do. He was a murderer from the beginning, and abode not in the truth, because there is no truth in him. When he speaketh a lie, he speaketh of his own: for he is a liar, and the father of it" (KJV). When a Baptist preacher once accused the *Christian Echo* of acting like Churches of Christ had a monopoly on God, a prominent black Church of Christ preacher gladly accepted the accusation, explaining that "denominations . . . have neither God nor Christ. The Church of Christ . . . assembles by Christ's authority and worships according to the New Testament pattern. And just so long as the church abides in the teaching of Christ it will keep that monopoly on God and Christ." R. N. Hogan, who followed Bowser as editor of the *Christian Echo*, dedicated an entire issue to the "New Testament Church" in the spring of 1956, wherein he stated the purpose in an editorial. "It is the policy of the Echo to save souls for the Master's work, [and] for this reason we are dedicating this issue to The New Testament Church with the hope of causing some one who is not a member of the 'True Church' to read their Bibles." The sermons and writings of Keeble, Bowser, and Hogan show how the ideal of restoration gave way to an exclusivism that not only discounted other expressions of Christianity, but also summarily dismissed them as fiendish ploys to distract seekers from the one, true church.[39]

These theological ideas and self-perceptions subordinated racial identities, at least to the extent that one's standing as a member of the church held more long-term significance than one's skin color. These dynamics stupefied outside observers. For example, in 1961 a white Church of Christ missionary named Thomas Tune sought and received support from several black churches in California, including one in Richmond that became his primary sponsor after their elders had several meetings with Tune. The local newspaper covered the story with a blaring headline: "NEGRO CHURCH WILL SUPPORT WHITE MINISTER IN HONG KONG." The *Christian Echo* encouraged its readers to support Tune and marveled at the local newspaper's reaction. "We know that we are not interested in the man's color but that the gospel be preached," the *Christian Echo* noted. "We trust that this will help to break down some of the prejudice in our own brotherhood that prevails among our caucasian [sic] brethren. May God help us all to look at a man for what he is rather than his nationality." Tune had been active in breaking down "the racial prejudice that exists among churches," and the *Christian Echo* gladly published his missionary reports from Hong Kong.[40]

Despite these examples of interracial cooperation, Churches of Christ still functioned within a wider culture that usually set distinct parameters that governed interracial encounters of all kinds. Individuals and churches might occasionally cross these boundaries, but only in the name of evangelism and never as a concerted challenge to the white supremacy that pervaded the United States. Churches of Christ or their colleges typically hosted lectureships in the South, where the laws of segregation slighted the spirit of the proceedings. Blacks were usually welcome and often attended, but they also suffered the stigma of segregated seating, confined to the balcony of the auditorium at DLC, for example. With the exception of Marshall Keeble, black preachers were rarely invited to speak at these events. By the middle of the 1940s, when integration was frequently the primary aim of civil rights organizations, black preachers established lectureships separate from their white counterparts.

Outside of the *Christian Echo*, blacks did not have an institutional entity or annual event around which they could rally for mutual edification, the exchange of ideas, or networking. Although the Nashville Christian Institute (NCI), a new grade school for blacks, was founded in 1940, its reunions would only serve these purposes in future decades. To compensate for their general exclusion, black Churches of Christ created their own annual lectureship, and the *Christian Echo* heralded its arrival in 1945 with a large photograph on its front page that included all of the attendees. Bowser was seated in the middle of the first row. "First Lectureship Meeting of the Colored Brethren" was scrawled across the bottom of the photograph, and the event was deemed a success. In 1952 black Churches of Christ initiated a youth forum where young people considered topics ranging from church doctrine to courtship and marriage. By the close of the decade, hundreds of young people attended a conference that now lasted several days. These endeavors were compelled by necessity more than separatism, and they showed how aloof Churches of Christ were from the broader agendas of mainline civil rights organizations, especially with regard to integration. As integration became more respectable in the coming years, black and white Churches of Christ ironically grew further apart.[41]

Instances of interracial cooperation and a shared theological outlook among Churches of Christ did not prevent blacks from chastising whites about racial discrimination, especially as the issue became prominent across the United States in the postwar era, but Church of Christ sectarianism did keep blacks from overtly endorsing the civil rights movement or associating with black pastors who served as some of the movement's leaders. Critiques of racism became more frequent and urgent in the *Christian Echo* after the Supreme Court's 1954 decision in *Brown v. Board of Education of Topeka, Kansas,* and references to the cooperation of white churches gradually decreased. Several black preachers commented in the *Christian Echo*. G. P. Holt described an encounter with a white preacher who claimed that "the members of the church of Christ would not stand for" school integration. Holt pointed out that he did not speak for Churches of Christ, a point conceded before the white preacher clarified that the church where he preached would not accept it. "Now is it not clear," Holt inquired, "where the trouble is where he preaches? It is not the church, but him, and he is trying to speak for everyone." Holt believed that racial prejudice was a learned behavior that conversion to Christianity should change, so he questioned whether anyone who expressed support for segregation could really be considered a Christian. This position was similar to that of A. L. Cassius, who asked, "Are we to allow the denominational churches of the world to prove their belief in and acceptance of the love and tolerance of Christ by the dropping of racial barriers within their churches, while we, ensnarled by apathy and indolence, do nothing? . . . Time is far spent and the day of reckoning draws near," he warned. A few months later, Holt again speculated, "God will do some segregating [between the saved and unsaved] and this should make a member of the Church both black and white feel right at home as they have practiced it [racial segregation] all along which is one of the most damnable curses of the church today."[42]

Holt and Cassius were two of several contributors to the *Christian Echo* who broached race relations in Churches of Christ, but R. N. Hogan issued the most prolonged and thorough critiques. Hogan's consternation was immutable in a series of editorials during the late 1950s and early 1960s, years that corresponded to increased civil rights activism across the country. The biblical literalism and primitivism that characterized the denomination as a whole also informed his writing on race. Hogan frequently employed the peculiar hermeneutic used by Churches of Christ against whites who resisted desegregation. A 1959 editorial began by observing that "most of our Brethren who are in high places in the church of our Lord, are going to lose their souls because they are respecters of persons." Hogan was angry that some white churches prohibited blacks or relegated them to "the basement, balcony or a dressing room," but he was especially appalled that racial discrimination persisted at the "so-called christian [sic] schools." Administrators had previously hidden behind the law but, by the time this editorial was published in June 1959, the Supreme Court's rulings against segregation in higher education were about ten years old. Hogan noted how "our government has informed the entire country that the practice of segregation because of race or color is unconstitutional. But christians [sic] shouldn't have to be told that." As he discussed Church of Christ colleges, Hogan inserted question marks into his text around the term "Christian," suggesting that he questioned the credentials of a nominally Christian college that excluded blacks. "The fact that Negroes are not allowed in these churches and schools is proof that God is not there; for where God is, no man is barred because of the color of his skin. Brethren, you may fallout with me because of this article, but you know that I am telling the truth and those guilty will do well to repent." A few months later, Hogan responded to the idea, popular among whites, that changes should be gradual and not forced. He exclaimed, "I think it is a terrible thing to tell people to take their time in obeying God. Take their time in repenting of their sins. Just as well to tell a man who has been in Baptist, Methodist or other denominational churches all of his life to take his time in coming out of that human institution."[43]

Charles Cannon, a white subscriber to the *Christian Echo* from southwest Arkansas, responded to Hogan's laments. His remarks showed how the Bible was a battleground for people who disagreed over providential intentions with regard to racial segregation. Cannon quoted Acts 17:26, "[God] hath made of one blood all nations of men for to dwell on all the face of the earth, and hath determined the times before appointed, and the bounds of their habitation" (KJV). Ironically, both segregationists and integrationists utilized the verse in a battle over biblical justification and authority for their respective positions. The latter noted that humans were "of one blood," while segregationists emphasized that God had prescribed boundaries for various peoples of the earth. Hogan responded in kind to what he called Cannon's "ridiculous arguments." He acknowledged that whites had helped blacks in a variety of ways, but this help was "nothing to brag about" because God commanded Christians to help each other. He also questioned how Cannon could speak of "their churches," a misnomer among the exclusivist Churches of Christ, and he cited a letter in his possession about "a sister who lives in a town that [has] two congregations of so-called White churches of Christ, but she is not welcome at either." Hogan concluded his rebuttal with an appeal: "I sincerely pray that my brethren, both White and Colored, will soon rid their hearts of hate, prejudice and pride and be satisfied with being simple New Testament christians, for regardless of the color of the skin, we are in the same kingdom, subject to the same King. Let's stop referring to other races as your brethren and to our own race as my brethren. Regardless of the race, if we are in Christ, we are all brethren."[44]

Writing about the momentous changes of the 1960s, church historian Richard Hughes has noted that "one scarcely would have known of them at all if one's only source of information during the period had been the *Firm Foundation*, the *Gospel Advocate*, or almost any other media outlet related to mainstream Churches of Christ." This same observation generally applies to the *Christian Echo*. Hogan's commentaries on race relations never made specific reference to the civil rights movement or its prominent leaders. He came closest in 1963, when he asked, "Where are the Churches of Christ . . . during all of those disgraceful racial struggles in these places?" He also engaged the popular rhetoric of segregationists who resurrected the age-old argument that integration would lead to miscegenation. The "Negro isn't interested in marrying the white man's daughter any more than the white man is interested in marrying the Negro's daughter," Hogan explained, before adding, "the white man doesn't seem to have any confidence in his daughter being able to take care of herself." His acerbic verbiage reached a crescendo when he urged his black readers "to love all white people, for you will go to hell if you hate them, like some of them are going to hell for hating you." The restorationist impulse that gave blacks and whites in Churches of Christ so much in common eventually became the means by which blacks questioned the persistent racism that pervaded the denomination and established their own programs independent of whites. As other Christian denominations and the federal government exhibited signs of change, Hogan and other black commentators were astounded at the obstinacy of many of their white brothers and sisters.[45]

By the mid-1960s, black and white Churches of Christ began forging paths more separate from each other than ever. While they shared a restorationist theology, the growing economic self-sufficiency of black churches enabled them to operate independently of whites, and white churches became less interested in sustaining relationships with blacks, especially on terms that asserted black equality and power. When Church of Christ colleges were finally desegregated in the South, the token efforts to recruit black students ensured that these institutions would remain almost the exclusive domain of whites. The damage of decades past was too much for whites to acknowledge and too much for blacks to forget.

3

LET NO MAN
DESPISE THY YOUTH

College students have long wrestled with competing interests for their time. In addition to attending classes and studying, students at Church of Christ colleges were often preoccupied with their social clubs (sanitized versions of fraternities and sororities), regular jobs, or romantic pursuits, confined as they were by curfews and dorm monitors. Civil rights were never a pressing issue for more than a handful of curious or thoughtful students. At the same time, current events away from campus inevitably became topics for discussion in history or political science courses, cafeteria banter, or late-night talks in dorm rooms. These discussions occasionally spilled over into the pages of student newspapers and, as the civil rights movement gained momentum in the 1950s and 1960s, some students at Church of Christ colleges became outspoken advocates for desegregation, even as college administrators stalled. Despite its multiracial membership, Church of Christ colleges were some of the last educational institutions, public or private, to admit black students. Fascinating glimpses into the evolving attitudes about race and segregation among whites can be seen in the desegregation of these colleges, particularly among students at Abilene Christian College (ACC) in Abilene, Texas, and Harding College in Searcy, Arkansas.[1]

As administrators cultivated a measure of insularity on their campuses, news of unrest in Little Rock, Oxford, and Tuscaloosa—flash points in the struggle to desegregate schools—spurred significant discussions in Abilene and Searcy about the degrees to which Christian colleges must transform or conform to the communities in which they existed. The desegregation of Church of Christ colleges highlights three significant points about the ways in which white southerners with strong religious commitments experienced the civil rights movement. First, racial attitudes were often demarcated along generational lines that exposed and exacerbated traditional tensions between college students and administrators. The strictures of campus life—curfews, dress codes, and chapel requirements—provoked the usual give-and-take encounters between students and their supervisors. Disagreements over the proper response to the postwar black freedom struggle arose in this context, as students sought legitimacy and respect from their elders, who might easily dismiss what they considered youthful idealism. Like their unlikely counterparts in the Southern Baptist Convention, some Church of Christ students publicly advocated the desegregation of their colleges in the 1940s and 1950s. Administrators were consistently less enthusiastic about the possibility, and student efforts to bring about change were often met with hostility.[2]

Second, a close examination of these white students reaffirms that racial attitudes were not dichotomous. Their perspectives existed on a plane of ideas about race and religion that cannot be easily labeled. Even desegregation, which most white students favored, was not an either-or proposition, as those same students often wanted desegregation with certain caveats. When desegregation was understood to mean the inclusion of black students in the classroom, then students sometimes became outspoken advocates for it. But white students could support the admission of black students and simultaneously oppose blacks and whites sharing the same dormitory room. Likewise, interracial romances were generally criticized, though not explicitly forbidden, and students expressed various opinions on interracial social clubs. These gradations of racial attitudes were most evident in the context of life on a college campus. Meanwhile, instances of racially motivated violence that often marked the desegregation of public universities were summarily condemned, and no comparable violence seemed to have unfolded at any Church of Christ colleges. Thus, the process of desegregation at Church of Christ colleges and the discussions of the civil rights movement that occurred there provide compelling insights into what these whites thought about the black freedom struggle of the 1950s and 1960s.[3]

The final point involves the competing motives behind the eventual desegregation of Church of Christ colleges. These institutions likely lagged behind other denominational colleges because the absence of a governing hierarchy precluded institutional debates and summary decisions. Although college administrators undoubtedly consulted with each other, decisions about desegregation were left with individual governing boards. At the same time, and unlike many adults, students came to view desegregation in moral terms. The inclusion of black students in class was perceived as a moral choice based on scripture, and students' newfound adamancy implied that segregation was wrong or sinful. Their insistence that Christians must desegregate dishonored and sometimes shamed their older brothers and sisters in the faith who had lived with racial segregation for all of their lives. Meanwhile, limited evidence suggests that college administrators ultimately chose to desegregate their colleges for financial reasons. Once the federal government stipulated that loan-seeking institutions not practice segregation, colleges caught up in the postwar competition for new facilities and students had little choice but to capitulate. Ironically, once the colleges began to enroll black students, administrators also began to speak of desegregation as a moral choice, the only option for a truly Christian college, just as their young charges had been doing for years.

Before these institutions desegregated, blacks in Churches of Christ had few options for higher education within the denomination. Seeking to correct this shortcoming, numerous blacks and whites cooperated in the creation of the Southern Bible Institute in Fort Worth, Texas. J. S. Winston, a former student of black educator G. P. Bowser, became the school's first president, and Bowser was asked to head the Bible Department. The institute opened in the fall of 1948 but soon relocated to nearby Terrell, Texas, when the opportunity arose to purchase the land and property of a military school. After remaining closed for one year, the school reopened in the fall of 1950 as Southwestern Christian College. By this time, Bowser was over seventy years old and suffering from cancer. He once visited the new school in Terrell before dying a short time later. Despite its association with Bowser, however, until 1967 each college president was white, and through its first decade of operation, 80 percent of its financial resources came from white churches or patrons.[4]

Another option for prospective black students was Pepperdine College in Los Angeles. Because of the cost and distance from the geographical concentration of Churches of Christ in the South, Pepperdine was usually not a viable option, so black preachers would either discontinue formal studies or attend a college affiliated with another denomination. This latter option was especially difficult to accept because it required one to study "denominational doctrine" instead of the teachings of "the New Testament church." For this reason, Norman Adamson applied for admission to Harding in 1953 and was initially accepted, until administrators learned that he was black and rescinded his admission letter. Black students affected by this discrimination were unequivocal in their protests, even as they maintained their loyalty to Churches of Christ. When Ernest Holsendolph was ready for college in 1953, ACC was an unlikely possibility, so he entered Columbia University, graduated in four years, and tried to enroll in ACC as a graduate student in 1957. Upon receiving his request,

President Don Morris replied with a letter that explained how the college had no plans to desegregate and that Holsendolph should try Pepperdine. Holsendolph subsequently berated Morris for presiding over a segregated institution. "I feel a deep sense of shame," wrote Holsendolph, "that an institution which bears the name of our Lord, should be an overt proponent of such an un-Christlike practice as segregation—even as secular colleges and institutions of the South, which are ignorant of God's truth, have finally yielded to the force of moral truth!"[5]

Floyd Rose was another black student who could not fathom the contradiction. He had followed the path prescribed for him by his mentors in graduating from both NCI and SWCC. He had close connections to Marshall Keeble and had thoroughly imbibed the denomination's restorationist theology. Determined to learn more Bible and become a better preacher, Rose submitted an application to ACC. When he received a rejection letter, Rose went straight to Morris's office for an explanation. He later recalled telling him, "If my application was rejected because I'm poor, Billie Sol Estes [his NCI patron] has already made arrangements for my tuition. If it's because I'm dirty, I can wash. But if it's because I'm black, there's nothing I can do about that. God made me the way I am." Unable to send a trite reply as he had to Holsendolph, Morris fidgeted in his chair, made uncomfortable now by the very presence of a person whose life was adversely affected by the college's refusal to admit blacks. "Floyd, I'm sorry," Morris said, before stammering through an explanation of how he was operating under the constraints of the board of trustees. Unfortunately, Rose left that meeting hating the fact that he was black more than the college's discriminatory admissions policies, but his attitude soon changed. While many white students were resigned to wait for desegregation to occur at the discretion of college administrators, Rose later became representative of a younger generation of blacks in Churches of Christ who were unwilling to accept the contradictions that came with claiming to be "the New Testament church" and practicing racial discrimination.[6]

For different reasons and in separate contexts, whites were having similar epiphanies. Whites at Harding were certainly aware of such contradictions, but their benevolent work often aimed to diminish the tension. Local churches in Arkansas, like most places, were usually segregated, although black and white churches regularly cooperated in evangelistic endeavors. Likewise, Harding students were actively engaged in activities with Searcy's black Church of Christ. In 1945, the *Bison*, Harding's student newspaper, reported that the "colored congregation . . . have [sic] begun work on a building for the use of the church in any way that is needed. The white brethren are assisting in the work." Volunteers were further solicited to assist with the construction of a home that was intended for "an aged negro couple," and the *Bison* later reported the completion of the project and the students' contributions.[7]

Similar sentiments could be found at ACC. As early as 1924, the student newspaper, the *Optimist*, voiced alarm at mounting racial prejudices. Perhaps these concerns resulted from the observations of a growing Ku Klux Klan or the violence that occurred when black servicemen returned home from World War I and asserted their rights as US citizens.[8] The essay declared that the "man who comes to believe that he is superior to any other men, by reasons of conditions of birth or place of residence or citizenship under a certain government, is sadly deluded. . . . A man is a man in God's sight for his Almighty hand created every man equal. Every man has a soul to be saved." Recalling World War I, the author closed with a stern warning: "Germany once believed that she was the only government on earth, and that her's [sic] was the only people on earth who deserved the joys of life. She has fallen. America shows signs of becoming, someday, a victim to the same sort of bigotry."[9]

Following World War II, a war that included an even stronger black presence in a cause that pitted Americans against an enemy that came to personify extreme racism, students at ACC registered concerns over the nation's claims of freedom and liberty and the practices of racial discrimination that characterized the United States, particularly the South. To be sure, opinions were not unanimous. In the fall of 1945, an editorial in the *Optimist* granted that blacks should have rights but that those rights, both spiritually and politically, did not necessitate social equality or full integration of public facilities. The editor consented to having black students at ACC but opposed integrated living and eating facilities because this "would do more harm in the white students lost, than good in the negroes gained." But this editorial would be the last to espouse any form of racial segregation or gradualist approaches to equal rights. One month later, the editor was criticized for making any qualifications to Jim Crow customs. A letter to the *Optimist* argued that "[s]piritual equality, if practiced, results in equal social, economic and political liberties. To say that 'all men were created equal' and then to deny equal liberties in any of life's relationships is to admit ourselves to be either tyrannical or unthinking." The writer concluded that the enrollment of black students "in the regular classes of ACC would seem to be a step forward in the fulfilling of the high and lofty purposes for which ACC stands." Like many others to follow, this letter supported its arguments through citation of biblical passages, in this case, the willingness of Jesus to associate with a Samaritan woman in the Gospel of John and his sharing meals with social outcasts in the Gospel of Luke. Ironically, the hermeneutic principles and tools that were stressed so adamantly by Church of Christ preachers and educators often became the means by which students questioned the status quo.[10]

In the fifteen years following World War II, ACC students became more strident in their challenges to the administration's maintenance of a policy that appeared both unchristian and undemocratic. In 1946, a group of seventeen students signed a letter to the editor of the *Optimist* that utilized more direct language. "Despite all of our preaching of Christianity, we have yet to practice it. We loudly cry at the injustices of other nations. Yet, here in America, we have granted freedom to the Negro—then dared him to use it." Tired of excuses, particularly those that warned of a possible exodus of whites should blacks be admitted, these students asked, "If any students were to withdraw from this Christian school because of the entrance of colored students into the classes, would it be a division in the school, or merely a weeding-out process? How can we teach Christianity in this Christian school unless we practice it?"[11]

The following year, another letter to the editor criticized those Christians for whom "public opinion [had] usurped the place of the Scriptures." The author invoked the names of heralded church leaders from the previous century, names that were revered in Churches of Christ as the ones who had helped restore New Testament Christianity. "The power of [Alexander] Campbell, [Walter] Scott, [Barton] Stone, and all other great Christians has lain in their disdain for 'What is the customary thing,' or, 'What will folks think about us,' and n [*sic*] a complete trust in truth." Even more damning was this student's assertion that denominations like the Baptists were leading the way in making necessary reforms. His letter concluded by sarcastically noting, "Maybe all we need now is for SMU [Southern Methodist University], TCU [Texas Christian University] and Baylor to admit a few negroes, and then it will be safe for 'Us Christians' to do the same." By citing three "denominational" colleges, the author hoped to highlight the irony in maintaining an exclusivist position toward other Christian churches while practicing discrimination, which, they contended, the Christian scriptures clearly identified as sin.[12]

Following judicial desegregation orders for public schools or the voluntary desegregation of some private institutions, students at ACC and Harding questioned the persistent inaction of their administrators. When Wayland College in

Plainview, Texas, a city some two hundred miles northwest of Abilene, enrolled its first black student in 1951, the *Optimist* took note. "Now if Wayland can take such a step," one columnist wryly observed, "surely a lot of other schools in Texas and the rest of the South can, too." This particular article hastened to correct those people who asserted that blacks were already granted equal opportunities. "If you think that this is so," the author opined, "visit some Negro public schools sometimes . . . and you will have to change your mind." After emphasizing the disparities in educational opportunities for blacks and whites in both public and private institutions and admitting that some problems might arise with the desegregation of ACC, the article expressed bewilderment over the college's obstinacy in allowing students "from every race under heaven except the Negro race."[13]

These comments appeared in the wake of significant Supreme Court rulings in 1948 and 1950 that dismantled the legal basis for segregation in higher education. Like most of their public counterparts, Church of Christ colleges in the South remained segregated long after these decisions. No organized protests unfolded, but the "Christian perspective" on race relations became a matter of dire concern. Amid the Supreme Court's rulings, and in response to what the *Bison* described as "much talk on the Harding campus . . . about the subject of race distinctions," a series of editorials appeared in the student newspaper in 1949. The *Bison* noted how "there are now a few isolated instances where some students are entering colleges and universities where they had been traditionally prohibited because of the racial group to which they belong," a likely reference to the recent admission of a black student to the University of Arkansas law school. Harding students were clearly intrigued by this development and, as the editorial mentioned, students from several foreign countries were already enrolled. In the fall of 1946, the *Bison* mixed several cultural metaphors in its profile of a music major from Hong Kong but also expressed a degree of enlightenment that reached beyond "the white man's burden." "When you see a black-headed, kimonoed figure lilting across the campus," the article concluded, "that, amigos of the West is the Yellow Flower from the East. Yessir, the twain have met, in spite of what Sir Rudyard saith." White students noted the irony of accepting students from other countries but denying admission to black Americans. For white students who were coming of age and formulating their world views in an exclusively "Christian" context, this denial posed unsettling questions. The 1949 editorial further explained how geneticists could not determine distinct dividing lines between racial groups, thereby dispelling

the popular notion "that God caused the racial groups to appear." The essay decried discrimination based on racial groups, while noting the presence of such
discrimination in various regions of the country.[14]

A more compelling editorial appeared in the *Bison* on the heels of a controversy at the University of Mississippi. In September 1950, Albin Krebs, editor of the student newspaper in Oxford, set off a firestorm of protest when
he wrote that black applicants should be admitted to the Ole Miss law school
because "[p]igment of skin must have nothing to do with measure of ability."
Shortly thereafter, an estimated eight hundred students in Oxford participated
in demonstrations that called for Krebs's resignation and included a cross burning. The *Bison* described these events as disgraceful. The author challenged
students and faculty by asking what kind of reception a similar editorial might
receive if written in the *Bison*. "Here at a Christian college, founded on the
beliefs of New Testament teachings," the editor wrote, "what would student-
faculty reaction be to permitting Negro students to enroll?" The column closed
with an expression of unequivocal support for Krebs and "his stand for freedom, toleration, and anti-discrimination." Reactions to these *Bison* editorials
did not appear in print, but the essays indicate that from the late 1940s, if not
earlier, some Harding students were certainly cognizant of racial injustice and
sympathetic to desegregation.[15]

The same could be said of students at ACC. One of the more provocative instances of raising the "race question" occurred during a chapel service in 1953.
Along with offering a regular reprieve from the daily grind of studies, chapel
services at Church of Christ colleges served as proving grounds for young men
honing their skills at preaching or song leading. The opportunity to speak was a
privilege not taken lightly. From the chapel pulpit, an aspiring preacher might
envision his future as a beloved minister with many congregants in churches
yet to be constructed and with a constant flood of invitations to conduct revivals across the country. In the moment, however, speaking at chapel entailed
admonishing schoolmates, impressing Bible professors, or perhaps even attract-
ing a young lady who knew well the Pauline passages about wives submitting to
their husbands. Rarely would one waste his appearance on a social issue, much
less one dealing with people who had nothing to do with the college or one's career aspirations. One could certainly discuss race relations within the confines
of a dormitory room or around a cafeteria table. The topic might even come up
during a government class, since it was, after all, of political rather than ethical
significance to many white southerners. But the pulpit was no place to expound
on such social and political concerns.

A student named Everett Ferguson came to believe otherwise. As a product of a small southeast Texas town, he was familiar with the region's racial prejudices. So it was with no small degree of trepidation that he walked to the pulpit at the appointed time to give a brief talk simply titled, "Race Relations." With the knot in his stomach characteristic of all young preachers, he nervously began, "If there are two things I hate, it's Niggers and race prejudice." A few people in the audience must have smiled in amusement. The irony was supposed to be humorous, but Ferguson was not trying to be funny. "This expression," he continued, "which has made the rounds on the campus in the past few weeks, is, I'm sorry to say, typical of the attitude of many." With that introduction, Ferguson proceeded to chastise his listeners who had blindly succumbed to the racism and discriminatory practices of their parents, their college, and their country. With his reputation at stake, he was careful not to go too far, including remarks that legislation alone could not improve race relations. But he did offer practical advice, admonishing his audience that their Christian duty required a certain response to racial prejudice: "[A]s Christians we should be in the lead in constructive programs for Negro welfare. We can treat them as equals; we can work to see that they receive equal treatment from others; and we can teach our less enlightened parents and friends."

Some schoolmates undoubtedly disagreed with these assertions but, for the most part, everyone would have affirmed that all people, regardless of color, should be treated with the dignity and respect becoming of a Christian. Yet Ferguson's closing remarks were not so agreeable. "I look forward to the day," he concluded, "when ACC will admit Negro students—when they will sit with us in the classrooms, participate with us in extra-curricular activities, eat with us in the cafeteria, and live with us in the dormitories—not because they are forced upon us, but because we as students, faculty, and trustees have matured in outlook to the point where we can voluntarily accept them on their own merit." A *Bison* editorial from the fall of 1953 posed similar questions, after noting the admission of a black student to Louisiana State University. "Just how far are you willing to go to lower your prejudices? Are you willing to have a Negro for a roommate? Are you willing to extend membership in your social club?" the editor asked, before poignantly concluding, "Surely our sins have found us out."[16]

Ferguson's opening quip illuminates an important point about many white southerners of that era. They could express disdain for racial prejudice while honoring traditional racial boundaries and sharing explicitly racist humor. Very few perceived any contradictions. While the most abusive forms of racism, such as violence or verbal assaults, might be abhorred, a milder prejudice that accepted segregation in both principle and practice was more typical. Thus, due to various understandings of what prejudice might entail, whites could claim to dislike racial prejudice, while their actions indicated that they wanted little or no association with blacks, unless perhaps the relationship was one of employer to employee.

White college administrators who opposed desegregation personify this perspective because they claimed to support education for blacks. Many made heavy financial investments in SWCC and NCI, gave time and resources to evangelizing predominantly black communities in the United States and Africa, and participated in benevolent programs to assist in the care of black orphans and senior citizens. These actions gave credence to the claims of many that they were not prejudiced, even though the methods utilized were at times demeaning to those people whom they were trying to help. The effects of institutional racism were rarely, if ever, addressed. In contrast, when the desegregation of schools became an issue of national concern, white students at church colleges heartily embraced the concept, if not the implementation.

Essays that advocated desegregation appeared more frequently in the student newspapers at ACC and Harding in the middle of the 1950s, even as students' attitudes about race continued to reflect the pervasive influence of white supremacy. As the nation awaited the Supreme Court's *Brown* decision in the spring of 1954, the *Optimist* ran a series of letters to the editor, each one calling for ACC to desegregate. Ten students signed one letter that cited a collection of Bible verses to support their arguments and addressed some excuses that had been proffered against enrolling blacks. "When we gather at the throne of God to sing praises to His name," the letter finally asked, "will God want us any closer to His throne than the Negro? Every race on the face of the earth is permitted to attend ACC except the Negro[.] Why?" At Harding, the *Bison* printed an editorial that complimented the students on recent interactions with black visitors to campus. The college's annual fall lectureship featured black evangelist Marshall Keeble, who "spoke to a mixed crowd of Negroes and whites." A chapel speech by a member of the Bible faculty had further challenged the status quo, and a young man from SWCC had led the singing during a chapel service. The editor felt assured that positive changes were underway. "Perhaps there is still much progress to be made, but nonetheless, we believe that the students of Harding College are fast approaching that enlightened state of mind when we can accept the Negro as a full equal, no reservations retained." In the months before the *Brown* decision, only one item appeared in the *Optimist* that obliquely questioned student enthusiasm for desegregation by urging readers to integrate churches first because "worship to the Almighty is far superior to the educational aspects of life."[17]

This apparent enthusiasm belied more traditional attitudes and practices that reflected the abiding influence of white supremacy on college campuses. Like many of their counterparts in public universities, students at Church of Christ colleges frequently participated in activities or communicated in language that perpetuated racial stereotypes. For example, at Freed-Hardeman College in Henderson, Tennessee, the student newspaper, the *Skyrocket*, frequently included racist jokes. Students at all of the aforementioned colleges enjoyed minstrel shows that caricatured blacks, but they seemed to be most popular at Freed-Hardeman, where they received prominent coverage in the *Skyrocket* and remained annual events through the spring semester of 1964, just before the first black students arrived on campus. Freed-Hardeman occasionally hosted black preachers, including Marshall Keeble, but no one seemed to perceive any tension between his appearance and the annual minstrel show. One issue of the *Skyrocket* described a Keeble visit on the front page before detailing preliminary plans for the celebrated minstrel show on the third page.[18]

Social clubs at these colleges hosted banquets with "Old South" themes well into the 1960s. These events might include illustrations of black mammies on programs and menus, activities that celebrated Confederate heritage, or guest speakers who were apostles of the Lost Cause. For a time at least, the term "nigger" was used frequently and loosely, too, as the name assigned by students to a local mule at DLC in the 1930s or as Ferguson remarked, in jokes or quips that circulated around campus. The sports page of the *Bison* once suggested that some intramural teams were "discriminated against like an Alabama Nigger after [an] election." And while ACC could sermonize against racial prejudice in a 1924 editorial, four years later, minstrel caricatures decorated the college yearbook, complete with slang racial terms and poetic verses that highlighted racial stereotypes.[19]

In the wake of the *Brown* decision, student newspapers continued to instruct their readers, both implicitly and explicitly, that racial prejudice was wrong and that by implication so was segregation. On the front page of an April 1955 issue, the *Optimist* celebrated the Texas Intercollegiate Press Association's decision to invite black colleges into the organization, a step made during an annual conference that was directed by ACC's press club and held on its campus. Not only was the three-day event a success, but the *Optimist* also radiated with pride in reporting that the momentous decision was made at ACC. An editorial included details of the delegates' discussions and the near-unanimous vote. "A small agate-type page in the solving of one of the nation's greatest social problems had fluttered and turned," the editor wrote. His description appeared below a cartoon depicting two people—one black, the other white—with newspaper print for bodies shaking hands and smiling broadly (fig. 4). In all capital letters, the caption read, "NO RESPECTOR [sic] OF PERSONS."[20]

Meanwhile at Harding, the *Bison* implemented a pedagogical approach in its comments about race relations. Two pieces from October 1955 demonstrated the point. First, one student began a column by describing the slave trade and slavery, "one of the worst blots in the history of our country." He briefly mentioned the Emancipation Proclamation, "a job uncompleted," before acknowledging the legitimacy of the *Brown* decision and the Supreme Court's subsequent instructions to desegregate "with all deliberate speed." "To accept these decisions and to take necessary steps to put them into force," he believed, "would be to exhibit the truly American spirit of cooperation and understanding." Knowing that Harding was the proud home of a right-wing American studies program and the primary impetus behind annual Freedom Forums held at Church of Christ colleges, readers of the column could not have missed the point. The author went on to castigate opponents of desegregation, especially those people who associated it with communism, and to one such proponent, he asked, "Shouldn't you, as an American citizen, be decent enough to accept the decision of a court which was established to make such decisions?" Not only was integration a Christian duty, but to readers enamored by the patriotism and anticommunism preached at Harding, this writer also sought to make obedience to the courts, and therefore, desegregation, the duty of a responsible American.[21]

A second piece, recalling the recent death of Emmett Till and his murderers' acquittal, urged Harding students to take personal responsibility with regard to race relations. The essay acknowledged that no court ruling or legislation could ameliorate problems. Solutions would only come "when every individual examines his own reasoning, rids his mind of prejudice and casts aside his faulty convictions that our racial problems will end." In language that now evokes thoughts of some of the most famous speeches from the 1960s, the author opined, "We seem to think that perhaps if we will forget about the Negro he will go away and leave us alone. But he will not go away, and our problems will never end as long as people have that attitude. Almost one hundred years ago

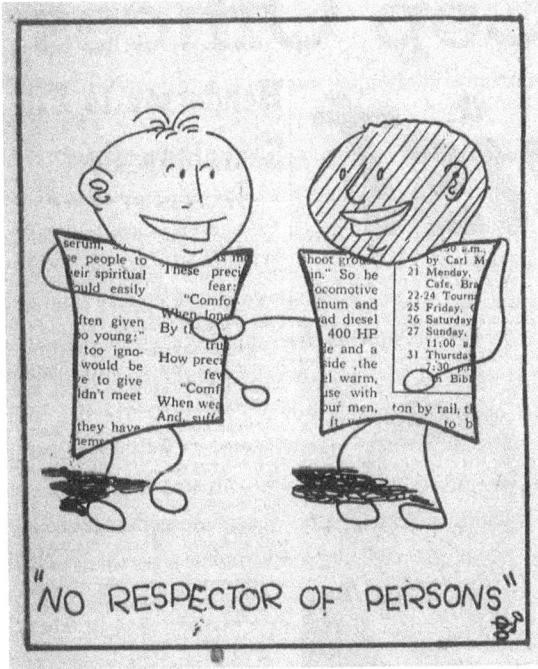

FIGURE 4. The student newspaper at Abilene Christian College published this cartoon in 1955 after the Texas Intercollegiate Press Association decided to invite black colleges into the organization.
Abilene Christian University Special Collections and Archives.

President Abraham Lincoln declared that the slaves should be freed. Although a century has passed, the Negro is still held in bondage in many ways. . . . Let us all look forward to the day when human beings are judged by something other than the color of the skin." Simple eloquence and noble aims notwithstanding, students were met with excuses from administrators who feared the financial and social implications of a decision to desegregate their colleges. Almost eight years would pass between the writing of this editorial and the admission of black students at Harding.[22]

Thus students found themselves in an increasingly awkward position. They were fiercely loyal to Churches of Christ and their educational institutions. In the minds of many students, most of whom were well versed in restorationist theology, Church of Christ colleges were the only truly Christian colleges. Plus, their administrators and faculty were respected Christian leaders, many also serving as elders, deacons, or preachers in local churches. But the schools were still segregated, and this seemed to contradict many of the most basic principles of Christianity. In the face of such a psychological and moral dilemma, students initially accepted that college administrators were wise men, aware of all pertinent circumstances, and eager to do the right thing. While desegregation might not happen immediately, many thought, it would happen soon. In the spring of 1956, after ACC students learned that their college would remain segregated, the *Optimist* remarked with resignation, "Under the present circumstances, it is the only decision that could have been made. The circumstances may change, and I feel sure that they will. When they do, the progress shall take its course. . . . Still we must remember that the students and their opinions will never dictate nor formulate the school's policy, but since they will be the ones most directly affected, their ideas will always be considered." While many students at ACC supported desegregation, they were not ready to take any steps to voice sustained opposition to administrative policy. Ultimately, desegregation did not seem to affect them. Students may have supported desegregation as an ethical idea, but it was nothing upon which they wanted to stake their educations, careers, or reputations. Meanwhile, as Harding students would soon be reminded, college presidents rarely made decisions based on careful consideration of students' opinions.[23]

By the fall of 1957, discussions of desegregation had become immediately relevant at Harding, as the eyes of the world fastened on Little Rock, fifty miles southwest of campus. The events surrounding the desegregation of Central High School and the school's subsequent closure are well documented, but the circumstances that unfolded at Harding offer a compelling addendum to the narrative. Harding students were well aware of the Pauline charge to Timothy in the New Testament—"Let no man despise thy youth; but be thou an example of the believers" (KJV)—and the chaotic events in Little Rock emboldened some to act. Over a year before the crisis, public discussions occasionally arose about what they might do. One letter to the *Bison* observed how some students believed "that we at Harding should be doing something in this question of segregation instead of sitting and waiting," before suggesting that students write letters in support of integration to the *Arkansas Faith,* a publication of the White Citizens' Council of Arkansas, whose leaders were "rather violent in their charges against the Supreme Court and those who are not pro-segregationists." Several months before the Little Rock crisis, a *Bison* editorial challenged students to let their actions match their rhetoric: "Let us make it a little more personal: though you verbally preach integration, would you be willing to follow what you advocate when the time comes for you to eat, ride, and directly associate with Negroes." The author also invoked biblical warrant for taking a stand. "Although the Bible does not specifically condemn segregation and it[s] results (as it does not specifically condemn many evils) it does set forth principles that, if followed, would eventually make people feel a brotherhood that can be attained only through a unity regardless of race."[24]

Several students decided to demand an immediate end to the policy of excluding black students. Student body president Bill Floyd was approached with the idea shortly after the Little Rock debacle and, while he cautioned students about demanding anything from Harding president George Benson, he did agree to circulate a "statement of attitude" that would adequately express the students' strong feelings. The decision to circulate the statement was relatively bold. Benson was an autocratic administrator and early champion of a political conservatism that emerged across the nation as the 1960s unfolded. He first came to national prominence in the 1940s after testifying before several congressional committees on the need to dismantle the New Deal, and he remained a stalwart among right-wing politicos throughout his lifetime. Benson was also the type of president who made decisions on his terms, with little regard to student input. His vice president, Clifton Ganus Jr., later remembered how "Benson called the shots, not the students. And even though there were many students that might want to be integrated, and even though there were some of us faculty members that were all for it, until he was ready for it, it didn't happen. . . . as I said, he ran a pretty tight ship and called the shots." Despite this stifling leadership style, or perhaps in fear of it, editorials in the *Bison* rarely leveled personal criticisms against Benson. One editorial from 1955 even blamed the students for the college's segregated status. "Probably the administration would be glad to [desegregate] if all the students favored it," this writer insisted, "but some of the Harding students wouldn't return to school if Negroes were admitted. Before any school can have successful integration, the individual prejudices of every student must be broken down."[25]

As the chants of "Two! Four! Six! Eight! We don't want to integrate!" echoed in the streets of Little Rock, those individual prejudices appear to have subsided at Harding. With Floyd's blessing and despite their fears of Benson, students circulated a statement in which signers affirmed "that they are ready to accept as members of the Harding community all academically and morally qualified applicants, without regard to arbitrary distinctions such as color or social level;

that they will treat such individuals with the consideration and dignity appropriate to human beings created in the image of God; and that they will at all times face quietly, calmly, patiently, and sympathetically any social pressures intensified by this action." More than 85 percent of the student body signed the statement, as did almost one hundred faculty, staff, and administrators. While its wording was tempered by the final paragraph's insistence that the statement represented "an expression of the internal readiness of the Harding community to end discrimination" and not "an attempt to precipitate action by the Administration," the message could not have been clearer: the overwhelming majority of people at Harding wanted to desegregate.[26]

Benson was neither persuaded nor pleased at this humble expression of dissent. He actually learned about the petition before a single signature had been obtained and immediately requested that the student council squelch it. The student body assembled to consider his request but eventually voted to circulate the statement as planned. Even an announcement at the following day's mandatory chapel service that discouraged students from signing the statement could not deter the effort and, after procuring nearly a thousand signatures, Floyd sent them, along with the statement, to each member of the board of trustees. Undeterred, Benson made another chapel appearance in which he made disparaging remarks about the statement. Floyd later recalled that Benson "told students in chapel that the action was improper and that the signatures were not an accurate expression of student feeling. I never understood how he determined this, when such a vast majority signed. His explanation was that 'they didn't understand what they were signing.'"[27]

Although they undoubtedly differed on what exactly desegregation might mean for Harding, the signatories fully understood the Christian principles that provided the foundation for the call to change. The statement specifically noted that Christians should not "make among people distinctions which God has not made," and it further affirmed "the principles of the fatherhood of God and the brotherhood of man." On some level, ironically, Benson believed in these same principles. Yet Benson also subscribed to a "theological racism" most commonly associated with justifications for slavery. Theological justifications for the subjugation of blacks had been around for several centuries, before experiencing a slow, uneven decline during the middle and latter decades of the twentieth century.[28] Floyd remembered how Benson "explained to us that God made some blue birds and some black birds and that they were not intended to mix." According to Benson, this observation proved applicable to blacks and whites as well. In classes on the Pentateuch, he taught that blacks were "under the curse of Ham," a reference to Noah's son in the book of Genesis that was proffered to vindicate racial segregation and black inferiority. Ganus later recalled, "I think he really probably believed that. He made a statement one time that indicated that. And then I've heard him make the statement, 'Well, it wasn't God's plan for them to mix and marry. Look at nature. I mean, you don't see blue birds and black birds mating.'"[29]

Benson certainly had pragmatic reasons for opposing desegregation, too. He feared the loss of students and financial support if Harding accepted black students. In the early 1960s, Harding administrators even received an offer of ten million dollars from an undisclosed donor to start a college in Mississippi that would forbid black students. But students remained skeptical of Benson's supposed misgivings, even as other administrators followed his lead. One Harding officer told Floyd that if he "wanted to crusade for integration [he] should go where everyone believes in it," while another intoned "that the student government should be an agency to indoctrinate the students with the ideas of the administration." These dismissive attitudes alienated both students and faculty. Bob Silvey, a student and budding author, remembered how race relations became the "issue more than any other that drove me away from organized religion. I had gone to Harding with the intention of becoming a missionary, but the blatant racism of President George Benson and his ilk nipped that idea in the bud. . . . a few of us thought it was a good time to demonstrate what Christian brotherhood really meant. We were quickly disabused of that callow notion." Benson's uncompromising position also discouraged Floyd, who had once aspired to be a preacher. Emboldened by the spirit of a righteous, though failed, cause, one student could not resist a final expression of protest. During the night following Benson's disparaging speech, he discreetly made his way to the administration building and the lily pond that adorned its front lawn. He quietly waded into the pond and the birdbath in the middle, where he hung a sign that read, "WHITES ONLY."[30]

To further dampen Harding students' interest in desegregation, Benson immediately commissioned one of the college's most popular and respected professors, James Bales, to deliver a speech on segregation during a weekly discussion group. Benson relied on Bales, a loyal supporter, to assuage students' concerns. To deflect criticism from Benson and the college, Bales explained to students that segregation should be viewed in the context of what was expedient with local customs and that racial strife was a centuries-old phenomenon

that spanned the globe. Following this line of reasoning, Bales removed segregation from the realm of moral discourse and placed it within a context of
cultural traditions over which Christians supposedly had little influence. He
reasoned that the apostle Paul might have abhorred slavery, for example, but
Pauline texts in the New Testament instructed slaves to obey their masters.
Likewise, Bales emphasized that the scriptures did not necessitate integration.
He suggested that God simply accepted all people regardless of their station in
life but did not, according to the New Testament, dismantle social hierarchies.
Bales also pointed the students toward the apostle Paul's instructions about
eating food sacrificed to idols. There was nothing inherently wrong with it,
but one should not partake if other church members might be offended. Bales
viewed desegregation in much the same way.[31]

Bales was a favorite professor for many students, but his arguments for acquiescence to segregation rang hollow. While conceding that his reasoning was
"as usual . . . very masterful," one student, Owen Olbricht, challenged Bales in
a personal letter by noting that "association with other races does not leave the
wrong impression as eating meats sacrificed to idols might . . . but rather association with other races teaches the truth of the gospel of Christ, helping others
see and know the principle we of all people in the world preach: the unity of all
believers." Olbricht awaited a reply for a year before writing again, asking and
hoping for a response, but Bales never mustered one. Harding students might
conform to admissions policies, but they were zealous in their fresh religious
training and not about to concede biblical arguments to anyone who sought
to justify segregation, no matter how benign someone like Bales could make
the policy seem. These episodes illustrate how debates about admitting black
students were not solely waged in the courts and streets. The Bible was an important battleground on which many white churchgoers based their arguments
for or against desegregation.[32]

The example of Harding both qualifies and supports scholarship on the religious beliefs of white southerners. Benson's and Bales's attempts to convince
students that the Bible did not require integration show that white southerners
made more concerted efforts to employ holy writ in defense of segregation than
what historian David Chappell allowed when he wrote of "how little southern white clergymen contributed to the record of the segregationist cause."
Furthermore, editorials and letters to the editor in the *Bison* clearly indicate
that students were combating the notion that "race" was divinely ordained.
Had this belief not been so common, the students' comments would have been
nonsensical.[33]

At the same time, Chappell's broader assertion that segregationists ultimately "failed to get their churches to give their cause active support" is vindicated by the position of students like Olbricht. Examples from other denominations also show that generational divides indicated theological proclivities that determined one's biblical position on segregation. In December 1954, more than three hundred Methodist ministers and laymen met in Birmingham, Alabama, to form the Association of Methodist Ministers and Laymen, whose express purpose was to "prevent either the sudden or the gradual integration of Negroes and whites," but a few months later, a national Methodist youth conference resolved that "the tragic fact of segregation is a serious detriment to the witness of the world Christian community." A similar statement was ratified by the Arkansas Baptist Student Union in the fall of 1957 by a vote of 359 to 1.[34]

The winter break did not curb Harding students' interest in desegregating. In the spring of 1958, actor Hal Holbrook appeared on campus to perform "Mark Twain Tonight," a one-man show that he performed throughout the country. The routine challenged audiences to rethink their attitudes about race relations, so his performance was welcomed by many Harding students who were "spellbound," according to the glowing review in the *Bison*. The show elicited comments, both positive and negative, in the newspaper. One humorously described the habits of the *ministerius bigotus* and its companion, the *homakus bigotus*. During the academic year, according to the writer, these creatures "gather in four large coveys, one in Texas, one in Arkansas, and two in Tennessee. Here they repress their instincts, and improve their techniques of feather ruffling and redundant trilling." These four locations referred to colleges affiliated with Churches of Christ. The *Bison* also included poems and essays that evoked images of intellectual and spiritual stagnation at Harding. Some readers might have missed the oblique criticisms of the college administration, but a close reading suggests that students were growing weary of Benson and his leadership. One poem, titled "Reign, Reign, Go Away," stated,

Thought was drowned in
The sea of time.
"Death!" "Death!" cried
The reign.

Another essay told of "a small man [who] was pleased with himself and with his great faculty, his magnificent ability to utter words. . . . He spoke on and on until only he from the fancied multitude was left to bask in the bubble of his own voice in the emptiness of his words." While comments explicitly directed at Benson would not have been tolerated, these artistic voices pointed to growing frustrations that students felt toward the administration. Yet the students' righteous indignation on this issue did nothing to undermine enthusiasm for a minstrel show that spring, an event featured on the front page of the *Bison*.[35]

Benson also continued to press his case, often by inviting speakers to Harding who vindicated his positions on segregation and other right-wing political concerns. Leon Burns, a segregationist preacher from Columbia, Tennessee, made several appearances at Harding's annual lectureship and was also invited to speak during a chapel service. His booklet, "Why Desegregation Will Fail," was widely circulated among segregationist Christians. "[I]f I believed that integration of the races was even slightly suggested in the Bible," Burns stated, "I would dedicate my life to bringing this about; but in the light of overwhelming evidence both in and out of the Bible, I cannot believe this, and so have dedicated myself—without prejudice toward any race or individual—to maintaining segregation in our schools and in all realms of social contact as the only Christian, logical, and practical way to promote peace and good will among all men." Students' reticence to directly criticize Benson did not extend to his guests. When one speaker rebuked the Supreme Court over its recent rulings against segregation, a student corrected several misstatements in a letter to the *Bison* and closed by questioning the speaker's motives. "I wonder if . . . seeing our proximity to Little Rock and knowing that feeling has been high against integration, [he] was not trying to scratch 'itching' ears. . . . He has misjudged his audience."[36]

Students at ACC also remained frustrated in the spring of 1958. The *Optimist* ran a series of five editorials that addressed desegregation, each one urging readers to maintain a Christ-like disposition toward all people and implicitly suggesting that ACC accept black students. The first editorial simply contained three quotations from the local *Abilene Reporter-News*. Each one described the enrollment policies at the three private colleges in Abilene, Texas, including McMurry's admission of blacks and Hardin-Simmons's partial desegregation. ACC had made no arrangements to accommodate any black students, so the *Optimist* editor closed by noting how "[s]uch attitudes toward integration indicate our lack of progress toward solving the problem. Let's begin to pray about it." The next editorial was slightly more discreet in its disapproval of the administration, as it simply noted the schools in Texas that had desegregated and how successful the black students had been. But the essay still closed by observing

that "Texas schools are beginning to break the pattern that makes the segregated South the nearest thing we have to Nazi Germany." The final editorial in
the series emphasized how Christianity should inspire unity among all people.
With bold font, the editor passionately argued that segregation "denies this
oneness . . . is based on prejudice . . . [and] breeds barriers of hate and fear and
suspicion." The staff of the *Optimist* could not have made the point with more
clarity.[37]

During the 1958–59 academic year, both the *Bison* and the *Optimist* toned
down their rhetoric under the heavy hand of administrators who refused to
tolerate ongoing criticism from their own students. President Athens Clay Pullias at DLC had already stymied potential discussions of race in that college's
student newspaper after the results of a student poll from earlier in the decade
showed that almost two-thirds of the student body favored desegregation. By
comparison, the *Bison* and the *Optimist* enjoyed fewer restrictions, but even this
freedom could be quickly curtailed with a directive from the college president.
In the years immediately following the Little Rock crisis, the *Bison* largely went
silent on the prospect of desegregation. This silence might have resulted from
an administrative decision to monitor closely the newspaper's contents.

An essay in the *Bison* from November 1958 lashed out at the administration
over several issues such as curfews and dating restrictions, immediate concerns
that weighed more heavily on the minds of most college students than calls for
desegregation, which were not specifically mentioned. The essay complained
of "subterfuge" and "totalitarian regimentation" and employed startlingly direct language in assessing the college. "It has been often observed that Christian and American ideals are continually preached here, but rarely practiced,"
the author opined. "If the Golden Rule and the Bill of Rights were less often
memorized and more often synthesized into action, Harding College would be
a freer, happier, more productive citadel of uninhibited truth." The next issue
of the *Bison* included a *mea culpa*, likely ordered from the president's office,
and subsequent complaints were issued in broad generalizations. Appeals "to
keep pace with the accompanying transitions of our society" now replaced direct calls for desegregation or straightforward critiques of Harding policies.
But such entreaties should not be dismissed lightly. Through their mention of
works such as Richard Wright's *Native Son* and their logical arguments against
closed-mindedness, prejudice, and provincialism, several members of the *Bison*
staff found a prophetic voice that could not have been missed by readers who
were aware of racial turmoil. If direct confrontations with Jesus and Paul could

not convince administrators to desegregate Harding, these students must have thought, perhaps Bigger Thomas or deductive logic could.[38]

If the *Bison* rarely mentioned desegregation, an opinion poll conducted in November 1959 by a sociology class indicated that 56 percent of Harding students favored the admission of black students, while another 15 percent would accept "qualified" admission. Opinions were split about desegregating social clubs—42 percent summarily opposed that idea. In 1960, the newspaper printed the text of a speech delivered by a white minister named Carl Spain at ACC that sharply denounced the denomination for not acting decisively to desegregate its southern schools. But aside from a brief article that announced the desegregation of ACC and an article deploring the unrest surrounding James Meredith's admission to the University of Mississippi in 1962, the *Bison* would not broach the subject again until it announced the arrival of Harding's first black students in 1963. Either interest waned in some of the most momentous events of the students' young lives, or Benson determined that discussions of racial discrimination were inappropriate for a student newspaper.[39]

The situation at ACC differed in several respects. Its proximity to SWCC, then only a two-year college and only two hundred miles east, meant that some blacks, especially ministers in training, would want to complete a four-year degree at the nearest Church of Christ college. By 1960, ACC had also become the premier college among Churches of Christ, both in faculty and enrollment. Situated in west Texas, on what might be considered the outer edge of the South, ACC did not encounter the same degree of strident segregationist opposition that places to the east endured, so if a Church of Christ college in the South were to desegregate, ACC was the most likely possibility.

President Morris was also burdened by the complaints of young blacks like Ernest Holsendolph and Floyd Rose, but based on extant sources he also faced more pressure to desegregate from concerned adults. In 1955, the same year that the Texas Intercollegiate Press Association had desegregated on the ACC campus, an annual lectureship featured four sermons aimed at improving race relations. In a collective sense, these sermons were simply a recitation of familiar maxims. The Golden Rule was standard fare, and all speakers emphasized that Christianity required love for all people because Christ died for all. To minimize any doubt, lines about Christ's apostles not becoming preoccupied with immediate social change or the Bible not necessitating integration were also included. Yet even within this cautionary rhetoric, some challenging thoughts, at least by white southern standards, were presented to the audience. One speaker suggested that, where segregation was not practiced, local congregations should be integrated. Another cited fifteen passages from the Bible that teach the unity of humanity. And the final speaker made his remarks even more practical. "Is it possible for me to practice the Golden Rule and refuse to allow a person created in the image of God to sit beside me on a bus, or in a restaurant, or in the worship of God?" he asked. "Is Christ living in us when we refuse to use our influence to secure for minority groups the rights of education and suffrage and those other privileges which we have come to consider as inalienable to ourselves? . . . We cannot excuse ourselves by a geographical accident of birth."[40]

But the public pressure on Morris increased dramatically when Carl Spain delivered a sermon titled "Modern Challenges to Christian Morals" in 1960. Not only was Spain a faculty member, but his eldest daughter was also a sophomore at the college. His comments included a broad, blistering attack on Churches of Christ for some of its racist practices, but he specifically referred to the segregated colleges, and in doing so, placed a glaring spotlight on his own institution. His remarks vividly illustrated how primitivism became a factor for faculty and students in segregation's demise in the denomination's colleges. Spain declared, "I feel certain that Jesus would say: 'Ye hypocrites! You say you are the only true Christians, and make up the only true church, and have the only Christian schools. Yet, you drive one of your own preachers to denominational schools where he can get credit for his work and refuse to let him take Bible for credit in your own school because the color of his skin is dark!' Our moral attitudes are so mixed up," Spain continued, "that we use the story of Philemon and Onesimus to justify refusing a Negro admission to study Bible." In that story from the New Testament, the slave Onesimus was sent back to his owner Philemon by the apostle Paul. At the time of Spain's speech, the board of trustees was already studying the logistics of desegregating, but he touched a nerve that brought unwanted attention to Church of Christ colleges and ACC in particular.[41]

Other faculty members and several patrons soon voiced their agreement with Spain, especially when the activities of the integration committee began to lag. When a 1941 alumnus sent a contribution of ten dollars, he included a note that said, "There could be more, but—I am ashamed to hear that ACC is tainted with . . . race prejudice. What kind of light to the world is this?" Others stopped contributing altogether. One person sent a letter to the board of trustees to explain the reason why she and her husband ceased their monthly contributions. "When the policy is changed, if it is," she frankly stated, "we shall plan to resume on contributions to it." The *Christian Echo* also registered a complaint with ACC's public information office. "Very often we receive news for 'immediate release,'" the letter stated. "Since the most of our readers are negroes, we are wondering why you would want us to run it in our Periodical." These complaints and warnings were accompanied by similar criticism from other members of the faculty.[42]

LeMoine Lewis, for example, a popular Bible professor who held a doctorate from Harvard and sent several students from ACC to study there, sent a lengthy letter to his dean expressing consternation over ACC's refusal to desegregate. While he confessed to once cautioning students about moving too fast with integration, Lewis was convinced that racial discrimination was wrong. Along with articulating his personal embarrassment, he indicated that some people were reticent to contribute money to a college that refused blacks. Lewis was grieved to belong to a Bible Department that was "most guilty, because we have kept quiet rather than following in the steps of prophets, apostles, and our Lord who preached boldly and courageously against the evils of their day." In his estimation, not only was segregation wrong and contrary to divine will, but it jeopardized the soul of a black preacher who chose to attend a denominational school and the "conscientious little colored girl of Abilene [who] went to Boston University because she could not enroll in Abilene Christian College, and while in Boston quit the church and was lost forever." This stark language revealed how segregation posed not only a problem for restorationist theology and the fiscal health of ACC, but also the spiritual vitality of people directly affected by the admissions policy. For a preacher in the Bible Department at ACC, the latter concern could not be overstated. Four months later, in a one-sentence memorandum, the integration committee recommended that "any applicant who meets the admission requirements to graduate school be admitted."[43]

When the first black student enrolled in the graduate school at ACC in the spring of 1962, the news was anticlimactic. In a brief article relegated to page three, the *Optimist* simply observed, "After more than half a century of segregation, the first Negro student is enrolled at Abilene Christian." The article closed by noting that the undergraduate school was still segregated, but by May, the newspaper could report that the junior and senior classes would be desegregated in the fall.[44] In another article gauging students' reaction to this news, the *Optimist* revealed how most students at ACC, like Harding, welcomed the idea of having black classmates but retained some reservations about what desegregation might entail. Student opinions revealed that old racial stereotypes would not die with the admission of a few blacks, and at least one person admitted to disagreeing with the decision. Even those who agreed with the decision expressed a variety of reasons for their assent. Believing that blacks were inherently gifted athletes, some whites could not contain their excitement over the possibilities for successful athletic teams. "A few outstanding and qualified Negro athletes could make ACC the leading track team in the nation," one remarked, "since Negroes excel in the sprints, hurdles and jumping events." More than one person conveyed mixed feelings about living arrangements. One junior said, "I wouldn't want to live with one but I wouldn't mind living down the hall from one." Yet the *Optimist* claimed the moral high ground in subsequent observations on race relations, commending crosstown college Hardin-Simmons for finally desegregating and asking, "What's the matter with Mississippi?" when mobs instigated a riot over the arrival of James Meredith on the Oxford campus. At the same time, however, desegregation caused some students to pause and wonder how the college would now operate. It was one thing to share a class with a black student, some clearly thought, but it was something different to share a dorm room. These reactions exemplified the gradations of acceptance that characterized many whites. Racial stereotypes often persisted, and even white students who believed that schools should be desegregated might not agree to more intimate levels of interaction, such as sharing a dorm room or belonging to the same social club.[45]

These divergent opinions also characterized the student body at Harding, although when Benson finally announced during a 1963 chapel service that Harding would accept black students, he received a standing ovation. With no sense of irony, the *Bison* invoked the well-worn scripture that "God is no respecter of persons" and then dubiously, or perhaps sarcastically, proclaimed that "Benson's leadership in the movement for equal opportunity makes us proud, even boastful; it makes us happy, even ecstatic." Extant records do not precisely indicate why Harding accepted three black students in the fall of 1963. By that time, Congress was already considering what would become the Civil Rights Act of 1964, which would soon ensure that institutions doing business with the federal government were at least nominally desegregated. Given Benson's political connections, relationships with other college presidents, and penchant for making sound fiscal decisions, the admission of a few black students at Harding was likely more about finances than divine inspiration.[46]

If student bodies, in the aggregate, favored desegregation, why were college presidents so reticent to provide the leadership necessary for change? Answers to this question would no doubt vary between individuals, but three factors were especially relevant. First, the ideology of white supremacy, buttressed by a theology of racism, maintained a formidable degree of influence among Church of Christ clergy and educators. Benson really believed that blacks were under the biblical curse of Ham, and the momentous changes that occurred through civil rights activism, Supreme Court decisions, and federal legislation did little to alter his opinion. In a 1966 sermon, Benson asked what the proper Christian attitude toward race problems should be. "Before God, all men are equal," he stated. But "in like manner there is no reason to think the Lord wants a mixing of the races and the creating of just one mongrel race." For many years, this sincere belief prevented Benson from entertaining the idea that Harding should desegregate.[47]

With good reason, a skeptic could claim that Benson and others who subscribed to similar racist assumptions simply used theology to substantiate their bigotry. This practice may have been common. A church member once wrote that a college president privately told him that "many Negroes have venereal disease" and that the students needed to be protected. Yet this perspective fails to adequately explain Benson, who seemed to genuinely believe that providence had ordained racial hierarchies. Benson's global humanitarian and evangelistic interests also suggested that he did not harbor stringent racial animosities. Indeed, Benson provides an example of how theology continued to inform the positions of some people whose racism and faith in God and scripture had become so entwined that maintenance of a segregated society was equated with seeking God's will.[48]

In addition to theological predilections, political expediency molded segregationist posturing. Benson enjoyed a good relationship with Arkansas Governor Orval Faubus, but he was especially close to Senator John McClellan. Although the former's antics during the Little Rock crisis of September 1957 are more infamous, the senator was no less defiant of the Supreme Court. By signing the Southern Manifesto in 1956, McClellan had already registered his opposition to the *Brown* decision. In the context of the Little Rock crisis, he sent a memo typed in all-capital letters to President Eisenhower that stated, "THE MISTAKEN BELIEF THAT THE PRESENCE AND USE OF FEDERAL TROOPS OFFER EITHER HOPE OR PROSPECT OF A RATIONAL OR PERMANENT SOLUTION TO THE PROBLEM IS, IN MY BELIEF, A GRAVE ERROR OF JUDGMENT." The following year, McClellan informed a constituent that he had "without hesitation or reservation severely criticized the Supreme Court for its school integration decision and others."[49]

Like other southern politicians, McClellan had drawn his line clearly in the sand, and doing so made him a heroic figure to Benson. Shortly after the Little Rock crisis, Benson telephoned the senator with an invitation to be the guest speaker at the 1959 Freedom Forum. While this particular forum was held at Pepperdine College, it was directed by Benson's National Education Program, a small, fiercely conservative think tank that complemented the college's American studies program. Benson and McClellan definitely saw eye to eye on most policy matters, and Benson never ran short on flattery for the senator. "Senator McClellan," Benson once wrote, "you are rendering a great service to your country and your many, many Arkansas friends are very proud of you and of your record." In 1963, the year that Harding accepted its first black students, Benson arranged for Harding to award an honorary doctorate to McClellan.[50]

Benson was certainly not alone in carefully courting prominent politicians. President Pullias at DLC was close to Congressman Joe Evins of Tennessee, who was also a member of Churches of Christ. Evins gave thousands of dollars to DLC, offered the commencement address in 1952, and became a member of its board of trustees in 1967. He also sent his daughters to ACC. Evins signed the Southern Manifesto in 1956, so his sympathies clearly lay with the status quo. Pullias often discussed policy issues with Evins. When Congress was debating civil rights legislation, Pullias told Evins that "some of the fundamentals for which this republic was originally established are threatened." Pullias was unapologetically racist, even complaining in a meeting once about having to shake hands with Marshall Keeble. While theological racism was a contributing factor to college administrators' reticence to desegregate, political and financial advantages could be found in supporting segregationist public officials.[51]

Administrators most feared losing donors and students once blacks were enrolled. As early as 1946, letters to the Optimist recognized the possibility and even likelihood that having a desegregated college would cause some whites to enroll elsewhere. At Harding, James Bales feared such a backlash. He was proud that people from various ethnic groups had been accepted at Harding, but he worried that the presence of black students might deter parents from sending their children to Harding and that doing so "might cut off other means of support." In private, one college president admitted to a church member that, if desegregation occurred, "the school might lose monetary support and not be able to teach 'Christian principles' to as many students." In his famous sermon at the 1960 ACC lectureship, Carl Spain made reference to "people with money who will back us in our last ditch stand for white supremacy in a world of pigmented people." While students were resigned to potential departures and the loss of revenue, administrators remained apprehensive but, by the time Church of Christ colleges desegregated, the threat of any white exodus was not nearly as great as the potential damage to a segregated institution's reputation. Administrators finally succumbed when federal loans were jeopardized if colleges refused black students. Thus, when the president of Freed-Hardeman finally announced in 1964 that black students would be admitted in the upcoming academic year, he said the change in policy was due "to the mistake of accepting federal funds."[52]

The desegregation of Church of Christ colleges slowly altered the dynamics of campus life. Minstrel shows ended, for example, as racist humor migrated from the spotlight to the privacy of dorm rooms or conversations among friends. As desegregation proceeded in the region's public life throughout the 1960s, Church of Christ colleges took pride in the peaceful desegregation of their facilities, even if the decisive factor was financial rather than a commitment to equal opportunity or racial justice. The editorial bent of student newspapers also evolved. Cartoons and essays suggested that the admission of black students meant that the work of the colleges was done. There was little abiding concern with racial justice. Meanwhile, blacks did not rush to enroll in institutions where they had never been welcomed as students, and initial efforts to recruit them were not zealous. When enrollment at ACC topped three thousand for the first time in 1965, only ten students were black.[53]

Blacks did not eagerly enroll at Harding either, although if the student newspaper is any indication, the student body remained more engaged with ongoing civil rights struggles than their counterparts at ACC. By 1970, blacks composed less than 2 percent of the Harding student body, so "integration" was something of a misnomer. And although Harding students had previously expressed overwhelming support for desegregation, like students at ACC, they often struggled with the details. When blacks were allowed to live in dormitories, Benson's successor as president, Clifton Ganus Jr., recalled, "you'd have to be sure that you got the right roommate. . . . you wouldn't just automatically place a black student in with a white student without permission of the other white student." Enrolling three black students into a student body of approximately twelve hundred in 1963 left many white students with a sense of finality about the black freedom struggle. A *Bison* cartoon from February 1964 communicated as much (fig. 5). Two male students, one black and one white, shook hands while standing atop a map of the former Confederate states. A trash can in the picture held four signs with the words "violence," "race," "discrimination," and

We can do it.

FIGURE 5. The student newspaper at Harding College published this cartoon in 1963 after the first black students were admitted.

Bison, 1963. Ann Cowan Dixon Archives & Special Collections, Harding University.

"groups." The caption, "We can do it," suggested that ending discrimination was as easy as shaking hands and throwing the past into the waste bin of history.[54]

Desegregation permitted white students to level more frequent criticisms of social activism in general and civil rights protest in particular. Such critiques illustrated how some white southerners who might have been sympathetic to a few of the aims of the civil rights movement, such as desegregating schools or securing the franchise, became increasingly skeptical, if not fully hostile, to the movement's evolution. One *Bison* editor expressed previous support for what he called "'passive resistance' as a legitimate method" in the fight for equal rights, but his opinion changed after witnessing firsthand a 1963 demonstration in Chicago. While noting that the "crowd was peaceful and nondestructive," the editor referred to the demonstrators as "a mob which required close supervision by policemen." "The demonstration was highly emotional and fear-inspired," he contended. "They marched on the streets and sidewalks chanting in a primitive manner, 'What do you want? Freedom! When? Now!' and other similar phrases." This assessment displayed an underlying discomfort that many whites exhibited about empowered black citizens. If incorporating a few black students into class proved acceptable to most white students, then sharing living space or watching "primitive" demonstrators proved more troubling, if not outright alarming.[55]

Just as previous contributors to the *Bison* had pressed readers to consider biblical teachings regarding equality to promote desegregation, some students invoked Jesus's teaching, "Judge not, that ye be not judged," to question the necessity of civil rights activism. In 1965, as the Student Nonviolent Coordinating Committee and Southern Christian Leadership Conference were organizing in Selma, Alabama, the *Bison* published an article that rebuked the state for its record of black voter registration. But two letters to the editor summarily rejected the essay's claims. One author insisted that the "majority of the people in Alabama do not deny the Negro the right to vote," and "relations between white and black in Alabama are not as bad as many would have you think. . . . the majority of both races have no prejudice or hatred toward the other." The writer sympathized with the local government in Selma, though the letters were published on Thursday, March 4, three days before "Bloody Sunday." "Dr. King has many good points," the letter continued. "Leading the world in promoting peace is not one of his strong points, however." The letter closed by instructing readers, "Do not cast a frown upon the actions of a man unless you have worn his shoes for a day. . . . Every state has its weak points, but we should be very careful passing judgment upon our neighbors without first knowing the other side." A second letter criticized the act of labeling white southerners as "prejudiced against the Negro" because this "labeling itself is prejudiced for it places the accusation on all Southerners while there is no proof that more than a minority are involved." This author closed by rhetorically asking, "Is the disrespect shown by the civil rights demonstrators for law and order (symbolized by the numerous encouraged arrests) contributing to racial peace?" An essay written in the fall by Ken Starr, later known for his investigation of President Bill Clinton's romantic dalliances, included more subtle criticism. Starr quoted Thomas Jefferson in lauding "the important role which sincere protest plays in society," but he cautioned readers not to lend a "seal of approval to any and all 'movements' of the day."[56]

Various expressions of paternalism, in which whites presumed to know what was best for blacks, became more prevalent. A letter to the *Bison* that castigated black activists also pled, without irony, "Please do not consider this letter a slam against the Negro race. Some of my closest friends are colored people." A 1966 article chastised Churches of Christ for persistent racial segregation but also remarked that the "times are making the Negro community potentially one of the most responsible segments of society. True revolution is going [on] among them. Great displacement, both physical and psychological, is making them especially susceptible to new ideas. But we cannot reach them by our old methods, smacking of Jim Crowism."[57]

Some of the most intriguing exchanges unfolded when black students were given the opportunity to describe their perspectives on racial injustice. They attempted to diminish white complacency by directing their classmates' attention to the persistence of racial discrimination. In March 1967, a *Bison* editorial briefly outlined two students' remarks, made during a chapel service. "They told of difficulty in finding apartments, of difficulty being accepted by their white neighbors. One of them even said that he was sure he would be shunned if he attended church services at many Arkansas congregations." One of the students also read a passage of scripture, James 2:1–9, remarkable for its disapproval of esteeming the rich over the poor. The reading likely reflected the changing emphasis of civil rights struggles in 1967, as these black students noted that the scriptures erased both ethnic and economic distinctions among Christians. The editorial concluded, "Maybe we err in concentrating solely upon men's souls without regard to alleviating the physical discomforts and scorn that many of our neighbors are forced to face daily." The *Bison* did not record other student reactions.[58]

During a Friday chapel program in March 1968, "one of the most listened to of the whole year," Elijah Anthony and Howard Wright, two black seniors at Harding were provided a forum for discussing racial bigotry in Churches of Christ. Each student described past encounters with racial discrimination, and Anthony explained how he avoided recent violence in Birmingham, his hometown. In the context of the chapel program, however, the two seniors wanted to convey that Churches of Christ had not adequately addressed racial discrimination. When the two were asked to speak, they determined "that we had some things we felt should be said." Anthony told the audience that churches have "been avoiding the issue of race; we just slid over, under and around it." Wright added, "We're worried about what the world will think. . . . How long are we going to say, 'don't buck society?' How long?" A *Bison* editorial lauded the program because "it demonstrated . . . that we are not so fearful of hurting 'our image' that we will not take a long, hard look at ourselves." This "long, hard look" included the observation that church preference cards, distributed to students at the beginning of each school year, omitted the local black Church of Christ, and the same church was excluded by local white churches from billboards along the highways that welcomed visitors to Searcy.[59]

The assassination of Martin Luther King Jr. on April 4, 1968, reinvigorated the urgency with which students discussed race relations. While Harding flew the US flag at half-staff for three days, not all students expressed grief. Apart from a black student's eulogy of King and a poem decrying ignorance, prejudice, hatred, and pride, two of the three essays in the Bison about the assassination scolded classmates for laughing at the tragedy. An editorial lamented, "This laughter came from the basest kind of humanity, if indeed it did come from human thought. . . . It might be surprising to some that 'Christians' laughed; 'Christians' said he got what was coming; 'Christians' said 'I'd like to pin a medal on the guy who did it.' Yes, 'Christians' laughed." One cannot possibly quantify how many people at Harding delighted in King's death, but expression of such alarm in the Bison insinuated that these incidents were not isolated.[60]

The other two essays, while expressing grief over King's death, were nevertheless careful to qualify praise for his life. One author wrote, "Although this writer has doubted the wisdom of King's application of the principle of nonviolence at times, he is in complete sympathy with the goals and aspirations which King so admirably strove to attain." The last piece traced racial inequality back to the curse of Ham and to the institution of slavery in the United States. After documenting key points in the history of race relations from the antebellum era to the civil rights legislation of 1964 and 1965, including the statement that the Voting Rights Act of 1965 "seemed to be the final answer" in efforts "to do away entirely with all racial barriers before the law," this article turned its attention to a collection of problems that exacerbated racial tensions. The author contended that, "if the Negro sits back and demands the fruits of equality without preparing himself educationally, economically and morally to shoulder [the] concurrent responsibilities it entails, he neither deserves nor should he expect equality. . . . Mass reactions of violence to King's death only emphasize the white racist's claim that the Negro is only one step removed from the black jungles of Africa, barely better than his cannibal ancestors." These last two essays show that, even among sympathetic whites, feelings of suspicion, impatience, and even disgust arose in the wake of demands for equality by King and other civil rights activists. These cautious appraisals also contrast with contemporary memory of King that, as one historian wrote, "has been distorted almost beyond recognition."[61]

Back at ACC, administrators kept close tabs on the few black students who enrolled after desegregation. ACC compiled reports every semester that included each student's address, classification, grade point average, total hours enrolled, and total hours earned. Although John Stevens was vice president during the latter years of Morris's tenure, his inauguration as president in 1969 brought concerted efforts to welcome black students more fully into campus life. Stevens quickly approved the creation of an Ethnic Studies Forum, a student organization whose purpose, in part, was to promote "a dedication to the actualization of Christian brotherhood on the campus of Abilene Christian College." Each officer in the new organization was black. Stevens and his wife also sponsored social events where black students were guests of honor, and he made sure that ACC made special efforts to recruit minority students, including the hiring of black admissions counselors. When ACC started granting honorary doctorates, Stevens wrote to his vice president, "I do not see how now I couldn't recommend anybody for an honorary degree if I couldn't include my good friend and esteemed colleague Jack Evans," the first black president of SWCC.[62]

Individuals occasionally shared concerns about desegregation with Stevens, and his responses disclosed a desire to atone for the college's past mistakes. Interracial dating still proved problematic for Stevens, but even when such a relationship came to his attention, he was usually a calming influence on worried, white parents. In 1972, one scared mother wrote to Stevens when she learned that her daughter was dating a black student. "We are all for the colored people," she stated, "but not to that extent." Stevens responded with two letters. The first promised to have the dean of women explore the situation, but his second letter informed the meddling mother that her daughter had indeed been with a black student but "only in groups. . . . She has sincere respect for him. . . . She plans to finish ACC before thinking about marriage with anybody." While monitoring romantic relationships should have fallen outside the purview of presidential responsibilities, Stevens apparently calmed a concerned parent without interfering in student relationships.[63]

When he received a letter that criticized the admission of black students, Stevens wrote firm rebuttals that appealed to biblical principles, just as many students had argued when the college was still segregated. In 1974, one parent complained about desegregation and suggested that the college could receive more money by reestablishing itself as a segregated institution. Stevens replied, "The fact is that all students, regardless of race or color, are welcome here. We believe this is what the Bible teaches and we would not want to go contrary to the Bible in order to gain a contribution from any human being." Stevens was also not above apologizing for ACC's past discrimination. When an alumnus turned minister told him about the lingering anger of one black applicant who was rejected before the college desegregated, Stevens wrote a personal letter of apology. "I must say that I do not blame you for having these feelings," he wrote. "A number of years ago we changed our policy on admission. It is regrettable that for so many colleges and universities, as well as for a great part of society, it took so long to come to this point of maturity. Nevertheless, that is the truth, and there is nothing for us to do but to confess our wrongs and endeavor to make things right from this point forward." The letter closed by inviting the would-be alumnus to campus. In some respects, his letter represented the assumption of many whites that, once facilities were desegregated, people should simply try to forget past injustices and focus on the future. But the very act of sending such a letter signified a dramatic change in the administration's disposition toward blacks. This small act foreshadowed a formal, public apology for past racism and discrimination that a subsequent ACC president would finally issue as the twentieth century came to a close.[64]

Battle lines in debates over desegregation were drawn between students and administrators, and each side found biblical justifications for their respective positions. With help from the federal government and the incalculable impact of civil rights protests, the students' position ultimately prevailed. However, the implications of desegregation proved challenging for both students and administrators. As the civil rights movement progressed during the 1960s, it renewed attention on economic injustices and institutional forms of racism that otherwise sympathetic whites felt uncomfortable addressing. Simultaneously, the thought of sharing dorm rooms, romantic interests, or playing time in athletic contests disturbed white sensibilities. "We're still not over that feeling," Ganus explained years later. Moreover, within the confines of colleges such as ACC and Harding, the seeds of a new political conservatism were sown. Desegregated colleges were acceptable; persistent demonstrations aimed at overturning institutional racism were not. While administrators adopted the language of equality that students had used in espousing desegregation, the students imbibed the wariness of their elders toward civil rights activism. Together, they honed the rhetoric and articulated the values that would come to characterize the ascendancy of political conservatism in the final decades of the twentieth century.[65]

4

HEAR THE WORD
OF THE LORD

While Churches of Christ often sought to avoid or ignore the civil rights movement, the momentous events of the era were difficult to summarily dismiss. Prominent pastors, such as Martin Luther King Jr., Ralph Abernathy, and Fred Shuttlesworth, became significant leaders of the southern civil rights movement, and black churchgoers frequently composed the nonviolent armies that marched, stood in line for voter registration, or enrolled their children in formerly segregated schools. Many calls for justice were rooted in biblical imagery and stories that challenged white southerners to reevaluate their religious convictions. Thus the essence of Christian praxis was hotly contested in the South, where Churches of Christ were most prevalent.

In many respects, people who participated in civil rights demonstrations were exceptional. White southerners were largely missing. "Most of the white people who appear in film footage of civil rights marches," historian Timothy Tyson once wryly noted, "were brave followers of Leon Trotsky or radical Catholic sisters or saintly kooks of one description or another, and almost all of them were from somewhere else." Most blacks were not activists either, at least if marching in the street or volunteering for arrest are the standards for determining involvement. In commenting on his own hometown in North Carolina, Tyson observed, "The majority of African Americans in Oxford and elsewhere had stayed on the sidelines, paralyzed by fear, indifference, or their inability to imagine a better world. . . . there were always black people too fearful, too attached to 'their' white folks, too pessimistic or too beaten down by white supremacy to stand up for themselves." With few exceptions, the same was true of Churches of Christ. If activists composed only a fraction of the overall black population, then participation of blacks from Churches of Christ was hardly measurable. Many people undoubtedly participated in private, subtle ways, but active involvement in the southern civil rights movement would have required close association with leaders of other denominations. Churches of Christ only met with other denominations for debating the finer points of baptismal theology or what constituted worshiping "in spirit and in truth." And perhaps more importantly, public black activism would have jeopardized relationships with white churches that had long provided the financial and physical means necessary for blacks to operate their own churches and maintain their evangelistic endeavors. While some blacks worked within the confines of Churches of Christ to enact change, few sought a public role in the broader black freedom struggle.[1]

Then what can be said of the vast majority of people—black and white—who mostly observed what became some of the most celebrated events in modern history? Clues to their thinking can be found in sermons that both reflected and shaped their hearers. Churchgoers sought a word from God about the civil rights movement, and preachers were occasionally expected to provide one. Before the 1950s, Sunday school lessons and occasional comments from the pulpit generally scorned racial prejudice, but the Supreme Court's 1954 *Brown* decision provided the impetus for whites to ask anew if refraining from racial prejudice necessitated sharing public spaces with blacks. Many whites tried to distinguish racial prejudice, a sin, from practicing segregation or harsh criticism of the civil rights movement.[2]

The words from God that Church of Christ preachers spoke varied widely. Whites were more likely to be critical of the civil rights movement and the denominational preachers who spent so much time on social activism, while blacks were more likely to be sympathetic to the aims, if not the means, of civil rights activists. But extant sources indicate that few blacks from Churches of Christ participated in civil rights activism, due to their exclusivist attitudes toward other Christians. Meanwhile, faith inspired opinions on all sides. Faith compelled some to spend their careers fighting segregation and institutional racism. Others utilized faith to justify their racist assumptions, while still others genuinely believed that faith had no place amid discussions of politics and social ills.

As the beneficiaries of white supremacy, whites in Churches of Christ had a vested interest in supporting the status quo, so their responses to the civil rights movement are more difficult to interpret. Some undoubtedly opposed civil rights activism because they fully supported white supremacy, but other whites, like some blacks, had serious misgivings about political engagement and civil rights activism. Some whites held both views. Our inability to precisely determine or measure these motives should not prevent us from considering what whites said as the civil rights movement unfolded.

After the *Brown* decision, preachers were called upon to address what the Bible said about segregation, the "origin of the races," and interracial marriage.

Ministers such as W. A. Cameron reverted to biblical narratives that supposedly explained racial origins and validated white supremacy. Cameron preached
about "The Origin and Development of the Negro Race" at the Disston Avenue
Church of Christ in Gulfport, Florida, on August 15, 1954. A nearby church invited him to give the same sermon a week later. Cameron's message began with
an intricate genealogical history of Noah and his descendants, with a special
emphasis on Noah's third son, Ham. A curious vignette from the book of Genesis
explains how Ham's son, Canaan, was cursed by Noah to be "a servant of servants
. . . unto his brethren." Like many whites before and even after him, Cameron
believed that "the descendants of Canaan would always be the servants of all
the other races of the whole world." The notion that the Bible contained the
explanation for white supremacy and racial origins had long been popular in
the United States, especially during the Civil War era. The idea that blacks were
divinely ordained to be subordinate to whites died a slow, uneven death during
the twentieth century, but Cameron illustrates its persistence in the 1950s.[3]

Cameron's assessment did not prevent him from criticizing the slave trade
that brought Africans to the Americas. "Today, had it not been from the lustful
greed of the unscrupulous class of white men infesting the earth, there would
have been no Negro's [sic] in America." Without the slave trade, he continued,
"the black man would be in his own country, where Jehovah put him, and left
him, and wanted him." Yet this critical evaluation of the planter class did not
temper his harsh racism. He told his audiences that if they wanted "to know
how to treat the colored people (Descendants of Ham)," then they should "read
Gods [sic] explicit instruction to the Jews on that particular subject [in] Deuteronomy 7:1–5." This particular passage is an excerpt from one of Moses's dis-
courses to the Israelites, after they had escaped from Egypt but before they had
reached "the promised land." Moses claimed that God would drive out the in-
habitants who already occupied the land, and then he gave these orders: "thou
shalt smite them, and utterly destroy them; thou shalt make no covenant with
them, nor shew mercy unto them: Neither shalt thou make marriages with
them; thy daughter thou shalt not give unto his son, nor his daughter shalt thou
take unto thy son. For they will turn away thy son from following me, that they
may serve other gods: so will the anger of the LORD be kindled against you, and
destroy thee suddenly" (KJV). As far as Cameron was concerned, these instructions also sanctioned modern segregation. He urged his audience to obey this
message and remain "on safe ground for time and eternity."[4]

Cameron's disdain for the ruling class did not translate into empathy for
oppressed blacks, and one could easily get the impression that black lives were

expendable based on his application of this passage. Transposing modern constructions of race onto the scriptures, Cameron's sermon also listed several incidents from the Bible that buttressed his belief in white supremacy or at least black inferiority. He mentioned the complaints that Moses faced from his brother and sister after marrying a descendant of Ham, and he asserted that King Solomon married a black woman who ruined him and led him "away from God and into idolatry." Cameron also cited a few verses in which Ham's descendants were described as servants. "Why prolong the line of evidence?" he asked. "Today, the negro is still serving the sentence placed upon him. Let us leave him where God and the Bible left him and all will be well."[5]

Having determined the origin of the races, Cameron's sermon closed by arguing that blacks were innately lesser people. "They have always been cursed with a sence [sic] of fear, ignorance, superstition and an inferior[ity] complex." In explaining exceptions to racial stereotypes, Cameron claimed that "all those negro's [sic] who have a generous fertilization of white blood have invariably left the evidence of it behind them. But the genuine negro article is just what he has always been." He suggested that whites who needed "a servant for any purpose" should hire blacks and pay them well. "Remember the Negro is not responsible for being here," Cameron stated. "Our progenitors brought them here, many of them against their will, which makes them the white mans [sic] problem." Before ending his sermon, Cameron hearkened back to Deuteronomy one last time, urging his hearers to "let the white people of every state in the United States solve that problem in harmony with the word of God."[6]

Cameron's sermon, preached three months after the *Brown* ruling, undoubtedly addressed questions that had arisen in the minds of many whites. His insistence that whites take ownership of racial conflicts reflects the era's lingering paternalism, but it also contrasts with subsequent white denials of any complicity or responsibility in the plight of blacks. Although de jure segregation was a post–Civil War development, preachers like Cameron taught that racial segregation originated with God and was validated in holy writ. Various efforts at racial integration, however sporadic and tentative by the mid-1950s, threatened the surety and sanctity of perceived truths about race and religion. Cameron's message assured his audiences that racial segregation was part of God's plan and, as such, it should be maintained at all costs.

A 1957 sermon by Leon Burns, titled "Why Desegregation Will Fail," reflected whites' skepticism about desegregation. Burns's remarks may have been prepared in response to events in the fall of 1956 when riots erupted in Clinton,

Tennessee, after segregationists rallied their forces to prevent the implementation of judicial desegregation orders. During the following March, shortly after the schools in Clinton reopened, Burns delivered his message to the West Seventh Street Church of Christ in Columbia, Tennessee, two hundred miles west of Clinton. Many of his remarks centered upon the politics of race, rather than on any biblical or theological issues, so in this sense his sermon was somewhat unusual for Churches of Christ. Burns has received attention from other historians, including David Chappell, who cited Burns as evidence that segregationists conceded the Bible did not support their positions. One of Burns's comments deserves special scrutiny because it was misinterpreted by Chappell. Burns stated, "The Bible does not give a positive command for or against segregation between Negroes and Whites, but it is clearly seen by necessary inference that segregation is an important part of Divine providence and purpose." A cursory reading would seem to vindicate Chappell's use of Burns, except that the phrase "necessary inference" bore a special connotation for Churches of Christ. "Necessary inference" was one part of a threefold hermeneutic that Churches of Christ traditionally used to interpret the Bible. They long believed that the New Testament gave instructions in one of three ways: direct commands, divine examples, and necessary inferences. Each component of this hermeneutic approach carried equal weight. Historian Richard Hughes noted that, within Churches of Christ, this hermeneutic had "harden[ed] into a virtual orthodoxy by the twentieth century." That the Bible, in Burns's view, taught segregation by "necessary inference" was just as important as if it explicitly stated that black and white people should never interact.[7]

Burns was even more explicit in other portions of his sermon. Like many other staunch segregationists, he insisted that "those forces behind integration" were not really interested in equal educational opportunities or in repealing segregation laws. "These are simply means to an end, and the end is free and unrestrained intermarriage between Negroes and Whites, and they will not be satisfied until they get it." Much like Cameron, Burns alleged that God condemned interracial marriage. "Any student of human nature should know that there has always been a strong sexual attraction in every nation for people of another nation," he claimed. "This was clearly demonstrated by the Israelites when Joshua lead [sic] them into the promised land. God knew this attraction existed and in order to keep the people from losing their identity completely, he gave them the solemn command not to intermarry with other nations." Reflecting the Church of Christ hermeneutic, the final two sections of the sermon were titled "Old Testament Examples of Segregation" and "New Testament Teaching on This Subject."[8]

In the former, Burns highlighted numerous examples that supported his belief that segregation was a biblical tenet that modern Americans should obey. Burns cited a verse from the book of Leviticus that prohibited livestock breeding "with another kind," sowing a field "with mixed seed," or wearing a garment "of mixed linen and wool." Then he asked, "If such elements in the lower order of God's creation were to be unmixed, does it not follow that the same principle would apply to human relationships?" From the book of Genesis, Burns reasoned that the descendants of Cain and Seth (the children of Adam and Eve) intermarried. The intermarriage of these two peoples "which God had by law segregated was the direct cause of the wickedness that brought on the great flood." These extraordinary leaps of logic proved acceptable to many people who simply accepted the Bible as the literal word of God and a Church of Christ preacher as its best interpreter. Like Cameron, Burns also mentioned Noah's curse and Deuteronomy 7. To these stories, Burns added vignettes from the life of the patriarch Abraham. "God's refusal to accept Ishmael, Abraham's son by an Egyptian woman," Burns imagined, "is further proof that God intended Abraham's blood line to be kept pure." The care with which wives were found for Isaac and Jacob, Abraham's son and grandson, "shows that God did not intend that they mix their blood with that of other nations," Burns said.[9]

The New Testament was more challenging for segregationists, and prophets of integration were more likely to draw from its pages. Now Burns's arguments for segregation became even more specious. Based on the book of Acts, he described how the Holy Spirit descended on the apostles on the day of Pentecost and caused them to speak in various languages so that people within earshot could hear the gospel in their native tongues. "If God had intended that in the Christian dispensation all racial, national, and language barriers were to be dissolved, this was the place to announce it," he intoned. Instead, God seemed to confirm linguistic distinctions and, in Burns's judgment, segregation. Proponents of integration regularly cited scriptures that promoted unity between Jewish and Gentile Christians, but Burns pointed to the dissension that arose between them. The apostles taught that "the Jew could remain a Jew, and the Gentile remain a Gentile, but they would be one in their spiritual relationship to one another and to Christ." Thus he distinguished between a spiritual relationship and any physical or social relationship. Finally, Burns described a scene from the book of Revelation where the redeemed souls of all ages are gathered around God's throne. "The appearance of all nations and races will not only enhance the praise given to God, but will demonstrate the love, wisdom and mercy of God's eternal plan for man's salvation," Burns proclaimed. "How could any sane person even think of demanding that all nations must be one before this great day comes[?] To do so is to rob Heaven of its praise and God of His eternal glory." Burns clearly wanted no part of heaven on earth. With this peculiar logic, Burns earnestly believed that the Bible required racial segregation. Unlike Cameron, he condemned any hint of violence and hatred, a notable assertion given his city's recent history. Eleven years before this sermon, Columbia experienced a race riot, or what might better be termed a violent, state-sanctioned assault on the black community, yet Burns urged whites to remove "all prejudice and hatred" from their hearts and to "deplore all acts of violence."[10]

Burns was a relatively popular preacher among Churches of Christ in middle Tennessee and Arkansas. His occasional speaking engagements at the Harding College Bible Lectures, both before and after his segregationist sermon was widely distributed, implied that he enjoyed a measure of respectability as a doctrinally sound, engaging preacher. He even appeared on the same program with the venerable black preacher Marshall Keeble. These details about Burns do not quantify the churches or members who subscribed to his perspective on race relations, but his good standing among peers confirms that he was not a marginal figure. "Why Desegregation Will Fail" was also broadcast over a local radio station and, in anticipation of the high demand, the West Seventh Street Church of Christ published a pamphlet with the full text of the sermon. The pamphlets were sold in bulk: one dollar for ten copies, four dollars for fifty, or six dollars for one hundred. In this form, the sermon was placed in church tract boards, available for church members or visitors to have. Thus, at least in some Churches of Christ, Burns's sermon appeared alongside pamphlets that discussed baptism, instrumental music in worship (a sin to the a cappella Churches of Christ), and the evils of alcohol and gambling. Members picked it up to learn what the Bible said about racial segregation and to vindicate what many already believed.[11]

Burns apparently inspired other preachers toward similar endeavors. On September 22, 1957, less than three weeks after nine black students attempted to desegregate Little Rock's Central High School, Guthrie Dean, a Church of Christ preacher in Judsonia, Arkansas, delivered a sermon over KWCB radio in Searcy that acknowledged Burns's efforts. Dean had previously served a church in Ruston, Louisiana, where he had broadcast a sermon on KRUS about "The Christian Attitude Toward Integration." Dean's radio sermon in Arkansas made little use of scripture, an unusual approach among Churches of Christ. He opted for a history lesson.[12]

Dean's commentary on US history and race relations was notable for its patriotism, defense of the Old South, and attempt to associate the plaintiffs and Supreme Court justices involved in the *Brown* decision with the Communist Party. In contrast to Cameron's description of "the lustful greed of the unscrupulous class of white men infesting the earth," Dean's rosy account of slavery in the United States emphasized how "early Americans are not to be judged too harshly for accepting this practice" and how "all slaves . . . would have been freed by the natural growth of a new nation in its efforts to live by its own Constitution." He contended that the Civil War had nothing to do with slavery and everything to do with states' rights, that Reconstruction was summarily disastrous, and that the Ku Klux Klan was composed of "a group of honest and sincere men who had no desire to harm the Negro." His veneration of the Lost Cause and its rhetoric was most apparent when he claimed that, from the end of Reconstruction, "the Whites and the Negroes in all sections of our country got along increasingly well." Ignoring the prevalence of racial violence against blacks, Dean insisted that race relations were fine until President Franklin Roosevelt recognized the Soviet Union and the Communist Party began fomenting racial strife. Religious leaders who claimed that racial segregation was wrong knew "nothing of the higher principles of Christianity, or of humanity," according to Dean.[13]

When he finally turned to the Bible, Dean claimed that it "abundantly proves that God intended that there be many nations and races upon the earth." In similar fashion to Burns, Dean suggested that Christianity "makes no provision for all men to be equal while in this material life." He pointed to Pauline texts from the New Testament that instructed servants to remain with their masters and masters to treat their servants well. Dean also addressed Galatians 3:28, a passage often quoted by integrationists. The verse states, "There is neither Jew nor Greek, there is neither bond nor free, there is neither male for female: for ye are all one in Christ Jesus" (KJV). "If this verse proves the scripturalness of desegregation," Dean exclaimed, "it also demands that there be no segregation between male and female. Hence the division between male and female in public restrooms and in dormitories would be unscriptural." These distinctions were important for Dean because he understood the civil rights movement as "theological drama" that pitted Christianity versus "godless communism." He stressed that there "should be no doubt in our minds that this desegregation battle will be fought along religious lines." Dean even insinuated the potential for physical violence. "[T]he bloodiest wars of human history have been religious wars," he warned, before noting that the newspapers had recently been filled with "mob violence, race difficulties, forced integration, [and] murmmering [sic] of another Civil War." His greatest fears were the atheism of the Communist Party and those people who espoused racial integration as a Christian principle. These two notions threatened not only "the southern way of life" but also Dean's entire worldview.[14]

Criticism of distant entities such as the federal government soon gave way to more localized attacks, and some preachers used the church's restoration theology to appeal to whites who were weary of social turmoil and racially charged issues. In this manner, Christian primitivism became a tool to highlight the shortcomings of civil rights activists, especially Christian pastors. The New Testament did not speak of social or political protest; Jesus did not organize marches against the Romans; and the apostle Paul even sent a slave back to his master. Thus, preachers used biblical narratives to disparage activists who claimed to find inspiration for social protest in their Christian faiths. White Churches of Christ in particular sought to capitalize on the discomfort of white southerners by emphasizing the church's plea for a return to New Testament Christianity. Implicit in that appeal was a desire for preachers and activists to attend to spiritual matters rather than political or social ones. By upholding Churches of Christ as a nondenominational church devoted solely to practicing New Testament Christianity, whites who disliked the social activism of other denominations offered Churches of Christ as a haven for people who wished to practice Christianity without the discomfort of having a denominational hierarchy pushing racial equality.

This mindset undoubtedly informed the Sixth & Izard Church of Christ in Little Rock, Arkansas, when they invited Marshall Keeble to conduct a revival after that city's infamous desegregation crisis. In keeping with traditional practice, local whites hoped to start a new church for blacks in the wake of Keeble's visit. The church must have also aimed to quell racial animosities that exploded with the desegregation of Central High School. With regard to race relations, however, Keeble remained enigmatic. On more than one occasion during his career, the Ku Klux Klan tried to run him out of town because his revivals often attracted both blacks and whites. But in addition to his preaching style, white churches liked Keeble because he refused to preach sermons about segregation. When asked about this omission shortly before his death, Keeble confirmed that he simply avoided the subject. "I don't recall speaking to an audience that I ever said anything about segregation much at all." In fact, Keeble was critical of other black preachers within the denomination who did broach the subject with white audiences. He thought that black preachers who talked about segregation would "just take it, and they couldn't talk or think of nothing else. . . . At the same time," he insisted, "I was bringing about unity among the races every day." A white church elder who once joined Keeble on a missionary trip to Africa reflected the sentiments of many whites when he recounted Keeble's position on segregation.

> Most of the time he's been very, very calm about this segregation problem, and he hasn't tried to take sides with anybody. He's tried to lay it on the line just exactly like it was, and he's really chewed out his black brothers in [the] flesh, maybe not in the church, but all over for the tactics and the attitude that they've used toward the white man. . . . And he hasn't been a one-sided affair. He's tried to look at the thing objectively from both sides and . . . hasn't tried to take sides with the colored people. Because if they had all been of the same temperament that Brother Keeble is, they would've probably gotten the same treatment that Brother Keeble has gotten over the years. But they had a grit in their craw and they had animosity in their craw, and rightly so the way they've been treated, but . . . this is all the unfolding of God's plan for the salvation of mankind.[15]

This appraisal of Keeble explains his popularity among whites during the civil rights movement, when preachers from other denominations were utilizing faith to attack racial injustices. Although Keeble was a captivating preacher, he was asked to come to Little Rock because he was a safe choice. Whites knew that he would not say anything inflammatory and, above all else, he would not criticize them for clinging to segregation. This assurance partly explains why Keeble estimated that whites outnumbered blacks by a ratio of ten to one at this revival, although there was enough of a response from blacks to create a new Church of Christ. Keeble's most striking memory of these events was a white husband and wife who wanted Keeble to baptize them. While Keeble had baptized whites in the past, he was sensitive to the heightened tensions in Little Rock and tried to convince the young couple to find a white preacher and a white church. "I tried to get rid of them [by telling them where the white church was].... He said, 'I want you to baptize me at the colored church.' . . . Well, I said 'alright.' And I go back in the pulpit and announce it, and before I could get down there [several blocks to the church from the tent], white people done beat me from the tent and the Negro couldn't get in to see the baptizing at all. They were just so carried away with it."[16]

The scene of a black man immersing a white woman and her husband in the South during the late 1950s seems almost unthinkable. To be sure, whites maintained firm control of the immediate environment. In the estimation of church leaders and the audience, Keeble was not threatening the racial status quo by baptizing this couple, although he was clearly participating in an activity that defied local custom. In other situations throughout the South, white churches refused requests from black preachers who sought use of baptismal facilities. Indeed, the image of blacks and whites sharing the same water was so disturbing to some whites that violence occasionally erupted when beaches or swimming pools were desegregated.

In a different context several years later, the demise of segregation and threat of black political power also troubled a white preacher from Montgomery, Alabama, named O. B. Porterfield of the Cleveland Avenue Church of Christ. On Wednesday night, March 24, 1965, approximately twenty-five thousand people were anticipating the next day's march up Dexter Avenue to the steps of the state capitol, the final leg of a trek that had begun for some in Selma and for others many years and heartaches before. The protest originated with the suppression of the black franchise in Alabama's Black Belt counties, particularly Dallas County and its county seat, Selma, where Alabama state troopers had repelled peaceful demonstrators with billy clubs and tear gas on March 7. Bloody Sunday, as it became known, inspired people from around the country to descend upon Alabama a few weeks later when another march was launched. Still disturbed by the negative publicity of Bloody Sunday and the Montgomery bus boycott less than ten years earlier, many whites in Montgomery, including Porterfield, were especially wary of what the following day might bring. Ironically, Martin Luther King Jr. and other civil rights leaders were planning the next day's activities at the home of Fred Gray, a civil rights attorney and preacher for the Newtown Church of Christ. Although he only participated in the last day's walk to the capitol, Gray had obtained the necessary court order to protect the marchers on their journey from Selma to Montgomery. On the morrow, he would be one of several civil rights leaders to meet with Governor George Wallace.[17]

Porterfield, who knew Gray from their days of working together as circulation managers for a Montgomery newspaper, appeared on local television station WKAB that night with a speech that warned of the impending march and the ministers who were participating. His opening remarks recounted the threat of communism, the rising divorce rate, and the increasing crime rate among young people, but he wasted little time in reaching the main point of his message. "We need a unity movement tonight," he pleaded. "Since the Church of Christ had its beginning about 2000 years ago we have been pleading for people to stay with God's word. . . . For a long time we have pleaded with preachers to stay out of politics and preach just the Gospel. For that reason neither I nor any Minister of the Church of Christ as far as we know has been seen parading up and down the street or praying on the street corners to be seen of men. Our job first and foremost is to serve Christ, save souls and not prove points." In the context of the Selma-to-Montgomery march, Porterfield used the restorationist rhetoric of Churches of Christ as a rallying cry for disgruntled whites. Marchers who journeyed from Selma and heard Porterfield might have recalled the sign displayed outside of the Selma Church of Christ: "When You Pray, Be Not As Hypocrites Are, Standing in the Street. Matt: 6:5."[18]

Porterfield further argued that preachers should focus on curtailing the aforementioned social ills by giving greater attention to the teaching of the scriptures. He urged "the so-called preachers from out of the state that have invaded this city and this state . . . [to] get off the streets, get out of the march, go back to your pulpit, but on the way back study to see what God said to do before you enter the pulpit again." Porterfield also noted several allegations regarding the conduct of a few marchers. He was so incensed that preachers would even associate themselves with some protestors, including a "single pregnant girl" and people who were "committing fornication on a street in Selma and also in Montgomery," that he asked, "Is this the type person that you ministers are upholding tonight and fighting for social equality for[?]" Porterfield complained about those people who were arrested for indecent exposure because, having no other choice, they "began to 'relieve' themselves . . . to the extent that it flowed down Dexter Avenue for approximately 1 or 2 blocks." Again, he demanded, "The least that you could do tonight is cease requesting so-called civil rights and social equality until you present to the people of Montgomery a higher type person and better morals."[19]

Porterfield's disdain for all of the protestors only escalated as his sermon progressed. He cited scriptures to validate the argument that the march and the ministers who supported it were displeasing to God. First, he mentioned the New Testament story of Onesimus, a slave who converted to Christianity and was sent back to his master by the apostle Paul. "Don't you think tonight," Porterfield opined, "that if Onesimus could live as a Christian as a slave . . . that anybody that wants to go home to Heaven whether they are white or colored can do so in the country and the state that we live in?" He reiterated the point by stating, "It is good to vote, yes, and it is good to be educated, yes, but neither of these things are necessary for salvation." Especially perturbed by the number of young people in the march, Porterfield exclaimed that "a large number of these boys and girls are the scum of the earth!"[20]

In the second half of his sermon, he encouraged viewers to visit a Church of Christ, where one could "go to hear the Word of God, and not a rabble rouser. You will not hear freedom songs," Porterfield continued, "but instead you will hear singing and praising to God. You will not hear bad things about the Sheriff . . . or the Governor but you will meet to take the Lord's Supper. . . . The Church of Christ deals with Godly things in Godly ways." He even took the time to describe how Churches of Christ were locally autonomous and did not belong to the National Council of Churches (NCC), an organization composed of numerous mainline Protestant denominations and devoted to civil rights. This distinction was intended to appeal to people who belonged to denominations that composed the council's membership. Porterfield explained that their money was being directed toward the council's activities, including its opposition to government-sponsored prayer in public schools and its heavy investment in the Delta Ministry, an effort to pursue racial reconciliation in the Mississippi delta. In a direct appeal to potential new members, he assured viewers that the "money given to a Church of Christ is used to preach the Gospel and to help the needy."[21]

In his closing remarks, Porterfield returned to the scriptures, seeking to further discredit the strong presence of the clergy in the march. A number of clergymen donned their collars during the protest, and Porterfield criticized this practice. He cited Matthew 23:5 and asked, "why is it you haven't seen a Church of Christ minister dressed in such a way?" Because, he answered, "the Pharisees and Scribes were condemned for changing their type clothing in order to be seen of men." Porterfield quoted the Golden Rule and promised to send a copy of his sermon to President Johnson, requesting that he "practice the Golden Rule and get this unholy, ungodly mess out of our streets, if he does not want it in his home." He turned to 1 Peter 4:16, an oft-quoted passage by overtly religious participants in the civil rights movement, and pointed out that the previous verse instructs the reader not to suffer "as an evil doer, or as a busy body in other men's matters," a clear description of the marchers in Porterfield's mind. He directed his audience to the Sermon on the Mount, instructing blacks or whites who might have been mistreated to "turn the other cheek" or "go the second mile." In the end, Porterfield wanted all of Montgomery, but especially its white citizens, to know that Churches of Christ were an alternative to the social discord, an alternative to belonging to a denomination whose ministers or money might have been aiding the march. "[W]e are humble as we possibly can be, we love one another, and the preacher does the very best at every minute to set a good example," he stated. "Ministers of the church of Christ . . . are striving to preach the word of God as best they know how, and not be entangled with the things of this world." In a final plea for citizens to oppose the march and stay at home rather than participate, he contrasted Martin Luther King Jr., the march's leader, with Jesus, the church's leader. "[T]he Leader we have will absolutely show us the right way. Isn't this what the Church really is to be, isn't this what the world is seeking for tonight, *a real restoration of simple New Testament Christianity?*" (emphasis in original).[22]

While each of the aforementioned white preachers utilized the Bible to sustain their arguments for segregation, Porterfield exemplified how restorationist theology could be used to oppose civil rights activism. He did not bother with the intricate details of integration as much as he fiercely denounced people whose Christian consciences led them to support the civil rights movement and the Selma-to-Montgomery march. With the battle over integration having been already fought and seemingly lost, Porterfield demanded that preachers focus on spiritual, not temporal, matters.

Similar sentiments inspired the publication of *The Martin Luther King Story* in 1967 by Harding College professor and anticommunist crusader James Bales. *The Martin Luther King Story* widened the growing chasm that existed between blacks and whites within Churches of Christ. Bales definitely perceived communism as a bigger threat than integration, equal access to public facilities, or voting rights, but he could not shake the idea that the Communist Party helped foment the racial discord that seemed more prevalent in the 1960s. He provides an excellent example of the struggle waged in the minds of many whites during the civil rights movement. In word and theory, Bales believed that freedom and liberty should be extended to everyone, and his practice of Christianity cultivated a desire to practice goodwill toward all people. He genuinely perceived communism as a direct and immediate threat to the country in general and the practice of Christianity in particular, so his patriotic zeal prevented him from recognizing the injustices born of institutional racism. When the country seemed to erupt in chaos, he began to view social protests as attacks upon those principles that he championed most. In sum, Bales's fear of social disorder made him suspicious of the civil rights movement at the very time when Christian faith and democratic spirit were inspiring others to work for the extension of civil rights to all citizens.[23]

These examples of white preachers illustrate how white resistance to the civil rights movement took different forms, but Churches of Christ included a remarkable number of blacks who also expressed opposition to civil rights activism.[24] Marshall Keeble, arguably the most prominent preacher—black or white—within Churches of Christ through the middle of the twentieth century, expressed his opposition to civil rights activism on numerous occasions. Floyd Rose was Keeble's student at NCI from 1950 to 1957, when Keeble also served as president. Rose recalled an occasion when Martin Luther King Jr. was scheduled to speak at Fisk University in Nashville. Several NCI students desperately wanted to hear King, but they were not permitted. Keeble told Rose that King was "the worst enemy that the Church of Christ had." NCI students also wanted to recruit Fred Gray, a school alumnus, to speak at their lectureship. A petition was circulated among them in an effort to convince Keeble to invite Gray to speak. Keeble refused, telling Rose that Gray had gotten "too smart." Gray, who greatly admired Keeble and was always proud to be associated with him and NCI, claimed to understand his mentor's position. "A portion of his preaching and work in the church had been sponsored by white members of the Church of Christ," Gray wrote in his autobiography. "I am quite confident that it was difficult for him to understand how one of his former boy preachers would now be standing in courtrooms fighting against racial discrimination."[25]

Gray was one of only a handful of blacks from Churches of Christ with a decidedly public role in the civil rights movement. The few who actively participated demonstrate the conundrums that blacks in Churches of Christ faced. Available sources suggest that the only black civil rights activists who were members of Churches of Christ and remained in the South throughout the 1950s and 1960s were Fred Gray and his family. In 1930, Gray was born to a carpenter and domestic in Montgomery where he attended Churches of Christ with his parents. "The church was the center of our early childhood," Gray recalled. In 1943, in an unsubtle effort to persuade her son to become a minister, Gray's mother arranged for him to complete his grammar school education at NCI, where he learned the Bible from Keeble and even accompanied him on fund-raising trips around the country. Upon completing his degree requirements in 1947, Gray immediately returned to Montgomery and enrolled in Alabama State College. At the time, he wanted to become a minister and history teacher, but his college experiences changed those plans. The daily indignities of riding a bus in Montgomery coupled with inspiration from several professors convinced Gray to aim for a career in law. After gaining entrance to Cleveland's Western Reserve University Law School in 1951, he privately pledged to "return to Montgomery and use the law to 'destroy everything segregated that I could find.'"[26]

Despite the rigorous demands of law school, Gray made time to attend church, including midweek services. He eventually became the assistant minister of the East 100th Street Church of Christ (now University Church of Christ) in Cleveland, learning the practice of ministry under the tutelage of J. S. Winston while preparing for his career in law. By the fall of 1954, Gray returned to Montgomery as an attorney, ready to keep the private pledge that he made as a student at Alabama State. From the outset, his personal faith inspired his legal endeavors although, in public pronouncements, he employed neutral language rather than the caustic tone struck by those who emphasized the sectarianism of Churches of Christ. In November 1955, one month before Rosa Parks refused to give up her seat on a Montgomery bus, Gray spoke to the Ten Times One Is Ten Club, the oldest club for black women in Montgomery. Even though Gray was only twenty-four years old at the time, his speech foreshadowed his entire career. "We must be strong, and we must be financially able and willing to carry our cases to court if our officials will not voluntarily desegregate our schools, parks, transportation system and all other public facilities," he told his audience. "During these crucial days, days of great decision, may the God of Heaven direct us, help us and may He through His divine guidance lead all men to realize that we were all made from one flesh, and that we are all God's children. May God bless us, assist us, and may He speed the day when all of our schools and all other public facilities will be completely integrated." A few months prior to this speech, Gray had represented Claudette Colvin, a fifteen-year-old who refused to obey a bus driver's instructions to give up her seat for a white patron. Colvin was found guilty of assault and battery by the juvenile court of Montgomery County, while the charge that she violated the segregation ordinance was dropped. The case gave Gray his first taste of the work necessary to attack racial segregation through the courts.[27]

A more decisive moment arrived on December 1, 1955. As he had many times throughout the previous year, Gray shared lunch with Rosa Parks. Later that afternoon, she was arrested and charged with violating segregation laws when she refused a bus driver's order to vacate her seat. Her defiance that day sparked what became the most popular bus boycott in history. Gray served as Parks's attorney, and he was also lead counsel in *Browder v. Gayle*, the Supreme Court decision that finally integrated public transportation in Alabama after a year of protest. The court determined that the Montgomery statute violated the Fourteenth Amendment. Gray's illustrious career as an attorney would include numerous historic victories, but he also took great pride in his work as a preacher.[28]

Soon after the boycott ended on December 21, 1956, Gray became the minister of the Newtown Church of Christ in Montgomery. He served in that capacity for sixteen years before he moved with his family to Tuskegee and became involved with a Church of Christ there. Although ministers were often bi-vocational, Gray was sometimes criticized for working as a civil rights attorney but, unlike most Church of Christ members, Gray believed that "having his life centered around Christ has assisted me in all of the cases that I have handled during my practice." In a 1985 interview conducted shortly after he became president of the National Bar Association, Gray emphasized, "The church has always been first in my life, and I feel my work [as an attorney] has been an extension of what the Bible teaches. . . . God made each of us from Adam and there is equal justice for all of us under Jesus." Gray interpreted his legal career in explicitly religious terms. He was also an advocate of nonviolence, though his reasons seemed to be more practical than philosophical. Gray recalled, "I always knew that there was the possibility of being hurt, but I never let it bother me to the extent of me being afraid of doing what I thought I needed to do. . . . I never had a [gun] permit, because I felt, one, if someone really wanted to kill you, they'll probably do it before you can use it. And secondly, if I had a pistol and used it even in the circumstances the average person would say are justified, because of my practice, they would put me under the jail."[29]

Gray was an exceptional attorney, but his callings to civil rights law and ministry were certainly unique within Churches of Christ. Gray may have been the first black person in the denomination to be an attorney and preacher but, even among his career choices, Gray and his immediate family were among only a handful of Church of Christ members who were actively involved in the southern civil rights movement. He was by far the most prominent Church of

Christ member within popular movement circles, and he was further unique in his involvement with the National Association for the Advancement of Colored People (NAACP), a civil rights organization that many within Churches of Christ, both black and white, considered a distraction from the cause of spreading the Gospel. Gray also dabbled in politics. He was likely cheated out of his 1966 bid to become an Alabama legislator, but he won a seat in 1970, becoming one of the first blacks to serve in that state's legislature since Reconstruction. Yet Gray's primitivist theology was otherwise orthodox among Churches of Christ. He never wavered from the tenets of the faith that he learned from Marshall Keeble or J. S. Winston but, unlike most others in the church, Gray's beliefs did not strictly prohibit his association with other ministers in a cause that many black activists imbued with religious significance. While Churches of Christ were known for their eagerness to debate the finer points of baptismal theology, for example, Gray could not recall any religious discussions with other ministers who were involved in the civil rights movement.[30]

Although Gray's activism was certainly unique, Floyd Rose may have stirred more controversy within Churches of Christ from his home in Toledo, Ohio. Like Gray, Rose was a black southerner whose life was marked by racial segregation. He was born in Valdosta, Georgia, to a sharecropping family in 1938 before moving to Atlanta at the age of six, when his father became minister of the Simpson Street Church of Christ. While Rose lived with the daily indignities imposed upon blacks in the South, one particular event in his childhood seared his memory and instilled a resolve in him that would impact his career as a minister and civil rights activist. During a church trip from Atlanta to Ensley, Alabama, Rose was seated beside an elderly lady who told him that she desperately needed to use the restroom. Since there was no restroom on the bus, he promptly walked to the front of the bus and told the white driver that a lady needed to use the restroom. Shortly after crossing the state line, the driver pulled over to the right side of the road, across the street from a gas station. Rose stepped off the bus and entered the station to request permission for this lady to use the restroom. What happened next would always haunt him.

This big, burly white guy, with a cigar hanging out of the right side of his mouth, looked up and said, "We ain't got no nigger restrooms." And I said, "But she's an old lady." He took the cigar out of his mouth . . . came around and opened the door, and put his big fat hand in the pit of my stomach and just shoved me back. And I went stumbling back, and my back hit the gas pump. And then . . .

I slid down, wearing my little blue suede suit my mother had bought me for the trip . . . grit and grime and dirt and oil [and] sand [got] all in it. And I turned and I looked toward that bus. Those black folk were staring out of the window, their eyes frozen with fear. [They] didn't move and didn't say a word when I got on the bus. And I looked in his direction and I looked in theirs, and I decided then that I didn't want to be like him and I didn't want to be like them. I didn't want to make people afraid of me, and I didn't want to be afraid of people who made other people afraid. I got back on that bus. Nobody said one word! Not one! And the old lady said she had soiled her clothes.[31]

Rose experienced problems in the public school system, and he was finally expelled for slapping a teacher. His parents sent him to NCI where he, like Gray, learned Bible and homiletics from Marshall Keeble. Rose also had other formative experiences that left lasting impressions on him. During a fundraising trip with Keeble in the early 1950s, he met a wealthy, white church member named Billie Sol Estes in Pecos, Texas. Estes gave Rose ten dollars and instructed the student to call his parents and ask if they would mind Estes financing their son's education. Rose took the money but never expected to see Estes again, so he never called his parents. A few nights later in Carlsbad, New Mexico, Estes appeared again. In spite of the segregated seating arrangements, Estes sat in the "colored section" next to Rose. After the services, Estes gave Rose another ten dollars and asked if he had telephoned his parents. Realizing what a tremendous opportunity this might be, Rose fibbed and told Estes that his parents would be delighted to have him sponsor their son's education. True to his word, Estes paid for Rose's education at NCI and sent forty dollars a month for living expenses. He also financed Rose's first two years at SWCC and tried, unsuccessfully, to have him admitted to ACC. On several occasions in hotels and restaurants, Estes and Rose would flaunt Jim Crow customs, and Estes, whose wealth accounted for his ability to act and associate with whom he pleased, spoke before numerous black Churches of Christ during the late 1950s and early 1960s.

As a man of great wealth, Estes was also well-connected. He maintained a relationship with Lyndon Johnson until the early 1960s, when Estes's fiscal and legal problems threatened to undermine Johnson's political credibility. Due to his fraud convictions (which were later overturned) and claims that Johnson facilitated President Kennedy's assassination, Estes quickly became a marginal figure in political and church circles. His 2013 eulogy in the *New York Times* characterized him as "a fast-talking Texas swindler who made millions, went to prison and captivated America for years with mind-boggling agricultural scams, payoffs to politicians and bizarre tales of covered-up killings and White House conspiracies." Nevertheless, his impact on Rose was tremendous. Rose named his first son Billie Sol and, later, the family asked Rose to deliver the eulogies for both Estes and his wife.[32]

While Gray was fighting legal battles to overcome racial injustice, Rose worked through his pulpit to coordinate protest marches and economic boycotts. As he finished his education in the early 1960s, Rose began showing more interest in the work of movement leaders Jim Bevel and Diane Nash. A few people, including Rose, who were associated with NCI once ignored Keeble's instructions, when he told them not to participate in a Nashville march led by Bevel and Nash. Rose, along with his father and Franklin Florence, also caused a stir on the campus of DLC in 1963 when he sought entrance there. President Athens Clay Pullias called the police, who escorted them off of the campus, while many white students gathered around and booed the officers.[33]

The assassination of Martin Luther King Jr. and the reaction of some of his fellow ministers in Churches of Christ inspired Rose to more radically alter his course. The epiphany began as he returned from Florida after learning of the assassination and hearing some of his colleagues use the occasion to publicly question the authenticity of the slain leader's faith. Conversely, Rose realized how much had changed in his lifetime. "As I drove back to Toledo," he recalled, "eating in desegregated restaurants and using the restroom facilities that were accessible to whites and blacks alike, I asked myself as I reflected on my Church's attitude toward Dr. King and the Civil Rights Movement, whether the light that was within us had itself blinded us to the true light." Rose still preached and practiced a restorationist theology, but he began to question some of the fundamental claims of Churches of Christ. "Although at the time I had not settled completely in my mind the question of the 'One Church,'" he later confessed, "*somehow I could not bring myself to believe that Martin Luther King, Jr. was outside the Will of God*" (emphasis in original). Over the next several years, he grappled with theological questions that arose in his mind shortly after King's death. "Like the Pharisees, we [Churches of Christ] were eager to cross land and sea to make one proselyte; to convert one Baptist or Methodist, but were less inclined to go across the street to feed the hungry or clothe the naked," Rose opined. "*While others were known for what they were and did, we were always known for what we said*" (emphasis in original). Rose was suddenly overcome with guilt and shame. Churches of Christ "became spectators," in his mind, "reapers of the benefits while others were participants in the making of a better America. Oh how ashamed I felt at times. While we emphasized the importance of baptism by immersion, weekly communion, liberal giving, the non use of instrumental music in the worship service on Sunday; we were humiliated and dehumanized by signs that read 'colored only' . . . on Monday."[34]

In the 1970s, Rose gradually began focusing his ministry more upon the life and teachings of Jesus, but he soon discovered that his growing disregard for restorationist thought ostracized him from other ministers. People became wary about whether he was a "sound preacher." SWCC and some churches rescinded speaking invitations. At the pinnacle of his popularity among Churches of Christ, when he was receiving nearly thirty invitations a year to hold revivals, he left the denomination. In 1979, he started a new church in Toledo that gave special attention to social activism. Success soon followed. He became president of the local NAACP in 1982, having only joined the organization one month earlier. Among other accomplishments, Rose succeeded with a program dubbed "Operation Fair Share" that used economic pressure to open up employment and business opportunities to Toledo blacks. At the time, Rose vowed to "turn in our charge cards where we can't turn in our time cards." The difference was profound, as agreements worth more than fifty million dollars were negotiated for minority businesses and employees. Along with his work through the NAACP, Rose participated in nonviolent demonstrations that resulted in numerous arrests. He brought renowned and often controversial figures such as Stokely Carmichael, Rosa Parks, Louis Farrakhan, and T. D. Jakes into his church to speak on special occasions. In the mid-1990s, Rose rejoined the church of his youth but maintained the beliefs that precipitated his break with Churches of Christ. He even returned to Valdosta, Georgia, in 1996 to work as a social activist.[35]

While Gray stayed in the South and remained with Churches of Christ and their theology, Rose made a name for himself outside of the South and, for a time at least, outside of the denomination's confines. Franklin Florence, a third black activist who was also educated at NCI, left the South like Rose but maintained his conservative theology like Gray. Florence moved to Rochester, New York, in April 1959 where he became the minister of the Reynolds Street Church of Christ. Like Gray, his Christian disposition and disgust at racism inspired his civil rights activism, but before he became a local leader in Rochester, Florence cultivated contacts with prominent white members of Churches of Christ. The restorationism and exclusivism that characterized Churches of Christ were an integral part of Florence's theology, and his interactions with whites reveal other ways in which blacks and whites cooperated within the denomination.[36]

In the late 1950s and early 1960s, Florence solicited donations for a new building for his Rochester flock, and many of his letters went to white Churches of Christ. More revealing is that he also requested their expertise in organizing church ministries and in clarifying certain biblical passages. For example, Florence asked Gus Nichols, a conservative white preacher from Alabama, about his understanding of issues surrounding marriage, such as whether a person from Churches of Christ could "marry outside the faith" (that is, marry someone from another denomination). Nichols sent a brief but cordial reply that addressed Florence's questions. The young minister also maintained a sizable collection of sermons, primarily those broadcast over Nashville's WLAC by notable white preachers from Churches of Christ. And like countless other Churches of Christ, the Reynolds Street church made financial contributions to the *Herald of Truth* radio program. Florence not only sought answers to theological questions, but he also used successful white ministers as a resource for his own ministry. At mid-century, the Madison Church of Christ in Nashville was one of the largest in the country and, therefore, other church leaders were interested in its methods for church growth. Florence borrowed organizational ideas from Madison and its minister, Ira North, to incorporate into his own church programs in Rochester. Florence and North exchanged personal letters, and North urged his young black counterpart to visit the Madison church.[37]

Through long letters, telephone conversations, or personal encounters, Florence worked tirelessly during the early years of his Rochester ministry to raise funds for a new facility. His letters gave a history of "the work of the church" in Rochester and outlined possibilities for numerical and spiritual growth. Florence attended the lectureship at ACC in 1961 where he made repeated requests for donations, and he also telephoned church leaders about his church's financial needs. He emphasized his church's independence and the progress that members, who numbered about one hundred, had made through their own efforts. "Everything that has been accomplished thus far has been done without outside help," he insisted in one letter, "but we are presently in need of assistance if our demands are to be met." Elsewhere he wrote, "Our wish is to ask the church, to help us help ourselves." Florence even sought help from Pat Boone, a member of Churches of Christ whose musical career made him one of the most popular recording artists in pre-Beatles America. Although white churches had often served as benefactors to black churches, Florence's requests often elicited negative responses, a fact that might have helped foster the sense of frustration that he would one day express toward Churches of Christ, which he would later describe as "reactionary and racist."[38]

While Florence grew weary of whites within the denomination, his relationships with blacks never faltered. The Reynolds Street Church of Christ regularly donated money to NCI and SWCC, and Fred Gray was a guest speaker for the church in 1962, sharing a message titled "The Church in a Changing World." In that same year, Florence was invited to speak at the NCI lectureship, where he had delivered a baccalaureate address in 1961. These opportunities certainly depended upon the approval of Marshall Keeble who, like other institutional figures in Churches of Christ, had a penchant for ensuring that only "sound doctrine" be spoken on his watch. In an era marked by sit-ins and freedom rides, Florence was noticeably silent on the issue of race relations at the baccalaureate service. His sermon was delivered exactly two weeks after white attackers firebombed freedom riders in Anniston, Alabama, but his words could have just as easily been spoken by a white preacher in any Church of Christ. The sermon was titled "This Critical Hour," and it included familiar harangues against sins—deteriorating families, juvenile delinquency, crime, liquor, and dishonesty in general—that preachers from all across the religious landscape lamented. Ironically, he cited a Bible verse—James 2:9, "But if ye have respect to persons, ye commit sin"—and urged his audience not to commit "the sin of respect of person[s]." This plea appeared alongside similar ones concerning greed and indifference. In reciting a list of things that could not save a person, Florence included legislation. "And Legislation," he cried, "that holds God's authority in contempt, oft 'loosing wild tongues that hold not God in awe,' forgetting that 'the wicked shall be turned into hell with all the nations that forget God,' says, 'It is not in me to save you.'"[39]

Florence remained orthodox among Churches of Christ, yet he also became increasingly interested in the civil rights movement and social activism in general. By the mid-1960s, Florence became an outspoken and well-connected activist in Rochester. After the Southern Christian Leadership Conference dismissed the possibility of extending its activities into Rochester, Florence, now a prominent member of the local NAACP, secured speaking appearances from Malcolm X and later Stokely Carmichael. In 1965, following the suggestion of Saul Alinsky, a self-described radical and community organizer who worked extensively with Cesar Chavez's United Farm Workers, a group of community and religious leaders from Rochester formed a new organization, FIGHT, an acronym for Freedom, Integration, God, Honor, Today. (In a revealing change, the "I" was later said to represent Independence.)[40]

Florence became the president of FIGHT and, under his leadership, the group enjoyed many successes. FIGHT focused primarily on improving housing conditions, job training, and employment opportunities for local blacks. Rochester enjoyed a low unemployment rate, but the rate for blacks was consistently over 10 percent. The disparity between black and white incomes was over two thousand dollars, the highest of any city in the state of New York. Cost disparities in housing also posed another problem, as gross monthly rent for whites averaged about twenty-five dollars less per month than for blacks. These problems remained unaddressed, in part, because political representation in the city was all white. FIGHT waged its biggest battle from September 1966 to April 1967 over the hiring practices of the Eastman Kodak Company. While Florence and FIGHT were not completely successful in their attack on Kodak, many of their employment goals for the company and for the city of Rochester were met by the early 1970s.[41]

Florence had much in common with Gray and Rose, but he displayed a greater interest in the politics of the black power movement. With numerous other cities across the nation, Rochester suffered a riot in 1964, and FIGHT leaders occasionally alluded to the threat of violence or social unrest to attain their goals. When Kodak attempted to undermine FIGHT's aims, Florence announced, "Black leaders in every ghetto across the nation are watching the Kodak-FIGHT controversy and several groups have offered any help [that] FIGHT request[s]." Alinsky once referred to Kodak as "a southern plantation transplanted in the north," and other leaders warned that ignoring Rochester's problems might escalate the conflict "to every negro ghetto in America." When compromise between FIGHT and Kodak seemed most unlikely, Florence warned, "The cold of February will give way to the war-in of spring and eventually to the long hot summer. What happens in Rochester in the summer of '67 is at the doorstep of Eastman Kodak." Despite Florence's successes in leading FIGHT and his prominence in the black community, the Reynolds Street Church of Christ gradually became disillusioned with his activism, and they asked him to leave in 1970. He complied and, with a few members from the Reynolds Street church, formed a new church in Rochester, the Central Church of Christ, where he served as senior minister for over thirty-five years.[42]

The careers of Gray, Rose, and Florence illustrate at least three options that were open to blacks within Churches of Christ, but for the most part, church members simply did not accept public roles in the civil rights movement. These three men were exceptional in maintaining their denominational affiliation and participating in sustained civil rights activism. To be sure, Churches of Christ have always included blacks who refused to accept the racism and segregation that seemed endemic to white churches and the general populace. In the first half of the twentieth century, G. P. Bowser turned away white patronage that relied on his acceptance of Jim Crow customs or laws. Likewise, R. N. Hogan, Bowser's protégé, frequently berated his white brothers and sisters for their racism in the pages of the *Christian Echo*. But these voices resounded only within the confines of the denomination. Bowser and Hogan neither attacked segregation through the courts like Gray, nor worked for economic equality like Rose and Florence. They certainly did not join forces with "denominational preachers." Ultimately, Bowser, Hogan, and most other black ministers were, like their white counterparts, more concerned with restoring New Testament Christianity than with fighting social injustices. They might preach or write about the evils of racism but, in their minds, Christian faith should not inspire a march in the streets or cooperation with other nominal Christians in a civil rights movement.[43]

Their misgivings about the civil rights movement should be understood in the context of white patronage, as Gray noted, and as a product of the exclusivist mentality that they shared with whites. Over time, restorationist theology led them to believe that they were members of the only true church and that other expressions of Christianity were misguided, if sincere. In this sense, many blacks felt closer to their white brothers and sisters in the faith than they did to King and other black activists who were ostensibly working for their social, educational, political, and economic improvement. For many blacks, the insular world of Churches of Christ prevented them from seeing the broader implications of the civil rights movement. When racial identities were subordinated under the guise of Christian unity, blacks and whites took comfort in their self-perception as the "true church" vis-à-vis "the denominations." Most civil rights leaders belonged to the latter and were, therefore, ultimately detrimental to the restoration of New Testament Christianity. Blacks in Churches of Christ preferred the security of pleasing God and receiving eternal salvation over the possibility of attending a white school, entering a front door, or voting.

Keeble was certainly aware of the arrangement by which he could save souls. There was no room for criticism of segregation. Rose once confronted his teacher at NCI about it. "Why don't you just tell them?! You got to know this [segregation] is wrong. Just tell them! . . . Somebody ought to just tell them. And they respect you. You're the only one they let in their pulpits. You're the only one they let speak in the universities. Tell them!" On this occasion, Keeble listened to Rose's rant in silence but, as his former student got up to leave, he finally responded. "Floyd, you want me to tell them?! Just tell them?!" Keeble asked. "Then . . . how these kids going to go to school? If I tell them—I hate this as much as you do—but if I tell them, what's going to happen to this school?" White church members who knew Keeble would have been surprised at even this level of frustration. For them, Keeble appeared to personify what blacks should be: content with their station in life and focused solely on the Lord's work. In fact, Keeble disliked the indignities of the Jim Crow South as much as anyone. Yet his manner of coping—immersing himself in preaching and working tirelessly to uplift black churches and to educate black youths—was an archaic and ultimately unacceptable response in the minds of younger blacks who were more enamored by freedom rallies, sit-ins, and marches. Despite their disdain for Keeble's compliance with white leaders, several of his students honed their leadership and speaking skills under his guidance before becoming strong voices for civil rights movements across the country. And despite the reticence or outright hostility toward the civil rights movement that marked most Church of Christ members, they were living amid broader social and legislative changes that they could not easily ignore.[44]

5

JUDGMENT DAYS

No year has produced as many iconic images as 1968. The Tet offensive, political assassinations, Olympic games, and a presidential campaign provided numerous dramatic moments. One standard history textbook even claims that the "Sixties reached their climax in 1968, a year when momentous events succeeded each other so rapidly that the foundations of society seemed to be dissolving." Many Americans witnessed such events unfold on their television screens, as breaking and live coverage lent an immediacy to drama that might have otherwise seemed distant. Amid these headlines, Churches of Christ wrestled with racial problems in new ways that suggested both the hopes and limitations of interracial dialogue in 1968. Long before media pundits and politicos spoke of a "national conversation on race" in the 1990s, several churches and individuals experimented with venues of open and honest communication among blacks and whites.[1]

These exchanges were inspired by a variety of events, including churches' general tardiness in confronting racial animosities, the assassination of Martin Luther King Jr., the death of Marshall Keeble, and a provocative sermon series on race that was broadcast across the nation by the *Herald of Truth*, a syndicated radio program financed by Churches of Christ. Responses to these events provide compelling materials for assessing black and white racial attitudes in 1968. They show how churches and individual members proposed to address escalating racial tensions and past injustices. But in many respects, these dialogues became the last of their kind, as black and white churches ironically became more estranged after the demise of legal segregation. While black and white churches continued to agree that racial prejudice was wrong, they maintained profound differences over what such prejudice actually entailed, even as more and more whites came to see racial segregation as sinful. Blacks and whites also differed over the legacies of racial injustice and desirable solutions to racial inequalities.

These were judgment days for the faithful, and many people wondered what repentance should look like.

The first such conversation in 1968 occurred during the first week of March at Nashville's historically black Schrader Lane Church of Christ. The church's young minister, David Jones Jr., organized what was billed as a "race relations workshop" for area churches and any interested citizens. Known as the Jefferson Street Church of Christ until it fell victim to urban renewal and Interstate Highway 40, the Schrader Lane church hosted the workshop, a week-long series of nightly meetings, in their new building across from Tennessee State University, a historically black public university. Both the building and the workshop were turning points in the church's history. While the Jefferson Street church had often relied on the beneficence of whites, the new building "was the culmination of a plan to change the image of the church," their self-published history explains. "No Church of Christ had taken such a bold step" in hosting such a workshop that was also "designed to launch the church into its new role as leader in self-government." These comments illustrated the competing motives that existed for the Schrader Lane church and served as a remarkable example of the changes that were unfolding among black and white Churches of Christ as black churches sought a more complete autonomy, one that the denomination had adamantly espoused as characteristic of its churches. A report on the workshop emphasized that the new building "was totally financed by the Schrader Lane brethren, and no appeals were made to white churches." The church paid for its new building; there was no need to ask whites for help.[2]

All Churches of Christ in Davidson County received invitations to participate in the workshop, and attendance averaged 548 persons each night (fig. 6). Eleven speakers were featured during the week, including six college students, and their remarks were followed by question-and-answer sessions. Following the custom in Churches of Christ, all of the featured speakers were men. Five were black, and six were white. Exact figures are unavailable but, at the time, organizers estimated that blacks and whites attended in equal numbers on the first two nights. As the week progressed, the ratio changed such that blacks outnumbered whites three to two for the week.[3]

Jones spoke on the first night and outlined the purpose for the workshop. First, he wanted to facilitate interracial dialogue and understanding because blacks and whites did not really know each other. Second, Jones stressed education. He knew that "biracial gatherings may be uneasy or even tense," but he was concerned about "Christians [who] have held up themselves as good exam-

FIGURE 6. An integrated audience listened intently to the speakers at the 1968
Race Relations Workshop hosted by the Schrader Lane Church of Christ in
Nashville, Tennessee.
Courtesy of the Christian Chronicle.

ples" but "somehow overlooked the forest while shooting into the trees." Jones
wanted to expose the hypocrisies that he saw permeating Churches of Christ.
The denomination had enjoyed rapid growth in recent years, but he suspected
that part of the growth was due to the dissatisfaction that some people felt
toward other denominations' official positions on race-related issues. Jones's
assertion cannot be proven but seems plausible. With no denominational hierarchy to issue pronouncements and no association with the NCC, black and
white Churches of Christ presented themselves as detached from the racial
tumult of the period. They might attract new members who disliked their denomination's membership in the NCC or their pastor's sermon on civil rights.
The relative silence in Churches of Christ bothered Jones, who asked, "Do we
really believe that bigots and racists and 'Uncle Toms' can flock to the Church
of Christ, continue their 'southern way of life,' and 'go sweeping through the
pearly gates'? I would hope [our growth] is because we are doing a superior
job in evangelism, but I wonder. Are we growing or simply swelling?" He con-

cluded with imprecise platitudes that became common of blacks and whites, re-iterating that people must follow "the position of Jesus Christ in the race issue" and "initiate actions that will correlate on practices with true Christianity."[4]

Jones's sermon contained elements that were directed to whites. He re-buked one white preacher who had represented a neighborhood organization that was resisting integration, but his sharpest barbs were reserved for black preachers. Jones acknowledged that, in contrast to his recent experience with Schrader Lane, the "majority of Negro Churches of Christ were either begun, or financed totally or in part, by white churches who were discharging their duty toward the 'colored' brethren." The white beneficence and paternalism did not bother him as much as blacks who "willingly accepted and depended upon the contributions of their generous benefactors and never learned to stand on their feet to demand equal treatment. So they never mentioned to whites their *real* feelings" (emphasis in original). Jones contended, "Negro preachers have especially perpetuated the subservient position of the Negro because the white church and its conscience-soothing gifts represented his *meal ticket*" (emphasis in original). Blacks despised racial slights within the church, he surmised, but would not openly oppose whites or publicly express their misgivings. While whites had plenty of shortcomings, Jones exclaimed, "We must repent of our dishonesty in dealing with one another."[5]

A white businessman and future Georgia state senator named Lawrence "Bud" Stumbaugh delivered one of the most scathing sermons of the week. Stumbaugh was a member of the Madison Church of Christ in Nashville, one of the largest churches in the denomination, and a former resident of Selma, Ala-bama, a hotbed of civil rights activism in the 1960s. His remarks, titled "Incon-sistencies in Dealing with the Race Problem," scolded the church for avoiding talk of the civil rights movement. Stumbaugh was incensed that many members criticized the presidential candidacy of John Kennedy in 1960 because he was Catholic but then ignored the civil rights movement because it was supposedly a political, not a spiritual, concern. Many Nashville-area churches had fought a liquor-by-the-drink referendum in the fall of 1967, yet "If historians a thousand years from now were unable to read any documents other than pamphlets, pa-pers, and magazines written by members of the Church of Christ, they would not be able to discern that America even had a racial problem in the middle years of the 20th century."[6]

Stumbaugh's most unlikely assertions affirmed civil rights activism and "black power," the slogan popularized after Stokely Carmichael, as new chair-man of the Student Nonviolent Coordinating Committee, invoked the phrase in Greenwood, Mississippi, during the March Against Fear in 1966. Referencing the popular legend from the nation's foundational narrative, Stumbaugh argued that, if Paul Revere's famous midnight ride "was a glorious and patriotic call for freedom," then whites should not "condemn blacks for calling for arms in order to fight for their freedom." Whites commonly complained that civil rights activism only heightened racial tensions, but Stumbaugh explained how activism had influenced legal changes that were leading to the demise of Jim Crow. "I believe that at every opportunity, Christians of color ought to use all proper pressure and every moral means of force to assure that white Christians begin to practice the love and justice they have been preaching for so long. . . . I am in favor of 'black power,' for it seems this is what it will take to make a degenerate society do right." His listeners must have been stunned! A white man supporting black power was unusual anywhere, but a Church of Christ pulpit in Nashville was the unlikeliest of places. Anticipating his audience's astonishment, Stumbaugh carefully defined black power to mean "the strength and ability to accomplish aims . . . the force and energy necessary to bring about change, whether that change be political, social, or moral." From this perspective, black power was "imperative, if the bigotry and prejudice of this nation and the church is to be eliminated," he said. Stumbaugh's explanation certainly did not match the rhetorical flourish or bravado of Carmichael, but few whites bothered to parse definitions. Black power was already rich with several meanings, all of them threatening to most whites. But Stumbaugh concluded with a plea "that black people use black power more humanely and morally than have white people in whose hands white power has resided for so long."[7]

Subsequent speakers expanded on these themes during the week, relating personal stories, reflecting on biblical precepts, and challenging both blacks and whites to mend their relationships in the name of "New Testament Christianity." Don Finto, a white minister and faculty member at DLC, confessed how he had long been a "quiet integrationist" who was "ignorant of the way people feel and the urgency of taking concrete steps to alter the situation." This ignorance, whether willful or not, proved characteristic of many whites who, in their personal interactions with blacks, might have practiced common courtesy, but they otherwise seemed oblivious to the structural racism that pervaded American society, as well as the daily indignities that many blacks endured. Other speakers shared a variety of anecdotes, too. One white student described an integrated youth rally that he organized in Huntsville, Alabama; another white student related how he once heard an employee from a church-affiliated orphanage explain why black children were not welcome in his facility. Perry Wallace, who enjoyed a small measure of fame as the first black basketball player for Vanderbilt University, shared his dismay at a local white church where someone asked him, after many visits, to postpone placing membership until "the older brethren could get used to me." Another black student reported awkward worship assemblies in which blacks and whites sat on either side of an aisle or whites greeted the black preacher but not black members.[8]

Jones and other organizers of the workshop were generally pleased with the week's speakers and discussions, even if they maintained regret that some churches refused to participate. Thousands of copies of the sermons were published and available from the Schrader Lane church, and a thirty-two-page booklet, *Report on Race Relations Workshop*, was distributed with the *Christian Chronicle* in May. The cover of the report featured a photograph of three-year-old Debbie Minor, a black girl whose parents belonged to the church. On the back cover, a portrait of David Lipscomb appeared behind a reprint of his 1878 article "Race Prejudice," in which he wrote, "it is sinful to have two congregations in the same community for persons of separate and distinct races." In addition to sermon transcripts, the report included numerous photographs of the audience, blacks and whites sitting among each other in rapt attention. An insert on page ten offered fifteen "Suggested Guidelines for Improving Race Relations" that included some of the most concrete suggestions to emanate from Churches of Christ. Several items referred to educating both church members and the general public through preaching and ad campaigns, "telling the truth of the matter. . . . A serious educational program on the truth of the gospel on race relations should be launched immediately in every congregation." One suggestion was simultaneously serious and sarcastic. It asked churches to clearly indicate whether they were "open for men of all races. . . . Negro Christians do not wish to force themselves upon anyone—so a clearly marked 'White Only' sign would be sufficient" if a church did not want black members or visitors. As this proposal indicated, most of the guidelines were aimed at white churches, but one echoed a point made by several black speakers: "Negroes should develop plans to be independent—building their own buildings, buying their own songbooks, refusing to buy church buildings vacated by the 'white brethren.'" However, the care and hope with which these suggestions were crafted did not translate into widespread implementation. In retrospect, Jones determined that the workshop ultimately had little long-term impact.[9]

A month after the workshop, on Thursday evening, April 4, 1968, the nation was rocked by the assassination of Martin Luther King Jr. in Memphis and the rioting that ensued. Less than three weeks later, Marshall Keeble also died. Keeble's death was hardly noticed outside of middle Tennessee or Churches of Christ and, apart from their chosen professions, he and King had little in common. Keeble died at age eighty-nine, came from more humble origins than King, and had little formal education. King was only thirty-nine when he was assassinated, hailed from the black middle class, and held a doctorate. Yet the coincidence of their deaths in the same month provoked heated debates within Churches of Christ over race, civil rights, and the "pure religion" that churches claimed to practice. Many ministers expressed some sorrow over King's death, but several whites issued subtle condemnation. His death was also used to initiate interracial dialogue about improving race relations within the church and society as a whole. People who disapproved of the civil rights movement and the social turmoil that it seemingly precipitated remained hostile and skeptical of such efforts. These skeptics appropriated Keeble's death to articulate ideas about "proper" ministerial behavior, making implicit references to King and specific comments about race. The inclusion of Keeble and King in the same discourse provides a further means of understanding why some whites were so critical of King, how Christianity could be used to justify the racial status quo within existing political structures, and how Keeble personified white conceptions of "acceptable" behavior for black preachers.[10]

Keeble clearly possessed the rare ability to effectively communicate with both black and white audiences and, if success can be measured in numbers, his success among Churches of Christ was unmatched. Keeble's popularity as an evangelist was due in part to his capitulation to racial norms in the South. He was neither a civil rights activist nor overtly political in any traditional sense. One oral history noted an exceptional occasion when Keeble publicly, and modestly, endorsed Lyndon Johnson for president in 1964, but historical sources are otherwise silent about any political activity.[11] Throughout his life, he was first and foremost an evangelist, obsessed with converting sinners or winning people to the "undenominational Christianity" espoused by Churches of Christ. Keeble was mourned and reverently eulogized by both black and white churches who recognized his immense contributions to the growth of Churches of Christ. But when contrasted with concurrent remarks about King, this adulation from whites demarcated two factions: those who used their deaths to advocate changes within the church and larger society and those who used their deaths to support institutional racism.

The most remarkable reaction to King's assassination came from what historian Edward Robinson called Keeble's "greatest legacy," namely "the company of spiritual sons he left behind who perpetuated his work of planting, edifying, and solidifying black Churches of Christ throughout the South." Many of these "spiritual sons" were assembled for their annual lectureship during the first week of April 1968. The event typically consisted of a series of sermons or workshops by prominent preachers from the denomination. The vast majority of attendees were black, as whites were more likely to attend one or more of the annual lectureships at church-affiliated colleges. The Golden Heights Church of Christ in Fort Lauderdale, Florida, hosted the event in 1968. When news of the assassination reached the assembly, the church's minister was handed a note with the solemn news. Between speakers, he entered the pulpit and made the grim announcement to the audience. "I just got a note here that says Martin Luther King, Jr. was shot and killed in Memphis tonight. That just goes to show you, sometimes you can push people too far." He casually put the note in his pocket and announced the next speaker on the program. Floyd Rose and Franklin Florence, two young black ministers with some experience in civil rights activism, sat stunned at the news and this crass announcement. They pressured leaders to send a sympathy telegram to Coretta Scott King on behalf of all attendees. Two days later, the lectureship's organizers finally relented but Roosevelt Wells, the preacher who read the telegram to the full assembly, closed his remarks by noting, "Of course we all know that Dr. King was *not* a Christian" (emphasis in original). Later, another black preacher entered into a discussion with Rose about King. "Floyd, I know you don't like it, but Martin Luther King is in hell burning now if this book [the Bible] can be trusted." These perspectives were not voiced by marginal figures. Wells was a popular speaker on the revival circuit and would be for decades. Whites would be hard pressed to match this brazen rejection of King as an activist and a clergyman.[12]

On the day after King's assassination, President Johnson proclaimed that Sunday, April 7, would be "a day of national mourning throughout the United States. In our churches, in our homes, and in our private hearts, let us resolve before God to stand against divisiveness in our country and all its consequences." On a limited scale, several Churches of Christ observed this day of mourning, as sermons or weekly bulletins poignantly grappled with the tragedy, as well as the unrest that followed in cities across the country. The assassination conjured a prophetic voice from numerous white preachers who found the courage to speak more forthrightly and positively about King and race relations. A white preacher named Robert Meyers of the Riverside Church of Christ in Wichita,

Kansas, titled his sermon, "Can We Understand? (A sermon delivered on Sunday after a murder)." Meyers surmised that his remarks would be controversial, a presupposition that he acknowledged in his introduction. But he used this sobering moment to endorse King, whose death, Meyers stated, "made it chillingly clear that we must do something about the poisons of racism or face unbelievable civil terrors in years to come." He pled with his politically conservative, white audience to understand the circumstances that gave rise to civil unrest. The rioters' "burnings and lootings and surly rebellions, however frightening or annoying, are in actuality one of the most sorrow-filled cries for help ever to sound inside the halls of human misery." Meyers may have belied his good intentions by comparing rioters to children throwing a tantrum, but his message of understanding sounded an unfamiliar refrain within Churches of Christ.[13]

Other white ministers expressed similar viewpoints. In Port Arthur, Texas, Cled Wimbish confessed, "many of us have thought that Dr. King was just a troublemaker. I have. We thought that if he hadn't stirred up his people, they would have been happy to leave things as they were. But I believe that we were very wrong in thinking that." His sermon included a lengthy quotation from King's "I Have a Dream" speech. Likewise, John Allen Chalk crafted a sermon about King that he delivered on April 7 in Abilene, Texas, and several other occasions during the summer of 1968. "The Continuing Message of Dr. Martin Luther King" did not "offer a blanket endorsement" of King or his civil rights organization, the Southern Christian Leadership Conference. Chalk emphasized that King was not "doctrinally sound." But he quoted a phrase from the Bible about Abel, who was murdered by his brother Cain: "he being dead yet speaketh." Chalk proposed that King could figuratively speak from the dead and that every concerned Christian should "allow Dr. King's life and teachings to help illuminate and emphasize Biblical principles he taught, spoke, and lived." Chalk believed that the "pulpits that overlooked the opportunity to speak God's Word to men seized by the demons of hate, prejudice, selfishness, and ignorance the Sunday after King's death were guilty of either inexcusable obscurantism or criminal neglect." The sermon described the qualities in King's life and writings that were worthy of emulation, and Chalk quoted extensively from King's speeches and books. A young preacher named Rubel Shelly, who would later become one of the most influential preachers in the denomination, included remarks about race relations in his Sunday sermon in Grenada, Mississippi. He was fired the next day, even though his comments were so benign that he was too embarrassed to share them nearly forty years later.[14]

White ministers who used King's assassination to initiate a dialogue about race relations with their churches also utilized weekly bulletins that were mailed to each member, usually once per week. Churches typically used these bulletins to keep members informed of church-related activities and provide encouraging thoughts during the week. Dwain Evans published an article for his church bulletin that echoed several sermons from April 7, but his language was even more direct. "The non-violence which was so much a part of the life of Dr. King even til the day of his death was first taught by Jesus Christ. Would that we of the white race had learned this lesson so well as Dr. King." Integration, he wrote, "can only be a small part of the answer" to racial conflicts. "The critical thing is that white man and black man must stand together as equals." King's assassination and the rioting that followed had clearly shaken some ministers and awakened them to opportunities that might bring about equality and harmony among blacks and whites.[15]

These sentiments were uncommon, however, among Churches of Christ. The denomination's most popular periodicals, with the exception of the *Christian Echo*, remained eerily silent about King and race relations in general, but Keeble's death broke that silence. A revered white preacher named B. C. Goodpasture, the longtime editor of the *Gospel Advocate*, was one of the first to eulogize Keeble in print. The two men had a close, complex relationship. They corresponded regularly for decades, and Goodpasture even performed the ceremony for Keeble's second marriage. Goodpasture described Keeble as an "inimitable" preacher who "possessed many noble qualities." A portrait of the deceased evangelist graced the cover of this issue, and Goodpasture's one-page editorial was a fitting tribute to a man with immeasurable influence among Churches of Christ. But this respectful tone proved transitory and, like several other periodicals throughout the summer and fall, the *Gospel Advocate* began to echo sentiments first expressed by black preachers in Fort Lauderdale.[16]

A weekly bulletin published by the fledgling South Williamsport Church of Christ in Pennsylvania on May 10 foreshadowed the Keeble-King dialectic that soon developed. The announcement of Keeble's death included a eulogy with disparaging remarks about black civil rights activists. "Brother Keeble was a Negro," readers were reminded, "who will not be remembered for the marches he led. He will not be remembered for the many speeches he made in interest of the poor, which Jesus said, 'will be with you always.' He will not be remembered because he pled for 'black power.' He will be remembered because he 'preached the word.'" The message could not have been clearer. Keeble's life was honorable as "a Negro" precisely because he was not a civil rights activist. He was lauded as a "sound preacher," not an agitator from a denomination who concerned himself with political advocacy on behalf of minorities or the poor.[17]

Popular and influential periodicals published by whites soon offered similar appraisals. An editorial written by Reuel Lemmons in the *Firm Foundation* used a eulogy of Keeble to make derisive comments about civil rights activism, associating it with all forms of social unrest. He wrote that Keeble "never led a riot; he never burned out a block of buildings; he never marched on Washington." With no hint of incredulity, Lemmons suggested that Keeble "traveled—without discrimination—for seventy years among blacks and whites alike. . . . If he ever knew there were segregation lines he never indicated it. Indeed, because of his life and work there has been an infinitesimally small amount of racial prejudice in the Church of Christ." Lemmons resisted any effort to extol King. When John Allen Chalk submitted an article for publication in the *Firm Foundation* that praised King, Lemmons simply refused to publish it, contending in a letter to Chalk, "I do not believe I have an ounce of racial prejudice in me. I never have. . . . I did not run the King article for this reason. A lot of people wanted to compare [him] to Jesus Christ. In reality King was a modernist, and denied the faith of Jesus Christ as taught in the Bible. I do not agree with praising him either in our pulpits or our papers. If he was not an outright Communist, he certainly advocated communistic causes." Lemmons's restorationist mentality, a key characteristic of most black and white Churches of Christ, enabled him to dismiss King and any worthy cause that he might have represented. Other ministers were quick to point out Lemmons's inconsistencies. One white critic told him that the "rather thinly veiled criticism" of King in a eulogy for Keeble was "absurd." For his part, Lemmons only regretted "that the criticism was veiled at all." His eulogy for Keeble initiated a feud that lasted several months and demarcated the future trajectories for many Churches of Christ.[18]

Lemmons also had black detractors, but they were puzzled over his assertion that Keeble experienced little discrimination rather than his criticisms of King. They recalled circumstances in which Keeble endured discourtesies or mistreatment. One critic was Roosevelt Wells, the same preacher who had publicly stated that King was not a Christian. Wells was comparably plainspoken with Lemmons. "[Y]our appreciation of black men is limited to those who do not actively and openly protest the shameful unchristian and unamerican and unhuman treatment [sic] the black people of this country have received." Wells charged Lemmons with being either explicitly racist or completely insensitive to the "color crisis" in America. "In the spirit of Christ," he concluded, "I recommend that you do some research, some soul searching, and some waking up."[19]

Not to be outdone by Lemmons and the *Firm Foundation*, B. C. Goodpasture published a special edition of the *Gospel Advocate* in honor of Keeble. One essay by Karl Pettus contrasted Keeble with King by listing characteristics that did not describe Keeble but did apply to King's life. Once again, King was not named, but the references were obvious. "No flag was flown at half-mast in his honor. He wasn't eulogized by our nation's political leaders and political office seekers. He never won the coveted Nobel Prize. He never led a march or demonstration, peaceful or otherwise. He was never connected with a riot. . . . He didn't march for school integration, but he worked and spent himself for most of his life for Christian education. He gained equality and universal respect by the life he lived and the work he performed before God and his fellow man, both black and white. No day or week of mourning has been declared in his memory." Chalk penned an illuminating letter to Goodpasture that expressed his displeasure over Pettus's commentary. According to Chalk, the article was simply "a backhanded slap" at King and another example of Keeble being "'used' by a white man to get something off his chest." He further alleged that Pettus should not be permitted to write an article about Keeble "because he operates a 'white-only' enterprise that denys [sic] the universal Christ," and Chalk criticized the implications behind Pettus's assertion that Keeble "gained equality." In Chalk's estimation, the article suggested "that more Marshall Keeble's [sic] will solve our nation's social ills. This says that other Black men, Christians and Gospel preachers, who do not happen to operate like Brother Keeble, who are nevertheless preaching the Gospel, are all wrong." A handwritten note on this letter indicates that Chalk never mailed it. Goodpasture was forty years older, and his imposing reputation may have been too intimidating for the young preacher.[20]

While the *Firm Foundation* and the *Gospel Advocate* channeled their criticisms of King through eulogies of Keeble, Noble Patterson was more explicit in the July issue of his *Christian Journal*. After briefly acknowledging how King's murder was deplorable, Patterson launched into a tirade against the civil rights leader and Church of Christ preachers who developed an affinity for him. King, Patterson wrote, "did not believe the Bible . . . did not accept the virgin birth and the deity of Jesus Christ . . . [and] adopted the philosophy of India's Ghandi [sic] more than he accepted the principles of Christ." These charges demonstrated how an obsession with doctrinal purity could be used to discredit the entirety of King's work. "It is beyond comprehension," Patterson fumed, "how any, especially some of our own brethren, could support the principles that guided the life of Martin Luther King." He was further appalled that flags were lowered to half-staff at a college affiliated with Churches of Christ when the same courtesy was not extended to Keeble, who was, in contrast to King, "sound in the faith, fruitful and law-abiding. . . . This school lowered the flag for a Baptist preacher, but not for a gospel preacher." Although he did not call him by name, Patterson also took aim at Chalk by commenting upon "one of our young and dynamic radio evangelists" who preached a sermon about the continuing message of King. "If there was ever a message that needed to be DIS-continued," Patterson insisted, "it is the message of Martin Luther King." Patterson's jeremiad became popular enough to be reprinted elsewhere, including the *Word of Truth*, a periodical edited and published in Alabama by another respected preacher, Gus Nichols. The West End Church of Christ in Birmingham printed Patterson's editorial (though it incorrectly attributed it to Nichols) because it "represents the thinking of many many people [sic] in this part of the country." West End's minister explained to Chalk how "it has been difficult to understand why any faithful Christian would use this non-Christian as an example of anything." Goodpasture, Lemmons, Patterson, and their admirers could not have been clearer: black activism similar to King's fell outside the bounds of acceptable behavior for blacks and for Christians.[21]

Chalk joined a number of black and white preachers who used these controversies to pursue racial reconciliation. The race relations workshop in Nashville, coupled with the assassination of Martin Luther King Jr., galvanized enough support for more interracial dialogue that a small number of preachers organized public forums to address racial problems. Prior to 1968, the cooperation of black and white churches in a revival, the use of white preachers by black churches or black preachers by white churches, and interracial evangelistic teams presented to outsiders a face of interracial cooperation and camaraderie. These practices had long been common among Churches of Christ, although the degree to which these activities represented racial harmony certainly varied. With the focus on evangelism, issues of racial justice were rarely, if ever, addressed. Yet Churches of Christ were uniquely positioned to facilitate interracial dialogue, and several churches came to believe that their efforts to proselytize required them to first address the proverbial beam in their own eye.

These forums were never widespread, but they still represented an important effort to address epic problems. Sensitive topics pertaining to race relations were discussed openly, and black ministers, many for the first time, frankly addressed the church's collective failures in the presence of whites and prescribed solutions for the future. In many respects, whites served as the captive audience, forced to recognize the laments of their black brothers and sisters and to admit the failures of their churches to fulfill biblical mandates for equality and unity. At the same time, many whites were defensive and prone to view racism as someone else's problem. With few exceptions these forums, while creating some measure of understanding and goodwill between black and white churches, marked the end of an era. Black churches and ministers no longer needed the patronage of white churches and, for the most part, white churches were not interested in associating with their black brothers and sisters in what might be deemed mutual relationships.

If King's assassination compelled leading ministers to organize several forums, then Churches of Christ were not totally indifferent to the quest for civil rights that King's life came to represent. Race relations forums in Dayton, Ohio, and Atlanta should be understood as direct responses by Churches of Christ to his assassination. On May 24–25, 1968, the Collegiate Heights Church of Christ in Dayton hosted an open forum on "Human Relations." The church's minister, Woodie Morrison, was a young graduate of SWCC, and he invited four popular preachers to speak and more than thirty panelists to participate in discussions. Keynote speakers included two white preachers: Dwain Evans, featured in a 1963 issue of *Time* as a prominent evangelist among Churches of Christ, and Chalk, whose voice was carried by over two hundred radio stations across the country on the *Herald of Truth*. Two black preachers, G. P. Holt and Zebedee Bishop, were also featured speakers whose names were easily recognized by readers of the *Christian Echo*, as was the paper's editor, R. N. Hogan, who attended and served as a panelist on the second night.[22]

The keynote addresses from Dayton offered insights into what organizers thought were the most pressing topics of the day and what these preachers wanted to convey to an interracial audience. Morrison's advertisement for the forum included a flier that emphasized the dire urgency of the situation. "We are caught up in a nightmare of despair and are probably approaching the threshold of a bloody war in this Country unknown to mankind, unless some sincere efforts are put forth to change the thinking of the peoples of our Nation and world," he warned. "[O]ppressed people," he continued, "are saying that time has run out, and they want in, they want to be accepted and treated like other men created in God's image." Given these circumstances, Morrison felt compelled to organize a forum as a way for "God's people to discuss these subjects in love, truth, and honesty."[23]

To this end, the forum was conducted over two nights. Each night featured two preachers, one black and one white, and their portraits appeared on Morrison's advertisements. These sermons were intended to be didactic, but they often slipped into a confessional mode that highlighted the racism of white churches or blacks' firsthand experiences with discrimination. The title of each address indicated the forum organizers' desire to discuss pressing social issues in a context that relied heavily upon religious perspectives: "A Christian's View on Open Housing," "The Black Church—The White Church—Why?" "Is Interracial Marriage Sinful?" and "The Other Wall," an exposition based on a New Testament passage that depicts Jesus as one who broke down a wall separating Jews and Gentiles. Away from the drama of the civil rights movement, people sought practical answers to questions that were directly relevant to their lives. They hoped to discover biblical guidance for racial division and healing.[24]

Dwain Evans, the first white speaker, admitted his own shortcomings to the audience: "I recognize that as I stand here even this evening that I must confess to you that the sin of race prejudice [is] in my own life, a race prejudice that has been both explicit and implicit, an evil which is so distasteful to me that I am completely overcome at the thought that I still find myself afflicted with it." Evans's candor epitomized how some white ministers were trying to come to terms with past racial attitudes that did not comport to their professional calling. He was by no means an angry or violent racist, but he expressed regret over his past silence on racial injustice and his paternalistic disposition toward blacks. The honesty of Evans's confession increased his credibility, as he tackled the thorny issue of open housing six weeks after President Johnson signed the Fair Housing Act.[25]

As Bud Stumbaugh did in Nashville, Evans acknowledged that open housing "immediately presents many problems for us white Christians because open housing, we say, is a political issue. We say this very piously as if to indicate that because there is a political issue involved then Christians have no part nor lot in the matter of open housing." He reminded his audience that Churches of Christ had taken strong stands on public referenda dealing with gambling or the sale of alcohol and thereby had, on rare occasions, cooperated with denominations in the process. Evans felt that Churches of Christ had gotten involved "in those things that were political when they recognized that there were moral implications . . . and I'm glad they did." Open housing, for Evans, was also a matter of moral concern. He asserted, "Jesus Christ our Lord took open housing out of the realm of politics when he said in M[atthew] 25, 'I was a stranger and you took me in.'"[26]

Evans also challenged the two principal excuses that Church of Christ members had proffered regarding their lack of support for the civil rights movement, particularly noting the inconsistencies in espousing restorationist theology and strictly adhering to laws that enabled racial discrimination. First, Evans noted that Churches of Christ, especially those with the most legalistic readings of the New Testament, were apt to favor "law and order" over the civil disobedience that sometimes characterized civil rights protests. "You know," he said, "one of the catch phrases that we use to immediately excuse our lack of activity in these areas is civil disobedience, and our opposition to civil disobedience. I submit to you that we're not real well acquainted with what went on in the first century when we do this." Evans was alluding to early Christians, like the apostle Paul, who were jailed for preaching about Jesus. Second, he mentioned the passage from the New Testament, Romans 13, that taught subjection to government powers, but he reminded the audience that the apostles Peter and John disobeyed governing authorities when they continued to proclaim Jesus's resurrection. "We ought to obey God rather than men," Evans insisted, as he echoed the apostles' remarks in the Book of Acts. The implication that Churches of Christ were failing to appreciate a practice of first-century Christianity was damning to a group whose utmost objective, at least according to its rhetoric, was the restoration of New Testament Christianity. Evans closed by explaining how his church in West Islip, New York, had circulated petitions that expressed support for open housing, an action inspired in part by two black church members who were unable to find housing in their community.[27]

Ivory James, the black preacher who spoke the first night, attacked the church's hypocrisy in proclaiming that it alone embodied New Testament Christianity while it generally practiced racial segregation. "[I]t is indeed strange," he surmised, "when one considers that we, as members of the Lord's true body and who accept the scriptures . . . only as our rule of faith and practice in religious matters react as we do when it comes down to race. All the while we preach very loudly that division is sinful." James mentioned how some people believed that the Bible forbade racial integration, an "old die-hard argument" espoused by people who were horrified by interracial marriages. He would not even bother refuting what he considered such a ludicrous idea. James also spoke of his personal experiences with white churches, including a recent visit to the Hillsboro Church of Christ in Nashville. When James arrived early for a scheduled service and waited, no member spoke to him or even acknowledged his presence. At the close of the service, the minister called on James to lead the closing prayer and proudly stated, "You know, probably five years ago, the only Negro minister in the Church of Christ that could've led a closing prayer here would have been [Marshall Keeble]." James was not as impressed.[28]

In his closing remarks, James addressed those whites who "say the colored people would rather be by themselves. . . . How in the world do you know this?" he asked. "Have you ever taken the time to ask some of us colored people?" His inquiry apparently struck a nerve with some whites in attendance. Sensing the tension, James left his prepared remarks. "Now, don't y'll [sic] be all tense, because I wanta [sic] say what I got on my mind. I want y'll [sic] to loosen up a little bit, loosen up a little bit." James's words could have only been offensive had they contained an element of truth. Whites who spoke on behalf of blacks—"they don't want to go to school with us" or "they don't want to worship with us"—commonly did so as a polite way of supporting racial segregation. To be sure, the assessment was sometimes correct, but rarely because whites had an open and honest conversation with blacks. "The Lord's Church is no longer fishers of men, but we have become keepers of the aquarium," James humorously concluded, before ending his sermon with his own revised version of King's "I Have a Dream" speech.[29]

The notion that the Bible forbade interracial marriage was not absurd enough to be lightly dismissed by the forum's organizers. This question was a real concern to many blacks and whites. Theological racism, or racism grounded in biblical interpretation, was a serious obstacle that these ministers hoped to overcome through clear teaching. On the following night, G. P. Holt tried to answer the question, "Is Interracial Marriage Sinful?" Indeed, Holt related a personal experience where "a brother . . . spent 15 minutes trying to point out that God made everything after its kind and this simply suggests that each race should marry its kind." Holt proceeded to show how this brother was mistaken, concluding that "it is our privilege as children of God to marry whomever we desire, as long as that person is in the Lord, and the thing that will hinder us from accepting a plain truthful presentation of this will be nothing more than plain old down to earth racial prejudice."[30]

Because of his nationally broadcast sermons for the *Herald of Truth*, Chalk was arguably the most recognizable voice on the forum's program. His sermon focused primarily on the text of Ephesians 2:11–22, a Pauline passage that explains the removal of figurative walls that separated Jews from Gentiles. But the urgency of Chalk's message was strengthened by several anecdotes that he shared about his radio ministry. These stories were intended to illustrate the presence of barriers that separated black and white churches, barriers that he hoped—like the apostle's walls—would soon crumble. When the *Herald of Truth* received response cards from listeners across the country, administrators processed the responses and sent them to Churches of Christ in the vicinity of the listener. Although churches were not compelled to cooperate, the *Herald of Truth* hoped to assist listeners in finding local churches that could meet listeners' needs, answer their questions, and invite them into the church. Chalk recalled one occasion when a lady wished to make contact with a local church near her home in Louisiana. The contact soon wrote back to report, "I made a call on the lady who wrote into your program. She is . . . a colored person. . . . We have no work among those people." On another occasion, the *Herald of Truth* heard from an elder in Kentucky who had not even bothered to visit the listener because he recognized the address and refused to make contact. Chalk also shared vignettes outside of the radio ministry. He explained how a black student activist on the campus of Pepperdine College was inspired in part because of an occasion from her childhood when she asked a white preacher for a drink of water. He obliged her request by serving her with water in his dog's bowl. Chalk described how the largest Church of Christ in Memphis chose not to distribute an issue of the *Christian Chronicle* to its members because it featured new developments at SWCC, and he noted how a presentation at one lectureship by a black preacher was the only one omitted from a published collection of the event's proceedings. A wall certainly existed, and Chalk had little trouble proving its existence.[31]

The final keynote speaker, Zebedee Bishop, closed the forum with a bleak assessment of the present and future prospects for interracial harmony among Churches of Christ. Bishop's speech, directed primarily at whites, was unequivocal. "Many of you speak tonight with the authority that you know the Negro. I imagine you know the Negro, but you don't know the black man. There is a profound transition taking place in our society right now," he continued, "and I'm afraid that the church of Christ, as usual, is going to be the last to understand what's really happening to this nation and to this world." Restoration of New Testament Christianity was still a goal, in his opinion, but he explained that it could not come at the expense of racial justice. In Bishop's mind, the presence of racial injustice indicated that the church was not present. A truly restored church would not permit racial discrimination. "Now it is time past for the church of Christ to renounce its historical and spiritual dishonesty. It is time to cease from frustrating the restoration of the universal church of Christ." Bishop spoke more favorably than many of King, noting "many times when God's people think they can fold their hands, lock their arms and forget all about it, God has a way of working through history and working through other mediums to bring about his purpose." According to this logic, King was still not considered one of "God's people," but he at least was the servant of providence.[32]

The question posed by the title of Bishop's address—"Where Do We Go from Here?"—offered the opportunity for concrete suggestions. His answer was typically vague but aimed directly at whites. It contained a hint of pessimism and a strong warning: "Unless white members . . . stand in their communities, schools, political groups, homes and the church, and let justice ring forth . . . Christianity and the church will become defunct. . . . As long as the white church maintains its exclusiveness, the black church will exist and it must exist." This admonition placed the responsibility for action—letting justice ring forth and ending exclusivity, or segregation in this context—with whites. In a sense, Bishop's solution disempowered black churches by crediting their existence and continuance to the actions of white churches that, he must have known, would not actively pursue the inclusion he demanded.[33]

One month later, Atlanta's Hilton Inn was the site of a second forum that included some of the most prominent figures in Churches of Christ. Preachers, elders, college presidents, and professors convened at the invitation of a white preacher and Harding College professor, Jimmy Allen, and two black preachers, Eugene Lawton and Roosevelt Wells. Their invitations quoted from President Johnson's National Advisory Council on Civil Disorder, noting that "deepening racial division" prompted this "meeting on improving race relations among our brethren in America." The invitation described how "The New Testament churches are facing this same critical problem. In many areas, there are two fellowships of our people, one is black and the other is white. We are interested in eradicating the barriers that divide us and setting forth CONSTRUCTIVE PROGRAMS to make us truly one in the colorless Christ" (emphasis in original).[34]

Some fifty leaders assembled for two days of lectures and discussions, but several absences were noticeable. B. C. Goodpasture did not attend, nor did any administrators from DLC, Freed-Hardeman College, and Alabama Christian College. Fred Gray, the most unmistakable figure from Churches of Christ who was active in the civil rights movement, did not attend, either. The only person

FIGURE 7. Only men were invited to participate in the 1968 Race Relations
Conference in Atlanta.

*Folder 48, Race Information—Miscellaneous 1968, Herald of Truth Records, 1950, Center for
Restoration Studies MS #305, Abilene Christian University Special Collections and Archives.*

with a reputation for civil rights activism who participated was Franklin Florence, and he was not invited to speak.[35]

No women were present at the conference (fig. 7). The autonomy of local churches and general suppression of women's voices effectively prevented
women in Churches of Christ from taking more public roles in the pursuit of
racial reconciliation. The fact that women were not invited to this event especially perturbed Ona Belknap, editor of the *Christian Woman*. In a letter to
Chalk, she frankly expressed her disappointment in terms that resonated with
the growing women's liberation movement. "I was told I could not attend the
meeting . . . because I am a woman," she wrote. "[W]hy, oh why, are we treated
like second class citizens?" Belknap surmised, "the men in the brotherhood still
prefer their women silent, stupid and pregnant. Such women," she sarcastically
warned, "will continue to raise hippies, radicals and atheists, for their own
intellect has been so stifled through the years they do well to be able to understand crochet instructions." Belknap's pleas were spurned, but the relationships
that she perceived between motherhood, social pariahs, and women's voices in
a strongly patriarchal denomination indicated the urgent, if muted, concerns
that women shared with men in Churches of Christ.[36]

Blacks and whites served as featured speakers on both days, but the lecture
given on "Spiritual Equality in Christ" by Andrew Hairston, the black preacher

for the Simpson Street Church of Christ in Atlanta, may have generated the most discussion. Hairston grappled with the presence of racial division among people who claimed the unity of Christians in one church as a significant theological precept. He reaffirmed his belief "in the one church" but also proposed, "no honest person or true christian [sic] should contend for the existence of the true church in the midst of known or acknowledged segregation." He also made a crucial observation about Churches of Christ when he noted that "the Church of Christ became more segregated than before" the Supreme Court's 1954 *Brown* decision. "Prior to this time," he remembered, "whites frequented Negro meetings and services. After this ruling, there came an abrupt lessening of this limited interaction which came to be a symbol of approval of equality and brotherhood rather than condescension and accommodation." From Hairston's perspective, the very meaning of an assembly of blacks and whites had changed since the 1950s. Whites generally did not want to associate with anything that might connote acceptance of racial equality and, although Church of Christ assemblies had never overtly espoused equality, the presence of blacks and whites together had been ascribed new meanings, especially in the South, where civil rights organizations like the Student Nonviolent Coordinating Committee had largely ignored, if not openly violated, local customs and laws that enforced racial segregation.[37]

Hairston's remarks were ironic in several respects because whites had long affirmed the spiritual equality of blacks, but this affirmation rarely challenged the practical effects of white supremacy. With their "us against the world" mentality, Churches of Christ cultivated a self-perception that they were the only true church. Other denominations could more easily tolerate division, racial or otherwise, because they did not constantly rail against it. Hairston identified how this tension affected blacks, too: "We condemned our black denominational brothers and denied them fellowship because they called their ministers reverend, had instrumental music or sold dinners to support their churches. However, we found ourselves rejected by whites of the church whom we thought were our brothers." For decades, Churches of Christ had attempted to navigate southern racial customs and laws through loose associations between black and white churches. These associations led whites churches to declare their unity with blacks while maintaining segregated institutions. Once segregation outside of Churches of Christ started to decline, whites were called to make good on their claims of unity. The momentous events of the civil rights movement and an awakening of black consciousness necessitated changes that many whites were either slow or simply unwilling to make.[38]

Hairston's assessment included some advice about how to proceed but, like Zebedee Bishop, he was not optimistic, concluding that the "church is presently competing for number one position as the strongest citadel of segregation." He lamented that recent victories in the civil rights movement were attributable to "the god of the courts, the god of economics, the god of the legislature, and the god of pressure groups," not "the god of the church." Hairston offered three proposals for Churches of Christ to improve. First, he urged whites to integrate into black churches rather than expect blacks to immediately join white churches and institutions. Returning to the title of his address, he contended that spiritual equality "must mean not only that you can open the door for me; it must also mean that I can open the door for you without either having any hesitancy toward entering because of who opened the door." Second, he echoed the remarks of David Jones Jr. from the Nashville workshop and admonished black churches to "repent of the sin of parasiteism [sic]," to become self-supporting rather than dependent upon the good will of white churches. Finally, he urged this group of influential leaders to remain vigilant about the image that churches and institutions project. "The self-respecting black of today and tomorrow does not and will not hear you when you talk of spiritual equality when every piece of literature, filmstrip, *Herald of Truth* speaker, and giant effort of evangelism set forth only whites." If Churches of Christ really believed in spiritual equality, Hairston insisted, then it should be reflected in every endeavor. Otherwise, a claim of "spiritual equality is nothing more than a clanking cymbal [sic]."[39]

By the close of the two-day forum, participants decided to draft a statement, a highly unusual step for a Church of Christ assembly, that acknowledged "the sin of racial prejudice which has existed in Churches of Christ and church-related institutions and businesses. Because we love the church of Jesus Christ," the prologue explained, "and want to see her fully committed to the principles of Spiritual Equality and racial justice for all persons, we plead for the end of discrimination in all of its forms in the life of the church." A list of twenty-eight recommendations was drafted in an effort to end discriminatory actions in local churches, church-related institutions and businesses, and individual members. These men had absolutely no power to implement these suggestions outside of their personal circles of influence, a point that they highlighted to the press. One local newspaper reported that this "integrated group of ministers . . . emphasized that they did not constitute a formal organization, but were 'a gathering of concerned Christians.'" Administrators from ACC and Harding College chose not to sign the statement.[40]

The recommendations provided tangible guidelines for tackling the denomination's racial divisions. In addition to educating its members about racial discrimination, local churches could reevaluate their evangelistic activities "to ascertain [if] they are based on genuine fraternity, and not paternalism." In a period when black separatism was growing in popularity, these black and white leaders encouraged local churches to integrate "as these opportunities exist, seeking to achieve the meaningful involvement of all Christians of all races in the total program of the church." Church-related institutions were urged to "totally integrate," including social activities at Christian colleges, orphanages, homes for the elderly, and youth camps. Church of Christ media were asked to include more black voices and to develop "Bible school literature, books, filmstrips and slides to include proper representation of all races—to aid in the process of identification for minority groups." Christian colleges and business owners were advised to hire and train minority applicants "for jobs other than dead-end jobs." In an effort to be comprehensive, the final section stated that all Christians should "Affirm without equivocation that equal opportunities in housing, jobs, and schooling should be granted to all persons in our democratic society." The list is a remarkable example of what blacks had always supposed should be true for the church, but now they had succeeded, for the moment at least, in showing whites how crucial these items were to meaningful fellowship. Blacks not only lifted a veil that had previously blinded whites, but they convinced several of the most influential whites in Churches of Christ to sign a document that confessed to the veil's existence and the need to have it permanently removed.[41]

In the days following the Atlanta conference, attendees exchanged assessments that were generally positive, but the circulation of the statement throughout the denomination also provoked negative reactions. Writing in his church's bulletin, Dwain Evans called it "a historical meeting" and "a step in the right direction." In his estimation, the occasion marked "the first time white ministers heard black ministers 'tell it like it is.'" Evans also shared a fascinating moment that he described as a "highpoint of the conference." After hearing a stirring message from David Jones Jr. that mentioned interracial marriage, a white administrator from Pepperdine said, "David, I want you to know that I would be proud for one of my daughters to marry one of your sons." The statement, apparently made without consultation with either sons or daughters, brought to mind the film *Guess Who's Coming to Dinner*, released just six months before this conference, and marked a rare moment in US history.[42]

John Stevens, who would become the president of ACC the following year, spoke favorably of his experience in Atlanta. Although he chose not to sign the statement, Stevens honestly wrestled with the challenges that the conference raised and circulated a memo to ACC administrators that summarized what he gleaned and suggested strategies for improvement. With regard to the proposals for "Local Church Activities" and "Church Related Institutions," Stevens recommended that ACC and local white churches take prompt action, but he reminded other administrators to take a "hands off" approach to black congregations and colleges. As Hairston had observed in his Atlanta lecture, whites should join black churches, just as blacks should be welcomed at white churches. Stevens noted that discussions among some whites of closing a black church in Abilene and having its members join a white one were "probably not valid at this moment." Then he pinpointed a dilemma that white churches often encountered: "The trouble is, of course, that they have always been a very weak congregation and probably could not exist at all without being subsidized by the College [Church of Christ], and yet every month that the subsidy continues increases the resentment toward paternalism."

Members of the black church might have disagreed with Stevens's appraisal of their strength, but his comment demonstrated perfectly how many whites began to approach issues relating to the integration of churches. "Would it be better for the College [Church of Christ] to cut the congregation adrift and let it see what it can do?" Stevens asked. "The impression I got in Atlanta was that it would be. Of course, probably the best thing would be for a number of white brethren to place membership with the congregation and help it grow." Here Stevens identified a problem that loomed larger than the strength or weakness of any particular church. Whites might gradually become comfortable with blacks joining their churches and schools, but would whites ever be willing to join black churches or attend historically black colleges? Blacks' desires to see their churches and institutions survive, coupled with the unwillingness of whites to integrate into historically black organizations, helped explain the persistence of some forms of segregation.[43]

To confirm his interpretation of the Atlanta conference, Stevens shared his memorandum with several whites, including Dwain Evans. His choice of Evans was curious—perhaps he could have chosen a black preacher instead—but Evans "was very impressed" with what Stevens shared, before offering his own brief evaluation. "The thinking men of the Afro-American church are more interested today in real equality of relationships between black and white than they are in token integration. I think we are going to see the emphasis on black power increasing rather than decreasing. . . . I think it is a good thing. I know that as white men, we will be tested in the years and months to come. I pray that we may be patient as we deal with excesses on the part of our black brothers. Surely, they have been patient with us for a long time." In the wake of the Atlanta meeting, blacks now expressed cautious optimism about the future of Churches of Christ. Hairston sent letters to each participant that described the meeting as a "blessing" and a "new field of meaningful spiritual interaction." He also included a photograph of the entire group, an *Atlanta Constitution* article that reported on the event, and a copy of his sermon.[44]

Negative reactions arose from people who did not attend the forum. In a widely circulated essay titled "A New Creed Appears," evangelist W. L. Totty of Indianapolis took issue with the conference and the statement that it approved. Churches of Christ had, in part, defined themselves as a group "with no creed but the Bible," and the statement issued in Atlanta might loosely be defined as creedal. Plus, it included suggestions for individual churches, and this feature of the document hinted at a violation of local autonomy. "We wonder how that group in Atlanta, Georgia, thought they could have workshops of any kind for the churches in every region of the United States. Every congregation is autonomous in its government," Totty reminded his readers. "I heartily believe that race prejudice . . . [has] no place among God's people. But we believe that the Bible is sufficient and that we do not need proposals (creeds) signed by certain men. What we need more than anything else in the world is to have the Bible taught just as it is without fear or favor—a thing that is not being done, I fear, in many sections of our country now." Thus, even though the statement expressed sentiments to which Totty supposedly subscribed, he deemed it unacceptable and "a denominational venture." His article undoubtedly circulated among some churches that had ulterior motives in opposing the forum's recommendations.[45]

Totty may have had a legitimate argument based on past practices and the theology of Churches of Christ, but other critics certainly had a less noble agenda. Foster Ramsey published an article for a church bulletin that bemoaned the emergence of what he called "ecumenical councils." He noted, "We have long been accustomed to councils and conferences among the denominations in which decisions have been made and fastened on those religious bodies. . . . Preachers and teachers of the church of Christ are beginning to meet in these ecumenical councils where they come to certain decisions and attempt to set up these decisions as the pattern for the conduct of the churches of Christ in the future." Ramsey proceeded to misrepresent several components of the statement, though he claimed to have learned his information from someone who attended. For example, he said that the signed statement insisted that churches that refused to integrate would be disfellowshipped and that preachers and teachers were to encourage interracial marriage. "And so grows modernism and liberalism in the church!" Ramsey warned. Ramsey was grossly misinformed and eager to distort the proceedings. Totty was careful to condemn racial discrimination, but Ramsey simply latched onto the mistaken notion that these church leaders had issued an edict.[46]

Bob Anderson, minister of the Mayfair Church of Christ in Huntsville, Alabama, showed even more contempt. He composed and distributed a satirical letter, typed on letterhead from the "Committee For the Escalation of the Eskimo," about some preachers who met in New Mexico to discuss "an area of concern," namely "that no real concerted interest has ever been demonstrated toward the Eskimo." According to Anderson, the assembled ministers "recognized that there is a trend toward 'speaking for the brotherhood.'" The recommendations arising from Anderson's imaginary meeting were clearly intended to parody and trivialize the Atlanta conference's proposals. One urged church colleges to design "a special course . . . to teach introduction to Eskimo culture."[47]

Through its church bulletin, the Getwell Church of Christ in Memphis also expressed disdain for the Atlanta conference and its recommendations. In September, the church outlined a few of the proposals and named some of the signatories. Then, in a section titled "Agitation and Division," the bulletin stated, "It seems that some brethren are determined to create dissension and division in the church over racial issues." No mention was made of the black and white participants and their intentions to foster interracial unity within the church. Instead, the article cited "statements of radicalism" recently made by Dwain Evans, who had urged his church to view open housing as a religious issue. Evans allegedly expressed occasional shame at being a white man. The Getwell bulletin noted that Christianity and slavery coexisted in the New Testament and that these "brethren have come dangerously close to an effort at creed-making for the churches of Christ." Foreshadowing future debates about affirmative action, the bulletin article closed by charging the men with "advocat[ing] racism in reverse. They oppose hiring white men just because they are white, but they insist on hiring black men just because they are black. What makes one right and the other wrong? Truly, the legs of the lame are not equal." This final assertion left little doubt as to the Getwell church's feelings about race relations in general and blacks in particular. In the wake of the Atlanta conference, Chalk was amazed that such misinformation abounded about the meeting and the statement. Listeners to his weekly radio sermon wrote letters asking for details of the conference and an explanation of the statement. "I have racked my brain and have talked with other participants in that conference at length as to the reasons why these misunderstandings would arise," he wrote to friends in Tennessee. "We have been able to arrive at only one conclusion: rank prejudice and racial animosity."[48]

As if they anticipated the suggestion by blacks, Chalk and the *Herald of Truth* radio program had already planned a series of sermons about race relations for July 1968. The *Herald of Truth* was the only cooperative evangelistic endeavor with a national reach among Churches of Christ. It could be heard on over two hundred stations around the country, and its television program appeared on more than fifty stations. The vast majority of funds for the program came from churches and individuals, many of whom were regular listeners or viewers. In 1967, the *Herald of Truth* amassed some $1.3 million from approximately three thousand churches and ten thousand individuals.[49]

Sermons usually focused on explicitly biblical topics and rarely broached issues of broader concern. Chalk had become the program's most popular evangelist and, in 1968, he delivered a series of sermons, "Three American Revolutions," around the topics of crime, race, and sex. Each topic was addressed in four separate sermons broadcast in concurrent weeks during the months of June, July, and August. While connections were not explicitly made, discussion of race alongside crime and sex echoed the fears that many whites had long voiced in opposition to the extension of civil rights to blacks. However, white fears remained a subtext in the sermons.[50]

The sermons and the unusually vocal response from listeners provide some of the most compelling insights into the racial attitudes of religiously committed blacks and whites in 1968. Although the sermons were national in scope, most responses originated with southerners. Those responses offered explanations for how white, Christian southerners diagnosed current racial problems and conceived of their solutions. At the same time, letters from black listeners reveal almost unanimous approval of the sermons' contents as a first step in the right direction. "They surely rank among the great sermons of the century," a black man from Macon, Georgia, wrote. The black president of SWCC reported that, in his "travels among the Christians, especially Negroes, I am hearing many favorable comments concerning the July sermons." Other black listeners expressed surprise that the sermons were broadcast, although in retrospect the sermons contain little by way of prophetic indictment or substantive suggestions.[51] They were characteristically filled with biblical quotations that seemed relevant to racial tensions and widely applicable, directed more toward the issue of racism than in addressing or correcting specific injustices. A few sections broadly summarized the history of racial oppression in the United States, but the sermons also represented white preoccupations with urban unrest. The sermon that introduced the series acknowledged that the "Black man has had a long, difficult struggle" before asserting, the "tragedy is that ignorance, prejudice, and deliberate exploitation for economic gain have so hardened many of us today to the point that some black men believe nothing short of destructive violence will speed up the slow rate of change in white attitudes and activities. But all sensible men know this will never work and all Christian men know this opposes everything Jesus Christ taught."[52]

Chalk's definitions of white racism illustrated its limited scope in the minds of many whites. He accepted that racism was a set of false beliefs and, by implication, a person was racist if he or she subscribed to these beliefs. Presumably, a person who stopped believing these things would not be racist. There was no notion that whites could benefit from social structures that were inherently racist. Thus, Chalk also decried "black racism" and cited Elijah Muhammad.[53]

Chalk almost never gave specific examples of discrimination or any implications—historical, structural, or otherwise—of racism. One exception from his first sermon involved housing. He challenged listeners with a series of questions: "[What] would be your attitude toward the first white on your block who sold his house to a Negro family? Would you stay? Would you sell? What would you vote for, if your church decided to leave such a neighborhood?" Chalk suggested the answer: "The courageous Christian will continue to live in a racially changing neighborhood demonstrating God's reconciling gospel to his white and black neighbors." But this was the only instance when he addressed a specific problem. During the third sermon, Chalk mentioned "centuries of oppression from men of my skin color" that prevented blacks from trusting whites and "centuries of ignorance and myth [that] have tried to teach me to believe that those who are not of my ethnic group are not capable of lasting human relationships and permanent contributions to mankind." In the final sermon of the series, Chalk vaguely spoke of a "deep conviction of my personal sin" and "a genuine willingness to make the contributions Christ enables me to make to the troubled world in which you and I live." But specific suggestions were limited to a collection of platitudes.[54]

The *Herald of Truth* collected and cataloged hundreds of responses from listeners that were tallied for reports.[55] Over five hundred people expressed relatively clear approval or disapproval of the sermons. More than 350 letters addressed the sermons about race. The numbers, while suggestive rather than conclusive, indicate that 80 percent of listeners, most of whom I presume to be white, approved of the sermons. For the sake of comparison, the sermons on crime and sex respectively garnered 92 percent and 95 percent approval, so the sermons on race were clearly less popular, even if they were widely admired. Additionally, 75 percent of writers from former Confederate states expressed approval, and the numbers continued to drop by isolating states in which Churches of Christ were most numerous. Over one hundred letters came from Tennessee, Arkansas, and Texas, where the approval rate was 73 percent. Twenty-six letters were sent from Alabama and Mississippi, but only half of them approved.[56]

While many listeners expressed appreciation and agreement with the sermons, the letters are particularly useful for what they reveal about the evolution of white racial attitudes in 1968. Historians have only recently begun complicating the image of a South composed primarily of uncompromising segregationists, replacing it with one that finds gradations of racial attitudes and competing ideologies among blacks and whites.[57] These letters contribute to this more complex picture, as they vividly illustrate the moral and intellectual dilemmas with which whites wrestled. A Florida man described how "I joined my friends and fellow students[s] in May, 1954 to shout 'never, never.' Thank God, and some excellent teachers and professors, my thoughts have completely changed." A woman from Georgia expressed hope that "other [C]hristians do what I am doing, a lot of soul searching to rid myself of prejudice and other feelings that must go if we are to solve this major problem in our nation today." Outside of the South, a preacher in New Jersey told his church that "there is some Geo. Wallace in all of us; let us get rid of it!"[58]

Such expressions of contrition and empathy hinted that a growing number of whites acknowledged and accepted that blacks had faced widespread, systematic discrimination that belied both American and Christian ideals. Their solutions, it should be noted, involved personal changes of the heart and mind. The impulse among the radio program's white listeners was to repair their own distorted views on race and hope other individuals did the same. Once these relatively small steps were taken, however, whites seemed to assume that the "race problem" would be fixed, while many blacks had always understood that justice, by definition, must involve some means of reparation. A black Church of Christ minister said as much when he read advance copies of the first two sermons. Eugene Lawton of Newark, New Jersey, commended the *Herald of Truth* for broadcasting the series but offered some constructive criticism, noting that Chalk "was quite theoretical with little practical application and illustrations to substantiate his ideas. . . . Both messages seem to be saying essentially the same thing with little movement in the desired direction."[59]

Several white listeners also described how the sermons provoked debates in their Bible classes or families. Patricia Griffin of Wichita, Kansas, described conflicts in her family in one of the most engrossing letters. Griffin had arguments with her mother, who said, "the Bible teaches that God commanded the races to be seperate [*sic*]," and her mother-in-law, who "hates all negros [*sic*] and says they are all uncivilized, dirty, filthy, people." Her mother-in-law worried about her grandchildren "growing up in a community of 'niggers,'" her description for the housing development near McConnell Air Force Base where Griffin and her family lived alongside many servicemen and their families.[60]

Griffin's six-page, handwritten letter requested the *Herald of Truth*'s position on interracial marriage, but disagreements with her mother and mother-in-law illustrate how white opinions were often marked along generational lines. Chalk's sermons provided an opportunity to settle generational differences, as young people sought divine guidance for raising children in a way that diverged from their parents. Griffin came to see the futility of racial segregation but, with two influential, older women maintaining the opposite position, she felt unsure. Her ten-year-old daughter and her black friend liked the same boy at school. Her five-year-old son claimed to have a girlfriend in kindergarten, and Griffin later learned that she was black. As a young mother with children growing up in an integrated environment, Griffin wanted urgently to know, as a practical matter, if she was right in cultivating relationships across racial lines: "If I am wrong in feeling the way I do, I want to know, because my children are involved—now. . . . All I have gotten is 'I don't know what to tell you,' etc. or I have been given the run around. This is a problem facing a lot of young people today." Chalk's reply commended her position: "I know of no Biblical teaching that condemns interracial marriages," he stated.[61]

Numerous preachers sent letters, too, most notably Ray Dutton, then a student at Alabama Christian College, who was employed by a small church about forty miles south of Montgomery. In a reflection of his exclusivist disposition and youthful zeal, Dutton wrote that he had recently come to believe "that all of the Negros [sic] around our congregation were dying without one finger being lifted to get the gospel to them. I confessed my sin before the congregation," he continued, "because I knew that because I had not tried to help these Negros [sic] I had sinned." He then pressed the church to evangelize among local blacks, so several members suggested hosting a black preacher who would conduct a revival and perhaps start a separate, black church. Dutton resisted the creation of a new church, but his congregants, he wrote, "said that some people . . . in our community would (or might) contemplate burning our building. . . . My brethren would not object to worshipping with the Negroes, and have told me that they would not mind this, but they feel that it would be more expedient to act in the other way that I mentioned." Now he wanted advice on how to proceed.[62]

Chalk's reply was straightforward, as he insisted "that a separate meeting house should not be built." He expressed appropriate concern for Dutton's plight and for the local differences that may have existed between Abilene, Texas, and rural, south Alabama, but Chalk also lambasted church members who "have spoken the truth and defended the faith against all denominational error to the point, in some communities, of creating hatred and strife between denominational people and members of the church, and yet, would now worry about public opinion regarding a move that is of totally Biblical nature and is required by the very nature of the church." The exchange illustrates how evangelistic concerns led some whites to discuss race relations in terms that were largely foreign to civil rights activists, politicians, or members of the media. But even this evangelistic priority proved difficult among whites, some of whom believed that violence might follow any effort, however small, to facilitate interracial Christian fellowship.[63]

Dutton's question also shows the practical dilemmas that racial segregation imposed. Nowhere was this more evident than in questions about interracial marriage. During the previous year in the case of Loving v. Virginia, the Supreme Court had declared that antimiscegenation laws were unconstitutional, but the ruling was hardly the last word on interracial romance, even as Americans' attitudes slowly changed.[64] Although he had elsewhere condoned interracial marriage as acceptable to God, Chalk's silence about the issue on the radio elicited a variety of responses from listeners. An elderly woman from Idaho wrote that she was "free of any racial prejudice" and "would just as soon live next door to a negro family." But one question continued to vex her: "Do we have to favor mixed marriages between these races, to be completely free of racial preju-dice?" She speculated that if she had a daughter who married someone who was not white, "I would be unhappy about it, but if she planned to marry a negro, it would especially trouble me. Does that make me a 'racist' at heart?" she asked. This hierarchy of racial preference combined faith and race in such a way that she "would rather see her married to a fine Christian colored man, than to a white who was an atheist, or a scoundrel," but marriages between blacks and whites seemed "unnatural" to her.[65]

Chalk also fielded inquiries from family members about his sermons against racism and his perspective on interracial marriage. His mother-in-law lived in Nashville, heard unfavorable remarks made about Chalk, and asked, through her daughter, what his opinion was of interracial marriages. Chalk responded with a thorough letter that outlined his general beliefs about race and racism. "After recognizing all the complications and all the problems," he explained, "I have to say that the Bible does not forbid such marriages." Chalk believed that scripture only taught that Christians should marry Christians; race was of no concern. Thus, using his own children as examples, Chalk posed a question to his mother-in-law by reversing what had often served as the segregationists' trump card. "Would you want your daughter to marry *one?*" Chalk asked. "Do you want Mary Beth or John to marry a non-Christian white instead of a Chris-tian Negro?"[66]

A few months later, a relative from Mississippi wrote to Chalk and admitted that he had questioned the content of Chalk's sermons on race. He, too, men-tioned interracial marriage: "John, I believe that if you could only know what I went through—and am still going through—with Markie, your attitude in the matter of interracial relationships would take on a marked change. Or per-haps I'm wrong about that too. Maybe you will welcome, without the slightest reservation, a son-in-law or daughter-in-law of a non-white race. If so, I have wrongfully judged you; and I beg your forgiveness." Chalk was mindful that he could not relate to individual circumstances, but he reiterated that "God's word does not condemn such relationships." In fact Chalk was keen to know why the specter of interracial romance was such an overwhelming concern. "Since we are all committed to the truth of the Bible, and since the truth of the Bible must guide all human relationships, some of the reaction to the question of intermar-riage is not in keeping with God's word," he surmised. The crucial point here is not so much Chalk's relatively progressive position but the preeminence of interracial marriage in the discourse on race among whites. As centuries-old barriers to interracial marriages were crumbling, whites in Churches of Christ were forced to reassess what they understood the Bible to say about the taboo of interracial romance.[67]

Listeners who disapproved of the sermons occasionally incorporated interracial marriages into their critiques. An older woman from Alabama feared "the day when one of my children brings home a colored companion," and a man from Texas recited the segregationist mantra that "GOD himself separated and seggrated [sic] the races. . . . But you and Martin Luther King have a better idea." Such assertions and the questions that listeners posed illustrated the abiding power of theological racism in shaping white attitudes about integration.[68]

While widespread disapproval of interracial marriage might have existed among the radio program's detractors, the most common criticism involved the program's sudden interest in the "social gospel." The elders of the Tarrant Church of Christ in Birmingham asserted that Chalk had "used the *Herald of Truth* to discuss a political issue." The director of a preaching school in Oklahoma explained, "Many of us are not at all thrilled about the 'Three Revolutions.' Sounds too much like the Social Gospel themes of the liberals! . . . People will listen to old fashioned Gospel preaching," he advised. "They have heard all they want of Crime, Race and Sex." One Tennessean wrote, "We have no business meddling in politics, social problems, etc." Then he echoed the thoughts of several listeners who approved of Chalk's sermons: "If we preach to men what to do to get right with God, they will also get right with one another." Such a myopic view of human relations and the history of racial discrimination in the United States vividly illustrated the racial divide that existed. Many whites contended that racism was a matter of the heart, and changing hearts would ultimately dissipate racism and its effects. They neither perceived themselves as racist nor did they sense any culpability or responsibility for the countless injustices that blacks faced, even as they enjoyed the material benefits of white privilege.[69]

In this sense, the letters sent to the *Herald of Truth* are significant for showing how whites experienced the transitions that came with federal civil rights legislation and Supreme Court rulings that required desegregation. Public memory is marked by fierce white resistance and violence and rightfully so, as heinous crimes were committed in defense of maintaining white supremacy, and segregationist governors like George Wallace enjoyed tremendous popular support. But, however reluctantly, most whites eventually acquiesced to some degree to the new legal order. In doing so, they situated themselves within the social and political drama of the civil rights movement, usually as innocent bystanders who watched a series of dramas unfold over which they had little or no control. The prologue to the first sermon on race told listeners that they were involved in the "Racial Revolution . . . whether you like it or not!"[70]

The *Herald of Truth* sermons presented whites with an opportunity to affirm a position that separated them from vigilante violence, segregationist politicians, and civil rights activists. In 1968, many whites did not want to be associated with any of these, and they had come to embrace new racial attitudes and ideologies. Their perceptions of race and justice had changed, and the sermons gave voice to what that change might entail: individual commitments to remove racism from one's life. From this perspective, racism was confronted as an immorality, alongside any other human frailty, and in this view whites were not solely to blame. Another letter from a young preacher and recent Christian college alumnus proved the point. He praised the sermons but felt that "Both races are to blame and both are guilty of sin and need forgiveness." This perspective explained the staunch resistance to subsequent attempts to compensate numerous victims of racial discrimination. Reparations and affirmative action programs never gained traction among whites who neither perceived themselves as racist nor appreciated how they benefited from centuries of white supremacy. Racism, in this view, was not systematic or structural but personal. Following this line of thought, both blacks and whites might possibly succumb to the "immorality" of racism, but whites were never solely to blame. Chalk's sermons invited such thinking. During the June sermon that introduced the entire series, Chalk exclaimed, "White and Black racists have formed sides and taken positions so that any thing short of radical solution holds little hope for racial harmony in our country."[71]

As many whites remained largely oblivious to the historical extent and legacies of racial discrimination, this disposition became increasingly popular both inside and outside Churches of Christ during the latter decades of the twentieth century. Indeed, the letters sent to the *Herald of Truth* are filled with ideas that soon gave the Republican Party control of the South, foreshadowed the ascendance of the Religious Right, and promoted the idea of a color-blind society without accounting for or trying to correct past racial injustices. One listener included a list of suggestions for helping the needy that asserted, "It is not the giving away of money or writing to Congressmen that helps that much, but trying to convert people with the gospel." Someone from Chicago wrote,

"I feel that the churches should have coordinated as a powerful political organization to see that effective laws be legislated to aid the minorities but not as an appeasement. The poor and aged can be helped in a dignified way and at the same time contribute something of a kind of service. I believe some poor people think the United States owes them a living, because of some prevailing socialistic attitudes—these people should be taken to task and our government should see that the poor contribute some services to the community, county, state, or country." Another Illinoisan complained of "certain things that you say would not be offensive if spoken to a white man. But, spoken to a colored man, all hell breaks loose. . . . We have all kinds of races and colors in the United States. I can't see where the color of the skin should have anything to do with it." The *Herald of Truth* counted these letters among those that approved of the sermons.[72]

The judgment days that unfolded in 1968 contained unique opportunities and contexts for Churches of Christ to evaluate race relations. The forums and workshops that year were rare occasions when blacks and whites from the same organization sat together and communicated their assessments of race relations in Churches of Christ. Reactions to the assassination of Martin Luther King Jr. and the death of the beloved Marshall Keeble show the denomination's persistent wariness of civil rights activism, even as numerous preachers admitted that King's advocacy profoundly challenged Christians to reconsider their acquiescence to racial apartheid. In addition to the responses to the "Three American Revolutions" sermon series, all of these events portray how Churches of Christ confronted racial prejudice in that remarkable year. The conclusions that they drew would resonate widely, as they adjusted to the new realities created by the demise of legal segregation.

6

EXORCISING DEMONS

If efforts toward racial reconciliation looked promising during the 1968 forums, the implementation of specific suggestions often faltered. Many Churches of Christ, both black and white, were simply uninterested in participating in processes that would likely entail conflict and dissension. Rather than actively and purposefully pursue racial reconciliation, most Churches of Christ permitted legal reforms to absolve them of any responsibility in facilitating ongoing interracial dialogue, understanding, and community. Over time, churches simply chose to ignore rather than discuss and resolve sources of distrust. Excuses such as "they don't want to worship like we do" became easier to recite than working to make unity a lived reality. It was the path of least resistance.

In this respect, Churches of Christ reflected trends that also characterized denominations such as the Southern Baptist Convention and the United Methodist Church. Historian Mark Newman noted that the issue of race relations "had virtually disappeared from Southern Baptist Convention and Baptist state convention resolutions and newspapers" by the middle of the 1970s, and apathy reigned supreme. The Methodist hierarchy offered measured leadership in promoting racial reconciliation, but the "typical integrated congregation," historian Peter Murray explained, "was . . . a church in transition from all-white to all–African American." These assessments indicated that white church leaders and laypeople in largely southern denominations quickly abandoned opportunities created by the civil rights movement to address longstanding racial tensions and disparities in their communities.[1]

The denomination struggled to exorcise its demons, evolving in the wake of the momentous legal changes that sought to equalize opportunity and treatment for blacks and whites. While black churches still prioritized evangelism, the social problems that blacks faced in urban areas drew their attention, as did those tenuous legal challenges to racial discrimination. In larger cities, black Churches of Christ responded to the growing popularity of the Nation of Islam by designing ministries that sought to diminish the Nation's critique of traditional black Christianity. Meanwhile, white Churches of Christ increasingly invested their resources into new buildings, often following their constituents out of the cities and into the "safety" of the predominantly white suburbs, and into youth programs designed to attract those same suburbanites. In several instances, black churches purchased the buildings and property that had previously belonged to white churches, literally filling the void left by their departing brothers and sisters in the faith.

The occasional sermon or lesson against racial prejudice was intended to fulfill whatever spiritual obligation existed to address race relations. The result of such piecemeal endeavors was that black and white Churches of Christ grew more distant in subsequent years than they had been before the 1960s, a trend further supported by whites who grew strident in their criticism of blacks whom they perceived as "blindly caught up in the spirit of the day." Whites also downplayed long-term effects of white supremacy by emphasizing how black churches had often benefited from white benevolence. In 1969 a white minister named John Waddey issued "A Plea to My Black Brethren" in the pages of the *Christian Echo* that noted, "Anglo and Black brethren have worked together for years. . . . The danger I wish to warn against is an attitude that would erect new barriers to brotherhood now that old ones are vanishing. A militancy is emerging in some areas of the brotherhood, akin to that in the world of politics and social reform."[2]

There were some exceptions to the ways that Churches of Christ succumbed to the broader pattern of white flight, exceptions that served as stark reminders that other options were available and occasionally pursued. In a few instances, black and white churches merged as an expression of their commitment to Christian unity and, perhaps unconsciously, as a reaffirmation of the exclusivism of Churches of Christ. This kind of integration even occurred in Alabama, Georgia, Louisiana, and Missouri, places hardly known for progressive race relations. Some churches also developed ministries and programs that incorporated both black and white members. These examples were somewhat rare, however, and even intentional integration unfolded amid many obstacles. Black churches were understandably wary of their white counterparts, fully aware that white churches had a long history of controlling nominally black institutions, subverting black leaders, and failing to appreciate the contributions and talents of black members. At the same time, some Churches of Christ offered conclusive evidence that the traditions of racial segregation did not immediately evaporate when laws changed. Segregation still thrived in many churches and persisted in nominally integrated institutions. Incidents at several Church of Christ colleges in 1969 inflamed racial hostilities, and questions surrounding interracial romance continued to incite heated debate.

Throughout its existence, the *Christian Echo* often lamented the presence of segregated Churches of Christ, while recognizing and to some degree affirming white benevolence. Efforts to promote church unity and, by default, racial unity, became more common during the 1960s. A few Churches of Christ attempted to create and maintain integrated churches, and these efforts, even if rare, warrant attention. Generalizations about these churches are difficult to make. They typically had a majority of white members, as whites appeared less willing to integrate into black churches or attend a church where the majority of members were black. But Churches of Christ also had no hierarchical pressure to practice "token integration" as many educational institutions did. No governing body could require a particular church to do anything, so outside of moral or theological motives, churches had few, if any, compelling reasons to integrate. In a 1968 issue of the *Christian Echo,* a preacher from Mississippi explained, "I am not writing to try and make someone believe that just worshiping with the White will get us to heaven. Not by any means, but its [sic] a good start." Three years later, R. N. Hogan assailed whites for fleeing when blacks moved into a neighborhood. He urged them to stay in order to create and embrace integrated churches. "A great contribution can be made to the growth of the Lord's Church if our white brethren will stop running and remain in the community regardless of who or what race comes into the community, [and] preach the gospel to them, for that is exactly what the Lord said to do." His comments illustrated how integrated churches were conscious, local decisions that defied prevailing trends within the fellowship and the wider culture.[3]

Primary evidence about these integrated churches frequently proves elusive, but the *Christian Echo* offered an account of black and white churches merging in Tucson, Arizona, in the summer of 1964. Leaders from each church discussed the feasibility of merging until "Finally," the article reported, "after many meetings, and the solving or resolving of every conceivable obstacle[,] the weeks and months of careful planning, visualizing and hopefulness became a reality as the two congregations merged [and] combined their talents and resources and became one, effective November 15, 1964." The new church continued to use the facilities of the white congregation, perhaps explaining why three black members refused to join the integrated church. Likewise, three couples from the white church moved to another congregation. "At the beginning of any work you will always have a Sanballat and Tobiah," the account wryly noted, referring to an obscure story in the book of Nehemiah about two cynical exiles who distracted from efforts to rebuild Jerusalem's walls. Despite the detractors, the merger was considered a success and an inspiration for more integrated churches. In Willcox, Arizona, some eighty miles east of Tucson, a revival hosted by a white church yielded the baptism of three local blacks. "[T]hat congregation is now intergrated [sic] and the possibility of even more conversions [is] very promising. There are other areas in Arizona where the same type of work is being contemplated. Not the establishing of separate congregations, but the conversion of individuals and their addition to the existing congregations."[4]

The story about these Tucson churches revealed some of the motivating factors. Seven specific "advantages and-or results" were listed. They included breaking down sociological barriers, dispelling racial myths, interracial cooperation in ministry, numeric strength, combining and more efficiently using resources, and "recognition of the fact that people of all races . . . are basically the same." The benefits of combined resources were further explicated as the author described how many smaller churches were "Serving no good purpose other than housekeeping for the Lord." Opportunities for ministry seemed more promising if smaller churches chose to consolidate, and the article departed from its theme of racial unity to admonish smaller churches to consider other possibilities. "Each day I am becoming more and more convinced that there is strength not only in unity alone but also in numbers, and that if we could lay aside our petty differences, combine our talent and resources[,] we could indeed reach many more souls who are groping in darkness."

The article carefully avoided setting the expectation that churches should integrate everywhere and instead focused on the benefits of smaller churches combining their resources. This account failed to provide details about the logistics and structure of the new arrangement, but the integrated church in Tucson was apparently thriving nearly a year after the merger. The church proudly reported that "we are one, and that the color line as such does not exist, that a spirit of love and oneness, togetherness . . . is exemplified by the congregation." In some sense, the newly integrated church exemplified what Churches of Christ had sought to create all along. By subordinating racial identities within the church—"the color line as such does not exist"—members could more easily ignore the presence and profound influence of "the color line" within the

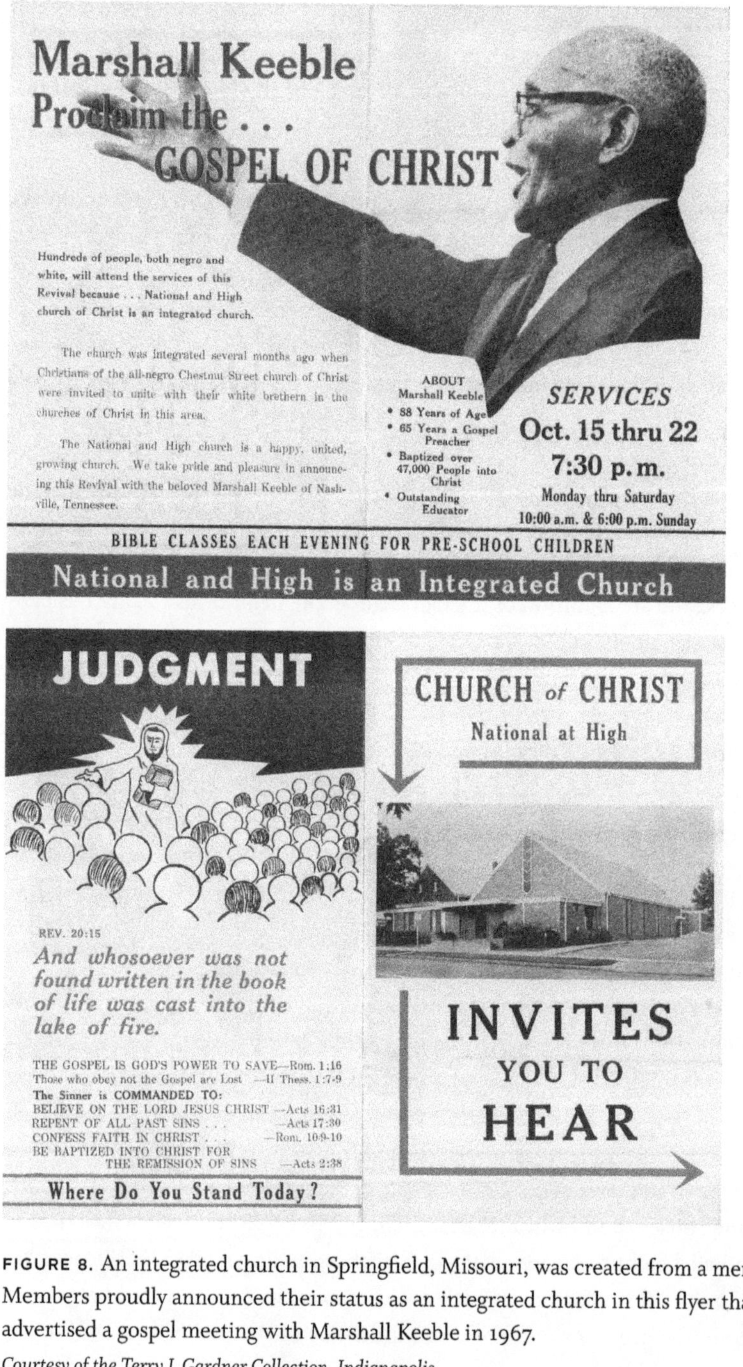

Marshall Keeble Proclaim the . . . GOSPEL OF CHRIST

Hundreds of people, both negro and white, will attend the services of this Revival because . . . National and High church of Christ is an integrated church.

The church was integrated several months ago when Christians of the all-negro Chestnut Street church of Christ were invited to unite with their white brethren in the churches of Christ in this area.

The National and High church is a happy, united, growing church. We take pride and pleasure in announcing this Revival with the beloved Marshall Keeble of Nashville, Tennessee.

ABOUT Marshall Keeble
• 88 Years of Age
• 65 Years a Gospel Preacher
• Baptized over 47,000 People into Christ
• Outstanding Educator

SERVICES
Oct. 15 thru 22
7:30 p. m.
Monday thru Saturday
10:00 a.m. & 6:00 p.m. Sunday

BIBLE CLASSES EACH EVENING FOR PRE-SCHOOL CHILDREN

National and High is an Integrated Church

JUDGMENT

CHURCH of CHRIST
National at High

REV. 20:15
And whosoever was not found written in the book of life was cast into the lake of fire.

THE GOSPEL IS GOD'S POWER TO SAVE—Rom. 1:16
Those who obey not the Gospel are Lost —II Thess. 1:7-9
The Sinner is COMMANDED TO:
BELIEVE ON THE LORD JESUS CHRIST —Acts 16:31
REPENT OF ALL PAST SINS . . . —Acts 17:30
CONFESS FAITH IN CHRIST . . . —Rom. 10:9-10
BE BAPTIZED INTO CHRIST FOR THE REMISSION OF SINS —Acts 2:38

Where Do You Stand Today?

INVITES YOU TO HEAR

FIGURE 8. An integrated church in Springfield, Missouri, was created from a merger. Members proudly announced their status as an integrated church in this flyer that advertised a gospel meeting with Marshall Keeble in 1967.
Courtesy of the Terry J. Gardner Collection, Indianapolis.

rest of society. A 1965 letter to the *Christian Echo* explained how black and white churches in Joplin, Missouri, had recently merged, and readers were promised that they would "find a cordial welcome" at the newly integrated church. Similar sentiments were expressed in a flyer produced by a church in Springfield, Missouri, that highlighted its integration and reported that it was "a happy, united, growing church" (fig. 8). A few years later, about forty blacks formally joined the white church in Sweetwater, Texas, a city some forty miles west of Abilene. "This of course has not come without its trials, tribulations, threats and moves," the white preacher reported to a friend, "but it has come, and it is here to stay!"[5]

In at least one instance, factors other than theology or moral imperative precipitated a merger. In the fall of 1968, Oldsmobile purchased the building that belonged to the Butler Boulevard Church of Christ, a black church in Lansing, Michigan. Rather than find or construct another building, the church sought to integrate into a white church, the Holmes Road Church of Christ. Occurring in the wake of so much tumult in urban areas, the merger caught the attention of Lansing's *State Journal,* which reported the story with a front-page headline that proclaimed, "Races Unite in Church Merger." Ministerial duties were split between the black minister, W. D. Wiley, and the white minister, Allen Killom, a 1930 graduate of Freed-Hardeman College. The *State Journal* interviewed both men. Killom contrasted Churches of Christ, who "have been quietly solving this problem among the members of the two churches," with "militants and advocates of black power and white segregationists [who] have been warring against each other and clamoring for their respective 'rights.'" Wiley called the merger "a history-making event" and expressed his happiness to participate. Killom shared the story with the *Christian Echo,* where he further explained, "Both congregations have shown a wonderful attitude. Not one criticism has been voiced." He displayed a bit of cynicism about the spate of race relations forums and urged other churches to follow Lansing's lead: "We feel that this is Christianity in action, a far more effective way than conducting 'Race Relations Workshops,' although these also may prove helpful, and we urge the whole brotherhood to consider this solution."[6]

Likewise, several southern locales saw Churches of Christ confront racial segregation with church mergers or purposeful integration. In the summer of 1968, a white preacher named Evans McMullen of Griffin, Georgia, converted Clarence Goodman, a black Baptist preacher, and his family to the restorationist faith of Churches of Christ. Located about forty miles south of Atlanta, Griffin was hardly a place where one would expect to find blacks and whites in the same church, but church members, buttressed by their exclusivist worldview, saw the potential benefits of having an integrated membership. Shortly after Goodman's conversion, the white Griffin church made arrangements for him to attend a preaching school, hired Goodman as an associate evangelist, and in the words of one observer, "the one church will continue its efforts to evangelize the total population," not just local whites. A comparable situation unfolded a few years later in Atlanta when the white West End Church of Christ, sensing the changing demographics of its neighborhood during the early 1970s, hired a black minister named Wesley Brown to attract black members to the church. The church's declining membership also contributed to the decision to hire Brown, who had ironically attended a revival at the church in his youth, at which time he was required to enter through a side door and sit in the balcony.

Now he was invited to become the full-time minister, a job that he accepted and held for more than three decades. A 1973 church bulletin announced, "Inasmuch as the community has changed so radically, the time has come when the elders feel that some changes in the church are mandatory. The decision to employ a minister from the Black race has been made. It is with much joy and a great amount of pleasure that we announce that the next preacher at West End will be Brother Wesley R. Brown. He is held in high esteem by both white and black Christians across the country." A black woman named Dorothy Griffin later recalled that the West End church had sought more black members before they hired Brown. "West End had made it known it was very interested in more black members," Griffin said. "And so I was one of several to respond. . . . But West End leaders made it plain, they would not be satisfied until they persuaded Brother Wesley to relocate." White membership continued to dwindle, as the church was directly affected by the broader white flight that occurred in Atlanta, and the West End Church of Christ would eventually become one of the largest black Churches of Christ in the country.[7]

Other concerted integration efforts occurred in Tennessee, Louisiana, and Alabama. In the fall of 1968, the Belmont Avenue Church of Christ in Nashville, Tennessee, hosted a revival in which six black and white ministers alternated as speakers throughout the week. Batsell Barrett Baxter, chair of the Department of Bible at DLC and a popular television preacher for the *Herald of Truth*, participated in the series. "The attendance was a full house each night," he wrote to a colleague, "and now it appears that this congregation will be able to continue in its present location with a mixed membership." Further away from the bright lights of a big city, a white church in Sulphur, Louisiana, hosted a gospel meeting with John Whitley, a black preacher from Houston, Texas. In contrast to the traditional practice of white churches hosting black preachers who would help establish a black church, Whitley agreed to preach "with the understanding that should any of another race obey the gospel, they would be welcomed, yes, even expected to worship with the existing church." Jim Brasher, the minister for the white church, urged his congregants to make the revival a success. In his weekly bulletin article, he reminded everyone, "When Jesus Christ commanded his people to preach the gospel to every creature, he included men of all races and colors. We have been negligent in the past, but with God's help, we hope to remedy that in the future. You can help by telling your acquaintances among the Negroes about this meeting." In a letter to the *Christian Echo*, Whitley deemed the endeavor a success. Four people were baptized, including an elderly black woman. The exclusivist disposition that was so characteristic of Churches of Christ was made apparent when Whitley wrote, "since the thrust of this meeting was to break down barriers which existed and to know that no Christians among Negroes lived in the Sulphur area to their knowledge, we were especially happy that the city witnessed this historic meeting and tremendous Christian fellowship."[8]

One of the more remarkable mergers of black and white churches occurred in Tuskegee, Alabama. Along with his work as a civil rights attorney, Fred Gray remained active in Churches of Christ. He continued to serve as the preacher for the Newtown Church of Christ in Montgomery throughout the 1960s, and he occasionally contributed articles to the *Christian Echo*, including one in 1966 about personal evangelism workshops. Gray resigned his preaching position in 1973, since he and his family had previously moved to Tuskegee and placed membership with the Tuskegee Institute Church of Christ. A white church, the East End Church of Christ, was also located in Tuskegee and, for a variety of reasons, both churches had experienced declining memberships. Allan Parker, the president of a local bank and a friend of Gray, served as an elder for the white church. Unlike other white denominations in Tuskegee, the East End church had always allowed black visitors. Meanwhile, Gray found Parker to be a reliable white ally amid local desegregation efforts. Historian Robert Norrell described Parker as one of a very small number of white liberals in Tuskegee, if liberalism there was defined as "open acceptance of the need for changes in race relations." About Tuskegee and Parker, Norrell further noted, "One might be a Goldwater Republican in national politics but, because of one's racial views, a liberal on Tuskegee issues." Parker not only cooperated during the desegregation process, but he also made a timely loan available to Gray as he prepared the lawsuit that sought redress for the abuses of the black men who were unwitting subjects of the infamous Tuskegee syphilis study. Parker was willing to wait until the case was resolved before requiring payments. After Gray and his family began attending the black church in Tuskegee, he and Parker met to discuss the possibility of having the black and white churches merge. Together they developed and implemented a plan that created a single Tuskegee Church of Christ, composed of black and white members. The new church had two white elders, including Parker, and one black elder, Gray. The relationship between these two men remained strong in subsequent years, even though the white membership gradually declined.[9]

Integrated churches were not particularly common within any denomination, anywhere in the country, but the exclusivism of Churches of Christ helped lay a foundation for interracial cooperation and fellowship. The fact that some Churches of Christ purposefully created integrated churches was alone remarkable, even though over time these churches typically succumbed to broader patterns of residential segregation that contributed to the racial polarization of churches and schools in the final decades of the twentieth century. In most communities, segregated churches persisted, and traditional practices of white paternalism survived the Jim Crow era. In Biloxi, Mississippi, for example, the aptly named Division Street Church of Christ was formed in 1966 when two black women settled there. The *Christian Echo* reported that they "began to search for the Lord's church, after being closely associated with some of the Caucasian brethren, they were encouraging [them] to have a gospel meeting." The white church helped conduct a revival with the aim of converting local blacks who would then form the nucleus of a new church. When no converts materialized, a few white members began meeting in the homes of these two ladies and their friends, rather than fully incorporating them into the church. Whites finally secured the services of a black preacher who accepted the task of creating a new church. When the black church, still "going from house to house," grew to fifty members, the white church purchased a building and parsonage for them. Without the slightest hint of irony, a member of the black church reported, "The work that these brethren are doing with the Negro brethren remind[s] me of what the Bible say[s]. How sweet and pleasant it is for brethren to dwell together in unity."[10]

A 1972 letter from a white church member in Alabama to the *Christian Echo* lamented the extent to which some churches maintained their racial exclusivity. The author, whose name was withheld by the editor, claimed to have promoted integration but no longer believed that he could take that risk, even though a black preacher was holding a revival near his home, because "the situation is bad here in Ala." He also described how an elderly black woman lived beside "the building of the white folks" but was apparently prohibited from worshiping there. "I think it is just awful that she can't just step out of her house and a few steps to get into the building . . . but there are so many looking for a chance to make trouble they just do not do that. What a pity!!"[11]

Several Churches of Christ in Memphis, Tennessee, demonstrated the reticence that whites felt about leaving their segregated past and the largely ambivalent efforts made by churches to address historic racial prejudices. The reputable Union Avenue Church of Christ consistently invited the denomination's most popular preachers to speak for its annual revivals and, in 1968, they sought the services of John Allen Chalk. Coming on the heels of Chalk's 1968 summer series, the decision was undoubtedly controversial, and the church requested that Chalk refrain from using sermon material that might "agitate the racial problem." Chalk refused the invitation to speak where his message might be censored, but he met with the church's elders about his recent sermons on race relations and his participation in various forums. He later sent a bound volume of the entire sermon series and urged them "to read these lessons carefully[,] watching for the sound, Biblical principles taught in them." Chalk called upon the primitivism of Churches of Christ to appeal for racial unity and healing. "At no point have we veered toward the 'social gospel,'" he wrote defensively. His thoughts about race arose from "the far-reaching implications of the gospel of Christ, and of the Biblical nature of the New Testament church."[12]

One elder from the Union Avenue church, M. A. Shelton, privately wrote to Chalk after he rejected their invitation. Shelton explained how he was favorably disposed toward Chalk and generally agreed with the preacher's sentiments about race relations. "Perhaps the thing that impressed me most in our meeting was your kind responses given with a smile to questions and statements, some of which were not made in the same spirit," he wrote. "I do not believe that your views on racial matters are significantly different to mine." Nevertheless Shelton was apparently in the minority among the church's elders and was deeply concerned that someone might learn of his admission. He asked Chalk to "keep this letter in confidence" and specifically noted that church stationery was not used. Shelton was clearly uncomfortable expressing mere agreement with Chalk's relatively benign sermons about race relations, and the invitation for Chalk to speak on anything besides race relations illustrates that the church's leadership remained committed to ignoring or resisting the civil rights revolution.[13]

A situation with the Highland Street Church of Christ in Memphis further illustrated how whites fiercely clung to traditional segregationist etiquette. In 1970, a student choral group from SWCC scheduled a summer appearance at the Highland Street church. Many historically black colleges traditionally maintained touring groups of singers who served as ambassadors and fundraisers. The Highland Street church elders agreed to host a performance but asked that no appeals for funds be made from the pulpit. Jack Evans, SWCC's president, consented to the request but also asked a favor of his white brothers and sisters. Since the group was set to perform on a Wednesday night, Evans hoped that members of the church might provide lodging and a few meals for the students. Small colleges like SWCC were perpetually cash-strapped, and the expenses of lodging and meals would diminish the effectiveness of the fundraising tour. The practice of boarding with allies and supporters was common, and the group consisted of only seven students. But the Highland Street church elders refused to assist, explaining to Evans, "Since your requests were not stated clearly in your first letter we feel that it [is] best to cancel your engagement at Highland Street."[14]

Evans surmised that the elders simply did not want their white church members to open their homes to black college students. "I feel that the *real* reason for the cancellation," he explained in a letter to them, "is *racism*. It is a matter of you not wanting any responsibility for lodging or asking any of the white members of your congregation to lodge eight *black* Christian young people. Not because those young people are immoral, violent, or militant, but because they are black" (emphasis in original). Evans noted that the choral program had long served as a means of bridging racial divides among Churches of Christ. White churches had often hosted them and cited their hospitality as evidence that they were not guilty of racial prejudice. Evans explained how "such programs as our singers are giving are helping the 'black' and 'white' churches of Christ to get to know each other. . . . [they] have sung in hundreds of white congregations all over the brotherhood and have lived in the homes of those who are converted and dedicated to Christ, and not to the mores of a racist society."[15]

Withdrawing an invitation to SWCC's singers was one of several racially charged incidents that haunted the Highland Street church in 1970. Earlier in the year, a Sunday school class of high-school seniors was encouraged by their teacher, Harold Bowie, to participate in the church's springtime evangelistic endeavors. Bowie later recounted how the students "asked if it would be permissible and desirable to include all the students of Memphis State University and the people of the immediate community near the Highland Street church building . . . without regard to race." Bowie shared the question with the church's elders and waited for an answer. Weeks passed with no response, so Bowie sought a meeting with them, at which point they explained "that it would [not] be expedient . . . to include black people . . . because the congregation had not been sufficiently taught to accept such a change." Bowie was disappointed but left the meeting with the assurance that "a planned effort be made to begin such instruction in a tactful but positive way in our Bible classes and from the pulpit." Months passed and the promised instruction never materialized.[16]

The church elders appeared to regress further. When several participants in the church's college ministry prepared a report of their activities for the congregation, they planned to include a black student who had been active in several programs in the church's Christian Student Center. Upon learning of these plans, the elders cancelled the student's appearance and reprimanded the people who made those plans without their approval. Although they issued a statement that all people were welcome to work and worship with the Highland Street Church of Christ, the elders' draconian actions suggested a strong animosity toward blacks and a desire to tightly control any circumstances in which a black person might be welcomed, however awkwardly, into their church. Bowie, who would later become a renowned leader in the private-school movement among Churches of Christ, decided to remove his family from the church in the wake of these events. He wrote a letter to explain his departure, emphasizing that he had not asked "for an immediate integration of the Highland Street congregation" but simply an educational program that emphasized racial inclusivity. He could neither "imagine that Jesus would have canceled the Negro student from his assignment to report on the Christian Student Center," nor "believe that he would have canceled the seven black [SWCC] students from appearing for a program in our building because housing was requested for them."[17]

Efforts at racial reconciliation came haltingly in Memphis, as elsewhere, and many whites were simply at a loss about how they might proceed. The 1960s had ripped off the facade of amicability that clouded the judgment of many whites in Churches of Christ. Finding themselves immersed in a culture with white-supremacist foundations, even well-meaning whites who had some understanding of church or national history had difficulty building mutual relationships that crossed the color line. An insightful exchange of letters in 1971 between John Allen Chalk and Harry Steele, a white elder of the Macon Road Church of Christ in Memphis, revealed these personal and communal dilemmas. Steele had organized a race relations forum in 1970 that brought few, if any, tangible results. Efforts to follow up with a leading black church in Memphis were not reciprocated, and even the *Christian Echo* omitted mention of the forum amid its usual assortment of reports from the field. Steele astutely observed how interactions among black and white Churches of Christ had become more strained. "It almost seems as if it went the other way and solidified both sides into a determination to go their separate ways," he noted about the forum. Steele lamented the lack of cooperation that he seemed to be getting from his black brothers and sisters in Memphis, while failing to appreciate the decades of mistrust that had only compounded with the ignoble decisions of prominent white churches in Memphis. Steele detailed some personal steps that he was taking to combat racial discrimination—hiring a black secretary "who has been with our company some time and passed over for promotion before because of her race," mentoring a black child, and visiting black churches—but "as far as church activity along this line," he confessed, "there seems to be little use at this time."[18]

Chalk was saddened by Steele's assessment but not surprised at the dilemma. He was more perceptive about blacks' wariness and tried to temper Steele's expectations. "Simply because spiritual principles are recognized, and even given lip service, the fact remains that most of us within the church are culturally dominated. . . . our attitudes and actions are those superimposed upon us by the larger culture outside," Chalk wrote. "We simply can't expect [black church leaders] to move in unfamiliar territory where, for the most part, they are not welcomed." His reply also foreshadowed the cleavages that would grow among Churches of Christ in the closing decades of the twentieth century. "Everywhere I go I see churches either dead or dying. . . . Yet, we have been content with being in 'the right church' and knowing intellectually what the Bible says without really experiencing a personal relationship with God." Black churches were increasingly likely to move forward, independent of any influence from, or relationship with, white churches.[19]

While younger black preachers might have avoided the most strident expressions of black power, they nevertheless imbibed its emphasis on self-determination and its rejection of white Christianity. Indeed black Christians were left to explain why they subscribed to a religion that had often served to justify white oppression of blacks. The very name "Church of Christ" was closely associated with white racism, particularly in Memphis and Nashville. David Jones Jr., black minister of Nashville's Schrader Lane Church of Christ, lamented how preaching "to Negroes is increasingly more difficult by Negro preachers because he is regarded as a traitor, an uncle tom [sic], a whitened black man, because . . . [of] the actions, disinterest, and racism of 'white' Christianity. Frankly, it is a burden for the black man to be a member of the 20th Century Church of Christ because of its racist policies." A black minister from Detroit assessed the situation even more frankly. In a letter written in response to the *Herald of Truth* series about race relations, Jesse Johnson felt that he spoke for "most black people" in describing the sermons as "(1) meager, (2) far too late, and (3) insignificant" without subsequent positive actions. "Once again," Johnson's lengthy letter stated,

the Churches of Christ are guilty of being 'the echo' and *not* 'the voice.' . . . After the whole of our society is discussing, debating, and condemning white racism in our american [sic] way of life, *one* of our brethren speaks to this point on nationwide radio. . . . What is tragic is the fact that we have procrastinated so long in speaking on the subject. But what is even more pathetic is that after such a long delay in addressing ourselves to this matter and after one of the brethren finally decided to speak to the issue, he then becomes the target of severe criticism [emphasis in original].

Johnson's primitivism and exclusivism crept into his critique—he warned of "the end of christianity [sic] in any form, in the black community" if white churches did not act promptly—but his urgent tone represented the passion and frustration that blacks felt. By the end of the 1960s, white Churches of Christ were showing only piecemeal and grudging recognition of black aspirations, and black Churches of Christ were feeling heat for associating with whites, for belonging to a predominantly white denomination that was largely silent during the momentous events of the black freedom struggle in the twentieth century. No church member could easily walk away from what he or she believed was *the* church, so black members found themselves in a bind. The solution was, in effect, to leave white Churches of Christ to wrestle with their own demons, distance themselves from any association with a predominantly white denomination, and forge a path as an independent church. This

approach was relatively easy without a hierarchical structure to impose strictures on liturgy or missions or to require formal integration. Facing pressure
from within their churches and the black communities to which they belonged,
black Churches of Christ further insulated themselves from their white counterparts who were simply too slow or stubborn to acknowledge the presence of
racial prejudice within the church and who showed no interest in addressing
past injustices.[20]

Black Churches of Christ and a few of their white allies were also confronted with new competition in the battle for souls, as various forms of Islam appealed to blacks who perceived Christianity as "a white man's religion"
and an instrument of contrived racial oppression. The actions of many white
churches seemed to confirm this assessment, so black members of Churches
of Christ not only had to justify their faith in Jesus, but also their commitment
to a predominantly white denomination. As whites practiced and supported
various forms of racial segregation, blacks were forced to explain this behavior
to potential converts who were often younger, well educated, and more prone
to question the restorationist claims of Churches of Christ. The Nation of Islam exploited this challenge. When a young man named Henry Stokes converted to the Nation of Islam, his mother feared for his soul. Stokes was once
a devout member of Churches of Christ who remained faithful during a stint
overseas in the Air Force but made some personal changes upon his return to
the United States. His mother attributed the changes to family difficulties and,
as devout mothers sometimes do, she pushed Christian reading material on
her son, including sermon transcripts from the *Herald of Truth* radio program.
After listening to a sermon titled "What Jesus Says for Himself," the younger
Stokes wrote a letter to Chalk to explain why he now rejected Christianity. The
sermon, much to his mother's chagrin, reaffirmed Stokes's "belief in Islam as
taught by the Honorable Elijah Muhammad." About Christianity, Stokes professed "that it is a religion established by white people, for white people, for the
purpose of dominating and enslaving Blackmen, the world over. . . . How a sane
Blackman can see Christianity in any other light today is a mystery to me."[21]

Chalk commended Stokes for his "pride of blackness" and readily conceded
the "many unfortunate, ungodly, and unscriptural things [that] have been advanced in the name of Christianity regarding race." Citing several passages from
the Christian scriptures, he countered Stokes's assertions about Jesus and asked
for more information about the Nation of Islam. Stokes's subsequent reply illustrated the wide communication gap between the two men. Chalk wanted

to discuss theology and Christian apologetics. He even purchased a copy of Elijah Muhammad's *Message to the Blackman in America* and a subscription to *Muhammad Speaks*, the periodical published by the Nation of Islam. But the time for theological debate had long passed for men like Stokes who were not as interested in theology as they were in social reform and justice. If Chalk wanted to discuss theology, then Stokes encouraged him to directly contact Elijah Muhammad who had "shown Black America the way to *real* freedom, justice, and equality here on this earth" (emphasis in original). Temporal notions of freedom, justice, and equality were largely lost on Churches of Christ. The denomination, with its past badly and perhaps irrevocably tainted by its historical apathy toward social justice, no longer appealed to Stokes. A church that urged unity and practiced segregation could not compete with the empowering messages offered by the Nation of Islam. Chalk was forced to admit as much in a separate letter to Stokes's mother: "Our problem today in America is that the church has not shown the way through to racial peace. We have remained in racial denominationalism, even within the church of Christ, rather than showing, rather than practicing, rather than preaching the one body seen in both groups of believers, as well as taught regarding the whole church of all the saved."[22]

Black Church of Christ preachers were better positioned to challenge the advances made by the Nation of Islam, and R. N. Hogan presented himself as a formidable foe of black Muslims. He publicly debated a Muslim minister and, in the winter of 1971–72, Hogan wrote a series of articles for the *Christian Echo* on what he termed "the Black Muslim Cult." His essays described the debate and evaluated what the Nation of Islam offered. Like Chalk, Hogan made theological arguments, but outside of the predictable rhetoric on whether Jesus was the son of God and speculation over the authenticity of Elijah Muhammad's teachings, the discussion hinged upon race. Hogan ironically employed an argument often used by whites to defend his willingness to associate with white churches. "My opponent accused me of defending the white man because I pointed out that the black man had something to do with enslaving black men," he wrote in the *Christian Echo*. "I still say that I do not condone the white man nor defend him in the atrocities that he has imposed on the black man and I do not condone nor defend the black man in the atrocities that he has imposed on other black men. . . . I am not going to hate the white man who is trying to live the Christian life, because of what his great grandfather did to my great grandfather. The greatest contribution to the growth of this Cult [*sic*] is that they continue to preach hate for the white man for what he did to our forefathers."

Regardless of the origins of the transatlantic slave trade, Hogan had to contend with his belonging to a predominantly white denomination that, on the whole, had shown little interest in the most pressing social issues of the era. Hogan had long tolerated white church members, even when they did not view him as their equal. Belonging to *the* church offered little alternative. Black Muslims were less willing to transcend white supremacy in the ways that Hogan had. Even if he spoke against racism, Hogan still belonged to a denomination that maintained segregated colleges into the mid-1960s and sometimes refused to integrate its churches.[23]

Muhammad Speaks described the debate as a victory for the Nation of Islam. The headline blared, "Wait-for-Heaven line of Christians smashed by debate of Muslim minister." Hogan's Christian rhetoric held little appeal, and his equation of black and white atrocities was met by "a loud groan of disappointment." Hogan's approach satisfied neither the members of the Nation of Islam nor the "youthful audience" and perhaps even frustrated members of the Church of Christ who attended. *Muhammad Speaks* noted, "THE DOUBT and disappointment by his own church members surprised many observers" (emphasis in original). Perhaps this assessment compelled Hogan to launch his series in the *Christian Echo* after the debate. The series was intended to educate readers and provide information for further discussions that were arising in the homes of black families. Hogan surely caricatured the Nation of Islam to some extent, but he also addressed those issues that were ultimately damning Churches of Christ and other Christian denominations in the eyes of the Nation of Islam and its converts. At the conclusion of his first essay, Hogan summarized the reasons that blacks should avoid the Nation of Islam, but he also admitted one of the group's strengths: "The Muslim organization is an organization that teaches hate, denies the Sonship of Christ, accepts human claims, rejects the inspired word of God and is carnally militant." But, he added, "I can commend them for [teaching] the young Black people to be clean, self respect and to do for themselves." These latter two points were especially relevant. Black Churches of Christ had long tolerated or even embraced white paternalism, which discouraged the self-respect and independence that young blacks longed to enjoy. On top of the white oppression that was endemic to the nation, they had to overcome notions of black inferiority that arose within their churches. The Nation of Islam offered a viable alternative.[24]

In the final essay of the series, Hogan made one of his strongest statements about pervasive racism across the country, not just within the church, attributing the growing popularity of the Nation of Islam to "the fact that the Negro has been exploited, oppressed and suppressed by the white man in every state of our country, in the North as well as in the South." He was not just castigating whites. Hogan now feared that blacks would be lost to the Nation of Islam, so he attempted to coopt their rhetoric to remain relevant. He surmised that the Nation of Islam "took advantage of the conditions into which the white man had driven the Negro." Its members speak "with increasing frequency of the atrocities imposed on the Black man throughout the major negro population centers of America. They are therefore, succeeding to bring into their Cult the militant, underpriviledged [sic] and exploited people who fall for their idea of a separate state." This observation suggested jealousy as much as criticism. The Nation of Islam attracted the very people who were the responsibility of Christians, Hogan realized. In the process of critiquing the Nation of Islam, he found it necessary to match the stringency of their critique of US history. Dealing with the Nation of Islam forced him to concede that Churches of Christ—his church, *the* church—had failed miserably in addressing what centuries of systematic racism had wrought.[25]

In this context, black Churches of Christ became more open to activities, literature, and programs that emphasized racial identity and pride. In the past, religious identity was the focus. Even if church members struggled with self-doubt because of their "blackness," encouraging black pride was almost never integral to a preacher's message or a church's ministry. A poem, composed by Lucy Mae Harris and published in the *Christian Echo* in the summer of 1965, evoked a moment when fostering racial pride warranted greater attention, as preachers did not want to lose their flocks to the ideologies of the Nation of Islam or the black power movement. "Did God mean to punish me, when He made my face black?" the opening line plaintively asks. "No!" the third line states, "God made me in His image, Equal to all other men." The poem ultimately found solace in Jesus who "was treated quite the same" as blacks who suffered discrimination and humiliation.

So no matter how much I suffer, because black is my skin,
I ask God to forgive them and give me courage to the end.
I'm proud of my complexion, for God made me this way,
I know He is with me, no matter what they do or say.[26]

Since the spread of Christianity among slaves in the United States, blacks felt solidarity with the persecutions that Jesus endured and stories of divine suffering, but they now turned to other alternatives for self-discovery. Several black Churches of Christ began coordinating black studies workshops for their members or interested local citizens. Classes typically focused on African heritage or "Blacks in the Bible," as noted in the history of the Schrader Lane Church of Christ in Nashville, Tennessee. The Schrader Lane church later developed an African studies class with a broader historical and political focus. In addition to studying some fundamental knowledge about the entire continent, classes delved into state formation in Egypt, Ethiopia, Sudan, Mali, Ghana, and Benin; the invasion of Africa by Europeans; the Atlantic slave trade; and American slavery. "We have to deal with the past only as we can make it useful to the present and the future," the church's official history notes. This renewed interest in black culture and history reflected broader cultural trends that were unfolding across the country. Perhaps the most notable personification of this evolution in Churches of Christ was Arthur Lee Smith Jr., a black man from Valdosta, Georgia, who matriculated at NCI, Oklahoma Christian College, and Pepperdine College, where he wrote a master's thesis about Marshall Keeble. Smith pursued an academic career after completing a doctorate at the University of California at Los Angeles in 1968. He eventually left the denomination and changed his name to Molefi Kete Asante before becoming the foremost scholar on Afrocentric thought.[27]

As black church members discovered new self-respect and solidarity through racial pride and self-awareness, their white counterparts felt increasingly ostracized. While some measure of unity, however perfunctory, existed before the 1960s between black and white Churches of Christ, whites who were apathetic or ignorant about institutional racism typically found no common cause with black churches who taught black history and empowerment. In this context, many whites left the denomination's apolitical roots and gravitated toward the political aspirations of Alabama's notorious George Wallace, who was running for president of the United States in 1968. Guy Woods, a popular white evangelist and debater, became an outspoken supporter of Wallace and critic of the *Herald of Truth* in the wake of its sermons on race relations. One preacher who hosted Woods for a revival noted, "Race he says is not to be discussed from the pulpit especially the radio pulpit. . . . He is a strong Wallace supporter and actively campaigns for him among brethren." A black preacher named Humphrey Foutz also made the connection between Wallace's burgeoning brand of conservatism and many white members. Foutz urged the *Herald of Truth* television producers to include blacks in the films that were used for evangelism because one "looked like a commercial for George Wallace or at best the John

Birch Society." They were "constantly harping on the 'Code Words' Law and Order. . . . They sound like the 'George Wallace' of organized religion."[28]

Indeed one of Wallace's closest advisors was Jimmy Faulkner, a former political rival and the namesake of Faulkner University, a Church of Christ college in Montgomery, Alabama. Faulkner was a businessman and journalist by trade, educated at Freed-Hardeman College and the University of Missouri, where he belonged to the Kappa Alpha fraternity, "largely because it was a Southern organization." Faulkner's relationship with Wallace began at the 1948 Democratic National Convention in Philadelphia, infamous for the walkout staged by southern delegates who broke with the national party over its civil rights platform to create the States' Rights Party. They would soon nominate South Carolina's governor, Strom Thurmond, for president of the United States. Wallace and Faulkner traveled together in a car to the convention as "anti-Truman delegates," committed to opposing President Harry Truman's newfound interest in civil rights. "I had qualified as a Truman delegate," Faulkner later recalled, "but had to change to anti-Truman in order to get elected." Both Faulkner and Wallace had future political aspirations to consider.[29]

Faulkner first pursued his gubernatorial dreams in 1954, when he narrowly missed a run-off with "Big Jim" Folsom. His next opportunity came in 1958 when he finished third behind Wallace and the winner, John Patterson, in a Democratic primary with fourteen candidates. Historian Dan Carter called Faulkner the "most racially moderate" in the field, and his biographer suggested that "Faulkner had a greater acceptance of integration than most Southerners, a trait that would work against him in a statewide election in the fifties." The election was especially contentious because of the civil rights movement. In the wake of the successful Montgomery bus boycott, Patterson had banished the NAACP from the state as attorney general, and other events such as passage of the Civil Rights Act of 1957 and the school desegregation crisis in Little Rock, Arkansas, forced candidates to articulate their positions on desegregation. Faulkner later claimed that the Ku Klux Klan worked for John Patterson, and Wallace's defeat in the runoff prompted his notorious pledge that "no other son of a bitch will ever out-nigger me again."[30]

Losing that election stung Faulkner about as much as it did Wallace. The Klan's support of Patterson, not to mention the attorney general's preposterous effort to ban the NAACP, did not deter Faulkner from using his campaign organization to raise money for Patterson during the runoff but, by 1962, Wallace sought Faulkner's support before pursuing the governor's office a second time. "Jimmy," Wallace entreated, "you claim that I cost you an election one time and I know that you cost me an election one time, can't we start all over again?" Faulkner agreed and later told his biographer that "from then on we were friends." Wallace relied heavily on Faulkner during future election campaigns. When Wallace ran for president in 1968, Faulkner spent considerable time organizing the collection of signatures in various states outside the South to ensure that Wallace's name appeared on their ballots. Faulkner oversaw the production of some of Wallace's campaign literature and was head of the Wallace campaign on the West Coast. When Wallace ran for governor again in 1970, amid one of the most notorious, race-baiting campaigns, Faulkner cosigned a note for $100,000 to keep the Wallace campaign financially solvent. In the presidential election of 1972, Faulkner served as an intermediary between Hubert Humphrey and Wallace, as the Humphrey forces contemplated sharing the Democratic ticket with Wallace.[31]

Perhaps Faulkner's role as a Wallace insider had more to do with politics than with faith, but the two were hardly separable. Faulkner's children later recalled their father's devotion. "When Sunday came around, you went to church!" one son exclaimed. "And Sunday night you went to church, regardless what else was going on. And Wednesday, too! It wasn't any use talking about it. . . . I don't care what ball game or something else was going on, you went to church. Even when we were traveling, we would find a church of Christ, and we'd go to church." The title of Faulkner's biography, *Faith and Works*, further suggested the significance of faith to his life, and his strong commitment to Churches of Christ included service as a song leader, treasurer, deacon, and elder. His generous financial assistance to Alabama Christian College in Montgomery led administrators there to rename the school after him in 1985. Thus Faulkner University bears the name of its chief benefactor and longtime chairman of the board, an Alabama politico with close ties to the state's most notorious segregationist, George Wallace.[32]

This political affinity for Wallace unfolded as a small but growing number of black students were learning to navigate predominantly white colleges. Events at Harding College during the 1968–69 academic year indicated larger trends within the denomination. The militancy that sometimes characterized the civil rights movement by the end of the 1960s appeared there in a relatively benign form. Weary of the vestiges of segregation in campus life and within the minds of many whites in the Harding community, black students organized a separate social club for themselves and became more vocal in complaints to administrators. The new club illustrated the presence of a small faction, including a few white students, who wanted the college to move away from its religious, social, and political conservatism. But dissent was not readily tolerated at Harding. Students who might challenge campus norms feared an administration that could strike hard and fast with the full support of the broader campus community. Events at Harding that year revealed that most whites in Churches of Christ failed to grasp the depths of segregation and its legacies, much less the persistent forms of racial discrimination that echoed in the daily lives of black students.

They named the new club Groove Phi, thereby acknowledging the cultural impact of the burgeoning black power movement and the incorporation of slang into mainstream usage. Although there is no evidence of a direct link, the Harding students adopted a name similar to a new club at Morgan State College, Groove Phi Groove, which was founded under different circumstances in 1962. The Harding students had a litany of complaints that illustrated how unwelcome they felt. They faced restrictions from other clubs in their intramural participation, for example, but hostilities were much more rampant than conflicts among competing organizations. They were incensed that derogatory terms such as "boy," "Nigra," and "colored" were still used frequently when whites spoke of or to them. Entities within the college, especially a conservative think tank known as the National Education Program, consistently derided the civil rights movement by claiming that communists influenced civil rights activists. During the previous fall, Harding professor James Bales published a controversial book, *The Martin Luther King Story*, with "A STUDY IN APOSTASY, AGITATION, AND ANARCHY" emblazoned across the top of the front cover. One black student had some of his personal property burned, and one of the most popular tunes that the pep band played at athletic events was "Dixie." In addition to a long list of grievances, various disciplinary measures taken by the administration against black students were perceived as unfair. Given these circumstances, it is easy to understand why black students questioned Harding's commitment to racial equality a few years after the first black students appeared on campus.[33]

The establishment of Groove Phi was simultaneously an act of protest, a means of organizing against the vestiges of white supremacy on campus, and a way to communicate that circumstances at Harding were unacceptable. Shortly after forming, members of Groove Phi started a petition that urged the band not to play "Dixie," and they arranged a meeting with Harding's president, Clifton Ganus Jr., to confront him directly with their concerns. Ganus recognized the need to improve race relations at Harding and within Churches of Christ. Jimmy Allen, one of his faculty members from the Bible Department, helped coordinate the race relations conference in Atlanta in 1968, and Ganus accompanied him and was the featured speaker at one session, although he did not sign the statement that issued from the conference. At a faculty meeting in February 1969, Ganus presented a summary of the suggestions from Groove Phi. Minutes from that meeting indicate that his remarks focused primarily on the social clubs; the relationships between himself, the faculty, and black students; and the playing of "Dixie." Ganus also noted that all but one of the twenty-eight black students at Harding were receiving some sort of financial aid from the college, a point that led him to conclude that some white students may have been mistreating black students but Harding College was not.[34]

Many white students resented the allegations made by Groove Phi and its few white allies. They perceived these criticisms as a summary attack on their beloved college and understood them amid the broader context of unrest across the nation, unrest that made many whites defensive of their nation and ways of life that often excluded blacks or diminished their civic and social contributions. The editor of the Bison, Harding's student newspaper, later recalled that most white students were initially unaware of any racial problems on campus but, as the spring semester unfolded, the newspaper stood firmly behind the Harding administration and defended the college against all critique. Subtle criticisms of the civil rights movement could easily be detected in the Bison's commentary about campus life, and the advent of Groove Phi elicited an editorial that the new club "may be a sign of their [black students'] desire to segregate themselves from Whites, but still to be treated as equal creations—a desire which some political leaders have obviously overlooked." About the controversy over "Dixie," the same editorial contended that, for the most part, the tune was "fondly recalled by Southerners without thought of slavery or freedom, white or black," although some people might "have malice in their hearts" when they listened to the song. The tenor of the Bison had changed markedly since the early 1960s when desegregation was the primary issue. Now black needs, demands, and aspirations upset white comfort zones and exposed the limits of the earlier, tentative support for core goals of the civil rights movement.[35]

As the spring semester progressed, rhetoric on campus grew heated, leading the Bison to lament that the "time has come when students must be either for or against civil rights. They cannot possibly harbor ideas which relate to the pros and cons on both sides of the issue. . . . At the risk of sounding trite, students today must either be with the 'in' crowd or with 'the establishment.'" The *Bison*, presenting opposition to civil rights as a viable option here, sided with the Harding establishment in the coming months. In addition to Groove Phi, one of the newspaper's targets was a psychology professor named Bob Gilliam. In class discussions and private conversations, he encouraged students to raise their voices against injustices on campus, and he urged students to consider alternative perspectives on current events. In February he chaperoned a group of students to a human relations seminar at Oklahoma Christian College, where the list of featured speakers included John Allen Chalk, Franklin Florence, and Howard Wright, a Harding alumnus. Gilliam had a profound impact on a few students within his circle of influence. One student returned from the seminar and admitted that "it was rousing to think that I could be so unaware. It motivated me to do something about the problem. It really made me aware of how stagnant my religion was." Neither Ganus nor the *Bison* were enamored with Gilliam, however. Without calling him by name, one editorial lambasted instructors "who have been guilty of destroying student integrity by promoting ideas through students which they did not have the courage to openly advance themselves. They have cultivated students for their own ego and popularity to the point of placing student against student. . . . And they have developed power cliques in students to offset their own weaknesses." Gilliam was clearly more open with his ideas about social justice than the *Bison* allowed, however, as Ganus later remembered him as "the one who was kind of leading the rabble." Ganus recalled "taking more abuse from him than . . . all of the faculty put together."[36]

A brief discussion series on campus was intended to be a first step toward tackling Harding's racial conflicts by giving space for black students to speak openly about the aforementioned hostilities and inviting white students to listen and ask questions. The student council and Gilliam coordinated the discussions on consecutive Wednesday nights in March, and some two hundred students attended each session. Ganus attended but did not participate, but his presence did little to curb any inhibitions that may have existed among the black students, one of whom called for "a change from a prejudiced administration, beginning with the president of the college." During the second session, students brainstormed for ideas about improving race relations at Harding, and a lengthy list of about seventy suggestions was printed in a special issue of the *Bison*. The list included correcting "inaccurate Biblical interpretations concerning race," banning Bales's book about King, incorporating black people into history courses, halting correspondence with parents about interracial dating, and hiring black faculty. Some black students had previously met to compile their suggestions, including a request for the administration to "take a definite stand on racial problems." An ad hoc committee of black and white students formed to refine the seventy suggestions and formally present them to Ganus.[37]

An editorial in the special edition of the *Bison* tepidly agreed that Harding had some racial problems, "but in doing so," it added, "we cannot blow it out of perspective." While it spared no criticism of both black and white students, little effort was made to carefully consider the issues that black students had raised during the school year or in recent discussions. Indeed black students were ultimately blamed for causing the tumult on campus. "The thought of 'talking things over' seems to infuriate some Blacks," the *Bison* opined. "They cry that the time for talking has long since passed. . . . Have the blacks actually talked or have they demanded? . . . The lines of communication have always been present, but the methods employed have been detrimental. It must be added at this point that abusive and false accusations do not constitute a means for solving problems." From the perspective of many white students, racial tensions arose because of insistent demands or criticism, not because of persistent forms of racial discrimination. The *Bison* failed to acknowledge that social clubs were discriminatory, that there were no black faculty members, that administrators closely monitored interracial romances, and that black students had no representation in the student council or the *Bison* staff. Indeed the editorial emphasized "that this problem is an individual problem and individual attitudes must be changed. . . . Both races must respect the other and lay aside prejudice; stereotyping must be eliminated and individuals must be accepted on their own merits." This emphasis on what amounted to simplistic, individual solutions to deeply ingrained, intransigent problems became increasingly popular in the last decades of the twentieth century. It absolved institutions of responsibility in perpetuating and benefiting from past racial injustices. This ahistorical approach to better race relations presumed that if people, black and white, would just follow the Golden Rule, then racial conflicts would be solved.[38]

The newspaper polled students to determine the causes of Harding's racial problems, and one white student aptly summarized a fundamental dilemma that whites perceived. Her comments positioned her white contemporaries as the arbiters of civil rights, as the next in a long line of whites whose economic and political privilege enabled them to dictate many of the terms upon which blacks lived. "We are so afraid that we might help the Negroes that don't deserve help that we won't go an extra mile with them in order to deal fairly with those that have not been treated fairly." She further deduced, "It would be contrary to Christian ideals to deny justice to those warranting it, by trying to avoid giving it to those that have continually abused it. I would much rather see some Negroes not making use of opportunities giving [sic] them than all Negroes with no opportunities." Her observations illustrated whites' limited conceptions of how to correct past racial injustices and white presumptions about setting the boundaries of black freedom and civic expectations. Simply opening the school doors to black students, many whites thought, would be sufficient to providing equal opportunity for all.[39]

The ad hoc student committee submitted its report to Ganus on March 19, 1969. It included a lengthy, perceptive analysis of why racial problems existed in the nation and a list of specific steps that could be taken to improve race relations at Harding. They also assessed the grievances that had been compiled by black students and urged the administration to address them. They were "concrete things the Whites (Harding) can do without compromising any principles in taking the first steps in this establishment of trust. Doing some of these things now may *look* like a capitulation. This is sad. Perhaps if we had already done some of these things we would not be in the position we find ourselves in because of our own inaction." Many of the committee's recommendations closely correlated to black students' suggestions, such as the hiring of black faculty, developing curriculum that included black history, and clarifying scriptures that were used to justify racial prejudice. The committee also asked Ganus to make clear statements about his positions on hiring black faculty, recruiting black students, and interracial dating.[40]

On the following day, Ganus appeared before the student body during chapel to respond to the committee's recommendations. At the time, Harding held two daily chapel services and required students to attend one each day. Many black students attended the first service, where they heard Ganus defend himself and Harding, while castigating students who had raised several pressing issues before the college community. In defending himself against charges that he was prejudiced, he said that he "had been prejudiced all right—prejudiced toward helping people regardless of their color." The evidence that he offered, however, was hardly convincing. He described how he let the "colored maid" eat at the dinner table with his family, helped desegregate Harding, and participated in the Atlanta conference. To his mind these activities confirmed that he was not prejudiced, and they formed the premise for the remainder of his speech.[41]

Ganus proceeded with mixed messages as he shared the committee's recommendations with the student body. He conceded some of their recommendations but spent a considerable amount of time in his speech chastising his detractors. In the process, he made a number of demeaning and insulting statements about Harding's black students. "I guess most [black students] are better fed and housed and better treated than at home," Ganus asserted, before reciting a list of grievances that he had with black students. "Irresponsibility is a terrible curse to any man," he preached, "and [for] too long it has been winked at in the Black man because his great grandfather was a slave." Ganus dismissed any special challenges that black students might face, adding that whites "have had a background of prejudiced teaching and bitter experience at the hands of the blacks," long before the concept of "reverse discrimination" entered common parlance. His remarks were met with widespread approval, as evidenced by the standing ovations that he received at the end of each presentation. During the second one, however, about twenty black students and a few of their white allies walked out of the speech in a mild protest that still garnered the attention of the Little Rock press. These students must have realized at that moment that they were powerless to change Harding. Although they were pictured giving a black power salute in the next day's *Arkansas Gazette,* their poses suggested defeat instead of victory. None of their fists were raised higher than their heads.[42]

Despite the hopelessness of their situation, the walkout would not be their last protest at Harding. A few weeks later, as Harding hosted its annual Freedom Forum, about thirty students gathered copies of a pamphlet, "The Communist Blueprint for the American Negro," that James Bales had provided to attendees. Led by black students Darryl Patterson, Travis Sanders, and Eddie Allen, the students burned the tracts and tossed the remnants into the lily pond in front of the administration building. Despite boldly telling onlookers that they could have burned a building instead, the demonstration was peaceful. "This is supposed to be a Christian institution," Patterson told the crowd that gathered, "and they allow this obscene literature." When a photographer from the *Arkansas Gazette* tried to take pictures of this protest, however, white students blocked his view. They were tired of black grievances, tired of the protests, tired of the bad publicity.

Protests were "definitely not winning any souls to Christ," the *Bison* opined. "Several faculty members and several students reportedly are leaving Harding College. But before these can be happy elsewhere, they seem to feel that they have to leave behind the smoldering ruins of what the rest of us still feel is a *great* institution" (emphasis in original). Letters sent by white students to Ganus in the aftermath of these events were also positive. One wrote, "I appreciate you and what you said in chapel today," before admitting that he was "a little apprehensive as to what your stand on race relations might be." There was reason for the student's uncertainty. To maintain the facilities and growth of Harding, to build on the legacy of George Benson, Ganus could not show too much concern for the special circumstances in which black students found themselves by attending a historically white college with a student population that was still 98 percent white. The words that he spoke in chapel on March 20 still incited some patrons to write letters requesting that he toughen his position. "Let this be remembered as the year of the *purge*, the *great purge*" (emphasis in original), one lady wrote and, in some respects, she received her wish. Gilliam left for another university, and another professor who espoused what some considered unorthodox opinions was fired. Black student activists Patterson, Sanders, and Allen were not allowed to return to Harding in the fall.[43]

Harding was not the only Church of Christ college that experienced such turmoil in the late 1960s. Pepperdine College underwent comparable tensions between recalcitrant whites and young black students who appeared militant by Church of Christ standards. Pepperdine had served as a staging area for the National Guard during the 1965 Watts riot, and a young black man died in March 1969 during a tussle with a white security guard that arose when some black teens were asked to leave the gymnasium. A series of financial and identity crises convinced Pepperdine administrators that moving the college to Malibu and serving as a bastion of political conservatism in southern California would ensure its future stability. By the early 1970s, however, black students composed 25 percent of Pepperdine's student body, a high percentage for any integrated college, so Harding was likely more indicative of changes unfolding in the parochial world of Churches of Christ. Administrators such as George Benson had maintained a segregated institution for theological, financial, and political reasons. Students seemingly had less at stake. In the years before their schools desegregated, whites were sometimes vocal proponents of welcoming black students. It was the Christian thing to do. However, as black demands extended beyond mere enrollment, white students grew increasingly defensive about the persistence of discrimination in their institutions. Neither white students nor administrators grasped the depth of segregation's effects, while black students knew firsthand how racial prejudice lingered and affected their everyday lives. Their justified impatience clashed with white incomprehension, indifference, and defensiveness.[44]

This clash was perhaps more broadly evident at DLC, where tensions within the denomination spilled into the courtroom. The lawsuit regarding the denouement of NCI and the liquidation and transfer of its assets to a scholarship fund for black students at DLC in 1967 has been well documented, but the college was threatened with further lawsuits for its discriminatory housing policies, which persisted into the 1970s. Integrated housing was just one of several issues that concerned whites as desegregation unfolded. Even Pepperdine College, which from its inception in 1937 had always accepted black students, refused to allow black students to live on campus during the first decade of its existence. When a white attorney and DLC alumnus made a direct inquiry to Athens Clay Pullias, the DLC president, he was told "that I didn't really understand the problem and that with more years I would better understand these kind of problems and whatever." Further inquiries yielded little results. Another administrator explained "that it would be unpopular to obey the new laws but that when they were 'inforced [sic] generally, we will be eagerly [sic] to comply.'" Thus the college practiced housing discrimination years after it became illegal, an unsubtle reminder that the "law and order" rhetoric of many whites during the era was much more about keeping the segregated order than following the law. The young attorney who approached Pullias did not miss the irony. "I hear so much today about law and order and as a member of the legal establishment have committed my life to that cause and yet I see here an institution that claims to be Christian [blatantly] ignoring the law of the land."[45]

Church of Christ colleges would eventually comply with housing regulations, but they often maintained close ties to a resurgent conservative political movement that arose as a backlash to the reform movements of the 1960s, especially at Harding College where, according to historian Bethany Moreton, "the process of wedding Christian vocational education to corporate concerns was most dramatically exemplified." By the 1970s, black and white Churches of Christ were moving in opposite directions, one embracing the civil rights victories and raised expectations of the black freedom struggle, the other seeking absolution in youth programs or foreign missionaries. Ironically Church of Christ colleges, the sites of protracted struggles to desegregate, became the most likely place where blacks and whites within Churches of Christ might interact. "I do not believe that God is happy or pleased with two churches," a black preacher wrote in 1969, "and believe me there are two Churches of Christ on earth today—a white church and black church. They are growing farther apart each day." Only the dawn of a new century and new assessments of the past would resurrect serious desires to pursue racial reconciliation.[46]

CONCLUSION
Repentance, Reconciliation, and Resistance

One Sunday morning a few years ago, historian John Hardin and I arrived in time for the morning worship service with a Church of Christ in Vicksburg, Mississippi. Today the church is known simply as the Bypass Church of Christ, a name based on the building's location beside the highway that skirts the eastern edge of Vicksburg. It was a relatively new church, founded in 1987 as the third predominantly black Church of Christ in Vicksburg. Eight weeks prior to our arrival, an event transpired that would have been almost unthinkable a few decades ago. A predominantly white Church of Christ merged into the Bypass Church of Christ, "uniting to form a new congregation of the Lord's church."[1]

We arrived on Father's Day and settled into a pew in the back of the sanctuary. Over two hundred people, about evenly split between black and white, had crowded into the small building for worship that day. The simple, A-frame structure included a small foyer that separated the sanctuary from the outdoors and, in this area, the sweltering summer heat and the cool air conditioner waged war each time the entrance doors opened. It symbolically called to mind "long, hot summers," "the heat," and a state with a long history of racial violence, oppression, and distrust competing against a collection of people who, at least for a few hours each week, seemed to forget and defy that past.

Churches of Christ are known for their a cappella worship, a characteristic that perhaps limits the aura of excitement that stereotypes some charismatic churches, so an up-tempo song or an occasional "Amen" during a sermon is about as exciting as it gets. The song leader that day was an elderly white man whose pace and song selection might well have disappointed anyone under sixty years of age. In keeping with Church of Christ tradition, the Eucharist was served, as it is each week, by a group of men who distributed the unleavened bread and grape juice between prayers that "those partaking of it will do so in a worthy manner."[2] (Churches of Christ are traditionally "teetotalers" who teach abstention from all alcoholic beverages.) The sermon was delivered by

Willie Nettle, the black minister, and he chose as his text 1 Corinthians 16:13–14, an excerpt from a Pauline epistle that simply states, "Watch, stand fast in the faith, be brave, be strong. Let all that you do be done with love" (NKJV). In lifting this text from the apostle's closing salutations to ancient Corinthian churches, Nettle found a message for fathers and their wives. "Women are to submit and obey their husbands," Nettle insisted, as he gave homage to another Pauline text. Contemporary fathers, he opined, were not "being men" because they refused to assert their authority in the home. Nettle extended this definition of masculinity to include "the denominations" when he suggested that "not being a man" could also refer to people with "denominational ties who refuse to listen to the Word of God [and are] being wishy-washy with the Word." He even made room in his homily for criticism of homosexuality and same-sex marriages in which the couple adopts a child. The sermon could have been preached in many Churches of Christ across the country, black or white.

These two churches announced their intention to integrate in a letter sent to the *Magnolia Messenger*, a periodical affiliated with Churches of Christ that includes didactic essays and reports on church events in Mississippi. One paragraph summarized their reasons for merging:

> Because of our love for Christ, his love for us, his pleas for unity of Christians and our love for each other, both congregations are convinced that worshipping and working together and following the principles and guidelines of God's word will make each of us stronger in Christ. We believe the blending of black and white cultures will not only glorify God, but also bless everyone involved. As one united body, we hope to have a stronger witness to the community and be better able to evangelize both populations in the Vicksburg area.

The letter further noted that both preachers would share ministerial duties. "We ask for your prayers for success as we embark in this new work," the letter concluded, "and we pray that our move to unity will be one of many over the next several years."[3]

This story is unique, however, because Churches of Christ, like several major denominations throughout the country, generally neglected opportunities for racial reconciliation and understanding that arose after the 1960s. Instead, the legacy of that decade became fodder for feel-good narratives about changes that were controversial and contested. For example, in 1998, Harding University published an informational volume about its institution and mission, titled

Against the Grain. Its most disingenuous assertion concerned desegregation. The story unfolded in three sentences, beginning with the note that the "South was still segregated in the early 60s, but Harding students and staff were ready to integrate and made known their views as early as 1957." The text then said that, "[q]uietly," the Harding graduate school in Memphis desegregated in 1962, followed one year later by the undergraduate school in Searcy. "Harding was the first private college in Arkansas to integrate," the text proudly explained, "and [President George] Benson received a standing ovation in chapel when he announced it." While much of the South was still segregated, the University of Arkansas law school desegregated in the fall of 1949, and with much notoriety, Little Rock's Central High School admitted nine students in 1957. Benson, of course, loathed having to desegregate his college; even after the first black students came on campus, he continued to teach that God intended the races to remain separate. Furthermore, "integration" had hardly occurred at Harding at all by the close of the 1960s, when twenty black students could be counted among a student body of almost two thousand.[4]

At the close of the twentieth century at least one formerly segregated Church of Christ college displayed a greater willingness to acknowledge and atone for its past. In 1999, Abilene Christian University (ACU) issued a formal apology to black members of Churches of Christ. Royce Money, president of the university, appeared at the fiftieth annual lectureship on the campus of SWCC, where he read a prepared statement. "We are here today to confess the sins of racism and discrimination and to issue a formal apology to all of you and to ask for your forgiveness," he said. "We understand from the Lord that part of repentance involves the resolve to go in a different direction in the future than we have in the past. But before we focus on the future, we need to confess the sins of racism and discrimination of the past against our African-American brothers and sisters in Christ." Sharing the stage with Money was Andrew Hairston, who had railed against the racism of white Churches of Christ during the 1960s. Hairston himself had been rejected by ACU before the school desegregated. By 1999, Hairston had enjoyed a successful career as an attorney and judge in Atlanta. He was also a minister of the Simpson Street Church of Christ and served as chairman of the board of trustees at SWCC. Hairston embraced Money after the apology was read. "I appreciate Dr. Money and ACU taking a lead on this, even if it's somewhat late," Hairston said. "The apology and reconciliation efforts are things that others couldn't bring themselves to do." The audience, composed primarily of black church members, stood and applauded at the close of Money's remarks. Many shouted, "Amen!" Some were moved to tears. A few months later, during the annual lectureship at ACU, a replay of these proceedings was shown during the opening session to a crowd of some four thousand people. Practical suggestions for encouraging racial reconciliation among churches were also discussed by a committee of black and white ministers whose October meeting had precipitated the apology.[5]

A few years later, administrators at David Lipscomb University sought to make amends with black churches through direct overtures to Fred Gray, who led the legal fight against the college when NCI was closed. In 2012 the university awarded Gray an honorary doctorate, and in 2016 the university renamed its Institute for Law, Justice & Society after him. A year later, the university announced the first recipients of a scholarship named in his honor.[6]

If they are not merging, numerous black and white churches are nonetheless finding enough common ground to venture into joint ministry efforts. The Schrader Lane Church of Christ in Nashville, for example, took the lead in a program aimed at helping welfare recipients achieve an education and gainful employment. Once a person graduates from the program, the church matches funds that the participants are able to save, thereby giving them some measure of financial security and independence. In this effort, the Schrader Lane church has been joined by a predominantly white church, the Woodmont Hills Church of Christ, also in Nashville. Other churches are consciously seeking to make their churches interracial by hiring ministers that reflect the ethnic demographics of local communities, especially in urban areas across the country.[7]

However, these initiatives, like the two churches in Vicksburg, appear exceptional. In contrast to efforts that honestly assess the past and seek to promote unity and justice, beyond the entrance to Harding's library is the George Benson Reading Room, complete with a large portrait and a sizable collection of plaques and other honors bestowed upon the former president. Benson was certainly a phenomenal administrator in the sense that he almost singlehandedly brought Harding out of obscurity. But reconciliation between blacks and whites is certainly impeded when a person with Benson's perspectives on race is so uncritically honored. Contemporary assessments of past race relations have also been hindered by the destruction of pertinent materials. Benson's files were thoroughly purged by his second wife. Even worse, the papers of Athens Clay Pullias, president of DLC from 1946 to 1977, and Hubert Allen Dixon, president of Freed-Hardeman College from 1950 to 1969, do not exist. Pullias took his papers with him, and school administrators were never able to recover any of them. The same can be said of Faulkner University, where sources that might illuminate the history of race relations at that school are no longer extant. Some years ago, I made several attempts to gain access to minutes of meetings of Lipscomb's board of trustees from the 1950s and 1960s but was refused.

Churches of Christ exemplified the many ways that whites have historically sought to minimize the perception of hardships that blacks have faced in this country. If the unconventional perspective of what constituted the church led some whites to associate more freely with blacks than they might have otherwise, this theological bent did not eventually lend itself to assessing and working to correct the gross injustices perpetrated against blacks throughout the United States, nor did it foster a spirit of equality between blacks and whites. The cry that the church had no business in politics rang hollow when more and more church members sought political office or worked diligently for temperance ordinances in their local communities. "Spiritual equality in Christ" operated as a phrase to downplay the demands of the black freedom struggle and to exonerate whites from any complicity in the apartheid system, especially in the South. Churches of Christ were exceptional, however, in that black members often echoed this same criticism of the civil rights movement. While they were outspoken against racial segregation, they did not champion the cause of Martin Luther King Jr., the Southern Christian Leadership Conference, or other civil rights advocacy groups. To associate with these ministers or groups would have been to align with "the denominations," something that both blacks and whites could not do in good conscience.

In the wake of the momentous changes of the 1960s, Churches of Christ were one of the few denominations that actually made conscious efforts to integrate individual, local congregations. This practice was not widespread, but those rare occasions when churches merged or labored to incorporate people from a variety of ethnic backgrounds have much to teach about the racial perspectives of some church members who defined church unity in theological, ethnic, and practical terms. Churches of Christ long acknowledged the theological unity of their denomination, even if that unity never "required" fully integrated houses of worship. In churches that made conscious decisions to pursue diverse members, however, one finds the rare occasion where words are met with deeds. Given this outcome, it is little wonder that subsequent generations have become increasingly cynical about faith questions, "the race question," and the denomination's answers to them.

Notes

Introduction

1. These divisions are explained most thoroughly in Harrell, "The Sectional Origins of the Churches of Christ," and *The Social Sources of Division in the Disciples of Christ, 1865–1900*; and Hughes, *Reviving the Ancient Faith*. Quotation appeared in Hughes, *Reviving the Ancient Faith*, 2.

2. Precise membership figures are notoriously difficult to ascertain for any religious body, but especially for one without traditional institutional structures. In the mid-1960s, an estimate of 2 million members was commonly accepted. This number may have been slightly exaggerated, as recent studies have suggested that Churches of Christ now have approximately 1.7 million adherents, with blacks composing over 13 percent of this figure. Whether membership numbered closer to 1 or 2 million at mid-century, at least 10 percent of church members were likely black. See Lynn, ed., *Churches of Christ in the United States*, 14, 17.

3. Among other instances, King made this remark on NBC's *Meet the Press* on April 17, 1960. See youtu.be/4MRYZ9RCmJs?t=6m48s (accessed May 21, 2013).

4. Hughes, *Reviving the Ancient Faith*, 2. Also see Allen and Hughes, *Illusions of Innocence*.

5. Historian John Hayes recently accepted this challenge when he wrote, "In the interstices of inequality in the early twentieth-century South, in a circumscribed world marked by intense poverty, poor blacks and poor whites listened to each other, borrowed from each other, and learned from each other about what it meant to be Christian in a hard world of toil and limit." See Hayes, *Hard, Hard Religion*, 1–19.

6. In addition to Harrell and Hughes, who are the foremost historians of Churches of Christ, studies of black and white Presbyterians, Episcopalians, Baptists, and Methodists nurtured my initial interests in this area of research. For these denominational studies, see Alvis, *Religion & Race*; Collins, *When the Church Bell Rang Racist*; Shattuck, *Episcopalians and Race*; Newman, *Getting Right with God*; and Murray, *Methodists and the Crucible of Race, 1930–1975*. Murray said that Methodists had the largest number of black and white southerners in the same church, a contention that is likely correct because they claimed over seven million members. However, blacks composed less than 5 percent of this figure, while the percentage of blacks in Churches of Christ was likely more than twice as high. Meanwhile, David Chappell and Paul Harvey published groundbreaking works that shaped how I conceived of race and religion in recent US history. See Chappell, *A Stone of Hope*, and Harvey, *Freedom's Coming*. Other notable denominational studies include Anderson, "Black, White, and Catholic," and London, *Seventh-day Adventists and the Civil Rights Movement*.

7. I am further indebted to historian Edward Robinson, whose timely biographies and edited collections of two prominent black preachers from Churches of Christ proved indispensable. His recent biography of Annie Tuggle additionally enhanced my appreciation for black women in Churches of Christ, whose voices were often difficult to discern. Robinson also examined the history of black Churches of Christ in Texas, providing insights into some remarkable congregational histories. See Robinson, *To Save My Race from Abuse*; *To Lift Up My Race*; *Show Us How You Do It*; *A Godsend to His People*; *The Fight Is On in Texas*; and *I Was Under a Heavy Burden*. More recently, Wes Crawford assessed black Churches of Christ in their quest for independence and theological evolution since the 1960s in *Shattering the Illusion*.

8. Hughes, *Reviving the Ancient Faith*, 51, 274–76.

9. Noll, *The Civil War as a Theological Crisis*.

10. Harvey, *Freedom's Coming*, 3.

1. Definitions of Racial Prejudice

1. A 2006 Gallup poll found that members of Churches of Christ were more likely than any other Christian group in the United States to attend a worship service each week. Sixty-eight percent of Church of Christ respondents reported that they "attend worship services at least once a week or almost every week." Mormons were second at 67 percent, followed by Pentecostals at 65 percent. See Bobby Ross Jr., "Poll: Church of Christ Tops in Weekly Worship Attendance," *Christian Chronicle* 63 (May 1, 2006), www.christianchronicle.org/article/poll-church-of-christ-tops-in -weekly-worship-attendance (accessed June 24, 2014).

2. Wilkerson, *The Warmth of Other Suns*, 33.

3. Hughes, *Reviving the Ancient Faith*, 272–73; Choate, *Roll Jordan Roll*, 6; Crawford, *Shattering the Illusion*, 61; and Campbell, *Race and the Renewal of the Church*, 29–30.

4. Hughes, *Reviving the Ancient Faith*,150, 273.

5. Elam and Boles, eds., *Elam's Notes on Bible School Lessons: 1929*, 280–85.

6. Ibid.

7. Ibid.

8. Hinds, *Annual Lesson Commentary on Improved Uniform Series of International Bible Lessons: 1932*, 304–10.

9. "Among the Colored Brethren," *Gospel Advocate* 106 (December 3, 1964): 782; Hughes, *Reviving the Ancient Faith*, 145–47; and Haymes, "Race & the Church of Christ."

10. H. Leo Boles, "Query Department," *Gospel Advocate* (March 10, 1927): 232; MacLean, *Behind the Mask of Chivalry*, 8; and Chalmers, *Hooded Americanism*, 87, 293.

11. *Annual Commentary on Improved Uniform Series of International Bible Lessons: 1944*, 256–70. R. L. Whitesides was the author according to Clevenger Jr., *Comprehensive Topical and Textual Lesson Commentary Index to Elam's Notes Annual Lesson Commentary Teacher's Annual Lesson Commentary*, 4. Some of the first works noting the significance of World War II to the black freedom struggle include Sitkoff, "Racial Militancy and Interracial Violence in the Second World War," and Wynn, *The Afro-American and the Second World War*. More recent assessments are available from Kruse and Tuck, eds., *Fog of War*.

12. Whitesides, *Annual Commentary on Improved Uniform Series of International Bible Lessons: 1944*, 269–70.

13. *Teacher's Annual Lesson Commentary on Uniform Bible Lessons for the Churches of Christ: 1949,* 139. Roy H. Lanier Sr. was the author according to Clevenger, *Comprehensive Topical and Textual Lesson Commentary Index to Elam's Notes Annual Lesson Commentary Teacher's Annual Lesson Commentary,* 4.

14. M. C. Smithers, "Let Us Open Our Eyes Brethren," *Christian Echo* 45 (June 20, 1949): 5.

15. *Teacher's Annual Lesson Commentary on Uniform Bible Lessons for the Churches of Christ: 1951,* 230–35. Roy H. Lanier Sr. was the author according to Clevenger, *Comprehensive Topical and Textual Lesson Commentary Index to Elam's Notes Annual Lesson Commentary Teacher's Annual Lesson Commentary,* 4.

16. Center Street Church of Christ bulletins, February 17, 1952; and December 6, 1959, Center Street Church of Christ Records, 1897–1986 (MC873), ser. 6, box 4, files 6 and 12, Special Collections, University of Arkansas Libraries, Fayetteville.

17. Center Street Church of Christ bulletin, [May 28, 1961], Center Street Church of Christ Records, 1897–1986 (MC873), ser. 6, box 4, file 14, Special Collections, University of Arkansas Libraries, Fayetteville.

18. *Newport* (RI) *Report,* January 10, 1954 James Bales Papers, Unprocessed, Special Collections, University of Arkansas Libraries, Fayetteville. The column from the *Dallas Morning News* was quoted by a church bulletin from a Church of Christ in Newport. After quoting the article, the bulletin concluded by noting, "As sincere Christians, we should be ever conscious of meeting the approval of God. The word of God plainly states, 'But if ye have respect to persons, ye commit sin.' (James 2:9)." This vignette is also recounted in Robinson, *The Fight Is On in Texas,* 47–48.

19. Ray Ferris to John Allen Chalk, January 10, 1958, John Allen Chalk Papers, Personal Correspondence, vol. 1, folder R, Special Collections, Harding University Graduate School of Religion, Memphis.

20. Rose, interview with author. I am indebted to James Beard of the Macomb, Illinois, Church of Christ for sharing the photographs from the 1950 gospel meeting in Abilene, TX.

21. Rose, interview with author; Mt. Sequoyah Encampment flyer, [July 11–19, 1953], Center Street Church of Christ Records, 1897–1986 (MC873), ser. 6, box 5, file 6, Special Collections, University of Arkansas Libraries, Fayetteville; and "Many Preachers and Guests Visit During Annual Series," *Babbler,* February 10, 1945. Also see Gray, *Bus Ride to Justice.*

22. Hughes, *Reviving the Ancient Faith,* 160, 183; Foy E. Wallace, "Negro Meetings for White People," *Bible Banner,* March 1941, 7; Robinson, *Show Us How You Do It,* 95–96; and Crawford, *Shattering the Illusion,* 74–75.

23. Foy E. Wallace, "Negro Meetings for White People," *Bible Banner,* March 1941, 7.

24. Ibid.; [A. B. Lipscomb], "'It's Not Keeble, but the Bible Is Right.,'" *Christian Leader* 45 (August 25, 1931): 6; and F. B. Shepherd, "The Goal for 1931," *Gospel Advocate,* January 1, 1931, 1.

25. [Foy Wallace], "From M. Keeble," *Bible Banner,* April 1941, 5; Haymes, "Race & the Church of Christ"; and Robinson, *Show Us How You Do It,* 95–96. Haymes referred to a passage from Proverbs 25:21–22, "If thine enemy be hungry, give him bread to eat; and if he be thirsty, give him water to drink: For thou shalt heap coals of fire upon his head, and the LORD shall reward thee" (KJV).

26. R. N. Hogan to James L. Lovell, April 18, 1941, James Lovell Papers, box 15, folder Historical (Church), Center for Restoration Studies, Abilene Christian University, Abilene, TX.

27. Ann Sewell to Clifton Ganus, March 24, 1969, Clifton Ganus Jr. Papers, Unprocessed, Office of Clifton Ganus Jr., Administration Building, Harding University, Searcy, AR.

28. Carl Spain to J. D. Bales, March 4, 1960, Unprocessed, Special Collections, University of Arkansas Libraries, Fayetteville.

29. Woodrow C. Whitten, "Race Relationships (I)," *California Christian* 9 (February 1953): 3; Woodrow C. Whitten, "Race Relationships (II)," *California Christian* 9 (April 1953): 1; and "Letters," *California Christian* 9 (February 1953): 3.

30. "Segregation—Or Christianity," *Christian Chronicle*, July 7, 1954.

31. James D. Willeford, "Call No Man Common" (sermon preached on January 29, 1956), Herald of Truth Papers, box 6, folder: Radio Scripts, 205–65, Radio Sermon No. 209, Special Collections, Brown Library, Abilene Christian University, Abilene, TX. The transcript of the sermon is misdated as 1955. This particular sermon, however, is found in a booklet containing a report of the program's activities for December 1955 and the program's sermons for January 1956. Information regarding the program's history is available at www.heraldoftruth.org/about (accessed August 7, 2014).

32. Ibid.

33. Ross W. Dye, "What Does the Church of Christ Teach on Segregation?" *Firm Foundation*, April 3, 1956, 213.

34. Crawford, *Shattering the Illusion*, 143–44.

35. James D. Bales, "The Christian and Race Relations" (unpublished manuscript), James Bales Papers, Unprocessed, Special Collections, University of Arkansas Libraries, Fayetteville; and James D. Bales, "To My Colored Brother," *20th Century Christian* 5 (August 1943): 15.

36. James D. Bales to Essin Essin, October 25, 1957, James Bales Papers, Unprocessed, Special Collections, University of Arkansas Libraries, Fayetteville; and "Assault African Student on Bus in Eastern Texas," *Plain Dealer* (Kansas City), August 30, 1957.

37. James D. Bales to David Lawrence, October 2, 1962; and James D. Bales, "The Christian and Race Relations," "Townsend Harris . . . ," and "Assembly," all unpublished manuscripts, James Bales Papers, Unprocessed, Special Collections, University of Arkansas Libraries, Fayetteville.

38. "Spain Backs Integration, Attacks College Practices," *The Optimist*, February 26, 1960; and "Segregation In Colleges Denounced: ACC Teacher Asks: 'Are We Moral Cowards?'" *Christian Chronicle*, March 8, 1960.

39. Carl Spain to J. D. Bales, March 4, 1960, James Bales Papers, Unprocessed, Special Collections, University of Arkansas Libraries, Fayetteville.

40. James D. Bales to Carl Spain, March 6, 1960, James Bales Papers, Unprocessed, Special Collections, University of Arkansas Libraries, Fayetteville.

41. "No Hate In His Path," *Christian Chronicle*, March 29, 1960.

42. "Readers Tell Own Opinions of Speech on Integration," *Christian Chronicle*, March 29, 1960.

43. Center Street Church of Christ bulletin, January 16, 1963, Center Street Church of Christ Records, 1897–1986 (MC873), ser. 6, box 4, file 16; and Pictorial Directory, 1966, Center Street Church of Christ Records, 1897–1986 (MC873), ser. 2, box 2, file 3, Special Collections, University of Arkansas Libraries, Fayetteville.

44. Rena N. Chaney to Bro. Bales, October 16, 1963; and James D. Bales to Rena N. Chaney, October 17, 1963, James Bales Papers, Unprocessed, Special Collections, University of Arkansas Libraries, Fayetteville.

45. James D. Bales to Editor of the *Arkansas* (Little Rock) *Democrat*, May 19, 1964; James D. Bales to Editor of the *Atlanta Constitution*, July 20, 1964; James D. Bales to Editor of the *Arkansas*

(Little Rock) *Gazette*, August 30, 1964; and James D. Bales to Editor of the *Arkansas* (Little Rock) *Gazette*, August 31, 1964, James Bales Papers, Unprocessed, Special Collections, University of Arkansas Libraries, Fayetteville.

46. James D. Bales, "Neither Race, Rank Nor Sex," *Gospel Advocate* 106 (August 27, 1964): 551–53.

47. Philbrick and Bales, *Communism and Race in America*, vii, 17, 67–68.

48. Mr. and Mrs. H. E. Jackson to Mr. Bales, January 7, 1965; James D. Bales to Editor of the *Arkansas* (Little Rock) *Democrat*, March 10, 1965; and James D. Bales to Editor of the *Nashville Banner*, March 18, 1965, James Bales Papers, Unprocessed, Special Collections, University of Arkansas Libraries, Fayetteville.

49. James D. Bales, "Massive Evangelism Needed in Negro Communities" (unpublished manuscript), James Bales Papers, Unprocessed, Special Collections, University of Arkansas Libraries, Fayetteville.

50. Edwin V. Hayden to J. D. Bales, October 15, 1965, James Bales Papers, Unprocessed, Special Collections, University of Arkansas Libraries, Fayetteville.

51. James D. Bales to Los Angeles County Grand Jury, May 2, 1966, James Bales Papers, Unprocessed, Special Collections, University of Arkansas Libraries, Fayetteville; William K. Floyd, "Why I Could Not Be a Career Preacher," in *Voices of Concern*, ed. Meyers, 169; and Bales, *The Martin Luther King Story*.

2. Made of One Blood

1. Hughes, *Reviving the Ancient Faith*, 271; Harrell, *Quest for a Christian America*; Hap C. S. Lyda, "African Americans in the Movement—Nineteenth Century," and Paul M. Blowers and Robert O. Fife, "Slavery, The Movement and," in *The Encyclopedia of the Stone-Campbell Movement*, ed. Foster et al., 11–13, 685–88. Portions of this chapter first appeared in Barclay Key, "Civil Rights Inactivism: Richard Nathaniel Hogan and the 'Enemies of Righteousness,'" in *Race and Ethnicity in Arkansas*, ed. Kirk, 111–22.

2. Stokes, *D. W. Griffith's The Birth of a Nation*; Cassius, *The Third Birth of a Nation*, 39, 94; Robinson, *To Save My Race from Abuse*; and Robinson, ed., *To Lift Up My Race*. The latter includes the complete text of *The Third Birth of a Nation*.

3. Cassius, *The Third Birth of a Nation*, 19–22; Harvey, *Freedom's Coming*, 45; and Haynes, *Noah's Curse*.

4. "Questions and Answers," *Christian Echo* 40 (August 20, 1945): 3; E. L. Turner, "The Christian Feast," *Christian Echo* 38 (January 5, 1943); and E. L. Barnes, "Miscegenation," *Christian Echo* 44 (December 5 and 20, 1948): 4–5.

5. Cassius, *The Third Birth of a Nation*, 17–25.

6. Ibid., 30–38.

7. Ibid., 49–50.

8. Ibid., 70–79, 86–88.

9. Ibid., 80–86, 95–96.

10. Ibid., 83, 86.

11. Ibid., 81, 83, 86, 88–94; and Barnes, *Journey of Hope*.

12. Robinson, "'The Two Old Heroes,'" 3–7; and Boyd, *Undying Dedication*, 26–27.

13. Boyd, *Undying Dedication*, 18–27; Goodpasture, *Biography and Sermons of Marshall Keeble, Evangelist*, 10; and Choate, *Roll Jordan Roll*, 6.

14. Robinson, "'The Two Old Heroes,'" 7–10, 12, 14.

15. Tuggle, *Another World Wonder*, 13.

16. Robinson, "'The Two Old Heroes,'" 7–8.

17. Ibid., 15–16; and Boyd, *Undying Dedication*, 28.

18. Choate, *Roll Jordan Roll*, 17, 21, 33–36; and Goodpasture, *Biography and Sermons of Marshall Keeble, Evangelist*, 10.

19. A. M. Burton to J. W. Akin, December 19, 1944, A. M. Burton Papers, Beaman Library, David Lipscomb University, Nashville; Shelly, interview with author; Ganus, interview with author; and Choate, *Roll Jordan Roll*, 48.

20. Marshall Keeble, interview by J. E. Choate, around 1967, Beaman Library, David Lipscomb University; Choate, *Roll Jordan Roll*, 53–54, 67–68, 78–79, 86; and Percy Ricks, "The Marshall Keeble I Knew" (unpublished manuscript), B. C. Goodpasture Papers, box 5, folder: Correspondence to and about Marshall Keeble, 1935, 1963, Disciples of Christ Historical Society, Nashville.

21. M. Keeble to B. C. Goodpasture, July 28, 1931, B. C. Goodpasture Papers, box 5, folder: Correspondence, Marshall Keeble, 1930–37, 67, Disciples of Christ Historical Society, Nashville; Letter from M. Keeble, *Christian Echo* 37 (August 5, 1942): 5; and Choate, *Roll Jordan Roll*, 77.

22. M. Keeble to B. C. Goodpasture, November 6, 1931, B. C. Goodpasture Papers, box 5, folder: Correspondence, Marshall Keeble, 1930–37, 67, Disciples of Christ Historical Society, Nashville; Letter from Russell H. Moore, *Christian Echo* 34 (November 5, 1939): 5; and Letter from F. F. Carson, *Christian Echo* 37 (May 20, 1942): 5.

23. Boyd, *Undying Dedication*, 15–29.

24. Tuggle, *Another World Wonder*, 46–47, 66; Boyd, *Undying Dedication*, 37–40, 57–67; and Evans, "The History of Southwestern Christian College, Terrell, Texas," 10–12.

25. Goodpasture, *Biography and Sermons of Marshall Keeble, Evangelist*, 37–39.

26. In Romans 6:4, the apostle Paul stated, "Therefore we are buried with him by baptism into death: that like as Christ was raised up from the dead by the glory of the Father, even so we also should walk in newness of life" (KJV).

27. Goodpasture, *Biography and Sermons of Marshall Keeble, Evangelist*, 46–48.

28. Holt, ed., *Life and Times of G. P. Bowser*, 47–48, 50, 54, 63–64; and Tuggle, *Another World Wonder*, 82.

29. Letter from Joanna Shackelford, *Christian Echo* 34 (July 20, 1939): 6; and Letter from L. M. Wright, *Christian Echo* 36 (April 20, 1941): 4.

30. Letter from A. L. Cassius, *Christian Echo* 34 (July 20, 1939): 6; Letter from Charles Henry Scott, *Christian Echo* 34 (August 5, 1939): 4–5; Letter from F. A. Livingston, *Christian Echo* 34 (September 20, 1939): 5; Letter from T. M. Sampson, *Christian Echo* 36 (August 20, 1941): 4; Letter from Robert E. Lee, *Christian Echo* 35 (November 20, 1940): 2; and Letter from Helen Baker, *Christian Echo* 37 (November 5, 1942).

31. "A Working Group in Oklahoma City," *Christian Echo* 35 (August 5, 1940): 7; and Letter from Sister Reuben H. Harrison, *Christian Echo* 35 (August 20, 1940): 5.

32. Minutes, [about July 1943], Center Street Church of Christ Records, 1897–1986 (MC873), ser. 1, box 1, file 1, Special Collections, University of Arkansas Libraries, Fayetteville.

33. Letter from R. E. Holt, *Christian Echo* 35 (May 5, 1940): 6; Letter from Berthina Martin, *Christian Echo* 38 (July 20, 1943); Letter from G. G. Jones, *Christian Echo* 38 (April 5, 1943): 4; and Letter from PFC Anderson Rall, *Christian Echo* 39 (May 20, 1944): 6.

34. Letter from Harriet Tucker, *Christian Echo* 37 (October 20, 1942): 5; Special insert by G. P. Bowser, *Christian Echo* 38 (August 20, 1943): 6; and Gussie Lambert, "Baptist Doctrine in the Light of Truth," *Christian Echo* 38 (November 20, 1943): 1.

35. Robert Lee Crawford, "The Harlem Tragedy," *Christian Echo* 35 (October 5, 1940): 2. The "tragedy" in the title involved the untimely death of Paul English.

36. Letter from G. P. Bowser, *Christian Echo* 42 (September 20, 1947): 8; Letter from Frances Douglas, *Christian Echo* 43 (July 5, 1948): 8; and Tuggle, *Another World Wonder*, 16.

37. Nancy Gray Arms, "In Memoriam," *Christian Echo* 52 (December 1957): 4.

38. Letter from Mrs. Vernon Collins, *Christian Echo* 42 (September 5, 1947): 6–7; M. C. Smithers, "Let Us Open Our Eyes Brethren," *Christian Echo* 45 (June 20, 1949): 5; [advertisement], *Christian Echo* 50 (January 1956): 7–8; [advertisement], *Christian Echo* 50 (April 1954): 7; Carroll Pitts, "You Need 'Power for Today,'" *Christian Echo* 53 (January 1958): 5; and G. P. Holt, "Put a Library in the Church," *Christian Echo* 54 (October 1959): 3.

39. "Sects of Perdition," *Christian Echo* 45 (October 20, 1949): 5; G. P. Holt, "I Disagree," *Christian Echo* 50 (April 1954): 1; R. N. Hogan, [editorial], *Christian Echo* 51 (April 1956): 2.

40. "Richmond, California Congregation Sends Missionary to Hong Kong!" *Christian Echo* 56 (June 1961): 1.

41. A picture in a 1945 issue of the *Babbler*, David Lipscomb College's student newspaper, shows a group photograph of black and white men who attended a lectureship there. See *Babbler*, February 10, 1945. Among numerous examples of Keeble's participation in lectureships, see "Keeble, Pullias Close Lectures Here Tomorrow," *Babbler*, February 2, 1939; "Lectureship Meeting, Oklahoma City, Okla.," *Christian Echo* 40 (May 20, 1945): 1; and Calvin Bowers, "The Seventh Annual Youth Lectureship," *Christian Echo* 53 (September 1958): 5. Historian Grant Wacker noted a similar trend of "unselfconscious mixing" followed by a tendency toward racial segregation among Pentecostal churches in *Heaven Below*, 226–35.

42. G. P. Holt, "If They Would Testify," *Christian Echo* 50 (October 1954): 4–5; A. L. Cassius, "'Colored Churches,'" *Christian Echo* 50 (July 1955): 4; and G. P. Holt, "The Greatest Meeting of All," *Christian Echo* 50 (July 1955): 5.

43. R. N. Hogan, "The Sin of Being a Respecter of Persons," *Christian Echo* 54 (June 1959): 2, 5; "Enemies of Righteousness," *Christian Echo* 54 (August 1959): 2; and Crawford, *Shattering the Illusion*, 97.

44. R. N. Hogan, "Brother C. A. Cannon of Saratoga, Ark., Replies to My Article on 'Segregation in the Lord's Church?'" *Christian Echo* 55 (January 1960): 2–4. Cannon's initial response to Hogan apparently appeared in the December 1959 issue of the *Christian Echo*, but I know of no extant copies.

45. Hughes, *Reviving the Ancient Faith*, 284; Houck and Dixon, eds., *Rhetoric, Religion, and the Civil Rights Movement, 1954–1965*, 385–97; "Race Prejudice," *Christian Echo* 55 (April 1960): 2; R. N. Hogan, "Racial Strife Continues," *Christian Echo* 56 (August 1961): 2, 4; R. N. Hogan, "Tradition Versus God's Commandments," *Christian Echo* 58 (July 1963): 1, 5; and Crawford, *Shattering the Illusion*, 134–36.

3. Let No Man Despise Thy Youth

1. Exact enrollment figures are imprecise. Abilene surpassed 2,000 students in 1955. Harding had approximately 1,500 students in 1965. See "ACU's History," www.acu.edu/aboutacu/history .html (accessed June 17, 2010); and "History," www.harding.edu/about/history.html (accessed June 17, 2010). Portions of this chapter first appeared in Key, "On the Periphery of the Civil Rights Movement."

2. Newman, *Getting Right with God,* 162–66.

3. For a comparable approach to a public university, see Cohen, "'Two, Four, Six, Eight, We Don't Want to Integrate'"; and Sokol, *There Goes My Everything,* 149–63.

4. Evans, "The History of Southwestern Christian College, Terrell, Texas," 12–20, 34, 51; and Boyd, *Undying Dedication,* 37–40, 57–67.

5. Adamson, interview with author; Ernest Holsendolph to President Don H. Morris, August 2, 1957, John C. Stevens Papers, box 222, Special Collections, Brown Library, Abilene Christian University, Abilene, TX; and Holsendolph, interview with author.

6. Rose, interview with author; and Don H. Morris to G. W. Cox, January 8, 1960, John C. Stevens Papers, box 219, Cox Proposal folder, Special Collections, Brown Library, Abilene Christian University, Abilene, TX.

7. "Colored Church Plans Building To House Aged Couple," *Bison,* October 23, 1945; and "Blind Couple Given Home," *Bison,* March 5, 1946.

8. MacLean, *Behind the Mask of Chivalry.*

9. "Race Prejudice," *The Optimist,* February 14, 1924.

10. "Colored Should Have Rights But . . . ," *The Optimist,* November 16, 1945; and "Letter to the Editor," *The Optimist,* December 14, 1945.

11. "Letter to the Editor," *The Optimist,* December 13, 1946.

12. Ibid., January 3, 1947.

13. Ed Broadus, "Informal Informer," *The Optimist,* November 30, 1951.

14. "Is It a Great Day for the Race?" *The Bison,* February 1, 1949; Nathan Lamb, "Silhouette on a Thumbnail," *The Bison,* December 5, 1946; and Kirk, *Redefining the Color Line,* 32, 60–61. Three Supreme Court cases related directly to higher education: *Sipuel v. Board of Regents of Oklahoma* (1948), *McLaurin v. Oklahoma State Regents* (1950), and *Sweatt v. Painter* (1950).

15. "What Would You Have Done?" *The Bison,* November 11, 1950; and Eagles, *The Price of Defiance,* 60–68.

16. Everett Ferguson, "Race Relations" (speech delivered at ACC chapel in 1953), Center for Restoration Studies, Abilene Christian University, Abilene, TX; and "How Do We See Segregation?," *Bison,* October 24, 1953. The Ferguson speech is also available at www.bible.acu.edu/crs /ItemDetail.asp?Bookmark=1588 (accessed August 13, 2010).

17. "Negro Discrimination Argued Against," *The Optimist,* March 19, 1954; "Harding Overcoming Racial Issues," *Bison,* February 27, 1954; and "Learn to Worship With Negroes First," *The Optimist,* April 16, 1954.

18. "Well, Are They?" *Skyrocket,* November 15, 1923; "Jokes," *Skyrocket,* November 15, 1923; "If he did?" *Skyrocket,* April 1935; "Lectures Draw Record Crowds" and "Minstrel Planned," *Skyrocket,* February 11, 1963; and Shelly, interview with author.

19. For examples of theme banquets, see "Down South In Dixie Scene of Annual Fete," *Sky-*

rocket, May 1946; "'Old South' Is Theme of Party by Sewall Hall," *Babbler*, October 19, 1951; "'Southern' Evening Spent By Ju Go Ju's," *Bison*, February 13, 1954; and "Old South Theme for Mohican Club Social," *Bison*, April 16, 1964. For examples of how "nigger" was used, see "'Uncle Bill' Spends 31st Year as 'Handy-Man' on D.L.C. Campus," *Babbler*, February 21, 1935; "One Man's Opinion," *Bison*, December 2, 1950; and Everett Ferguson, "Race Relations" (speech delivered at ACC chapel in 1953), Center for Restoration Studies, Abilene Christian University, Abilene, TX. The yearbook is mentioned in Hughes, *Reviving the Ancient Faith*, 288.

20. "TIPA Votes to Admit Negro College Press" and "TIPA Takes Step Forward," *The Optimist*, April 28, 1955.

21. "News, Views and Previews," *Bison*, October 12, 1955.

22. "Segregation: A Personal Problem," *Bison*, October 26, 1955.

23. "Staff Deserves Thanks, Credit; Segregation Needs Discussion," *The Optimist*, April 20, 1956.

24. Kirk, *Redefining the Color Line*, 106–38; Jacoway, *Turn Away Thy Son*; Eugene Bailey to the Editor, *Bison*, February 29, 1956; and "Then, How Will You React?" *The Bison*, April 24, 1957. The biblical quotation is from 1 Timothy 4:12.

25. William K. Floyd, "Why I Could Not Be a Career Preacher," in *Voices of Concern*, ed. Myers, 166; "Segregation: A Personal Problem," *The Bison*, October 26, 1955; Hicks, *"Sometimes in the Wrong but Never in Doubt"*; Barclay Key, "'Out-Democratin' the Democrats': Religious Colleges and the Rise of the Republican Party in the South—A Case Study," in *Painting Dixie Red*, ed. Feldman, 38–54; Moreton, *To Serve God and Wal-Mart*, 164–68; and Ganus, interview with author.

26. "Results Of Recent Poll On Racial Integration Show Student Attitudes," *The Bison*, November 14, 1957; and Floyd, "Why I Could Not Be a Career Preacher," in *Voices of Concern*, ed. Myers, 166–67.

27. Floyd, "Why I Could Not Be a Career Preacher," in *Voices of Concern*, ed. Myers, 166–68.

28. "Results Of Recent Poll On Racial Integration Show Student Attitudes," *The Bison*, November 14, 1957. See also Bill J. Leonard, "A Theology of Racism: Southern Fundamentalists and the Civil Rights Movement," in *Southern Landscapes*, ed. Tony Badger, Walter Edgar, and Jan Nordby Gretlund, 165–81; Haynes, *Noah's Curse*; Chappell, *A Stone of Hope*; Harvey, *Freedom's Coming*; Noll, *The Civil War as a Theological Crisis*; and Kidd, *The Forging of Races*.

29. Floyd, "Why I Could Not Be a Career Preacher," in *Voices of Concern*, ed. Myers, 166–68; Haymes, interview with author; Ganus, interview with author; and Haynes, *Noah's Curse*.

30. Floyd, "Why I Could Not Be a Career Preacher," in *Voices of Concern*, ed. Myers, 168; Ganus, interview with author; Robert Silvey, e-mail message to author, July 29, 2008; and Haymes, "Race & the Church of Christ."

31. Owen D. Olbricht to Bro. Bales, November 13, 1957; and Owen D. Olbricht to Bro. Bales, October 6, 1958, James Bales Papers, Unprocessed, Special Collections, University of Arkansas Libraries, Fayetteville.

32. Owen D. Olbricht to Bro. Bales, November 13, 1957; and Owen D. Olbricht to Bro. Bales, October 6, 1958. James Bales Papers, Unprocessed, Special Collections, University of Arkansas Libraries, Fayetteville; and Ganus, interview with author.

33. Chappell, *A Stone of Hope*, 112–17.

34. Ibid., 6; Collins, *When the Church Bell Rang Racist*, 19, 58; Murray, *Methodists and the Crucible of Race, 1930–1975*, 74; and Newman, *Getting Right with God*, 164.

35. "Mark Twain Proved Treat to Audience; Petty Also Approves," *The Bison*, March 20, 1958; "Assignment Harding," *The Bison*, April 10, 1958; "Reign, Reign, Go Away" and "From Under The Editor's Door," *The Bison*, May 1, 1958; and "Chapel Program," *The Bison*, April 17, 1958.

36. Leon C. Burns, "Opportunities Presented to the Church by Religious Conditions in the World," in *Harding College Bible Lectures, 1959*, 21–25; Burns, "Some Dangers Which Faced the First Century Church," in *Harding College Bible Lectures, 1961*; "Chapel Schedule," *The Bison*, November 19, 1959; Leon C. Burns, "Why Desegregation Will Fail" (sermon preached on March 24, 1957, at West Seventh Church of Christ in Columbia, TN), copy in possession of author; Chappell, *A Stone of Hope*, 109; and Jack D. Harris to the Editor, *The Bison*, May 15, 1958.

37. "Integration Attitudes," *The Optimist*, April 11, 1958; "The Pattern Maker," *The Optimist*, April 18, 1958; "Who's Funny Now?," *The Optimist*, April 25, 1958; "Segregation Is Painful," *The Optimist*, May 2, 1958; and "'If I Be Lifted Up,'" *The Optimist*, May 9, 1958.

38. "Over 65% of Student Body Favor Admitting Negroes," *Babbler*, February 1, 1951; "Innovation," *The Bison*, November 13, 1958; and "*Dear Readers*," *The Bison*, November 20, 1958. For comments written after the apology, see Gary Ackers and Bob Silvey, "Innovation," *The Bison*, December 4, 1958, March 13, April 9, and April 16, 1959; and David Finley, "Finley's Findings," *The Bison*, April 14, 1960. Student journalists experienced similar pressures at public universities. For examples, see Clark, *The Schoolhouse Door*, 160–62; and Eagles, *The Price of Defiance*, 60–68.

39. Grace Davis, "Opinion Poll Reflects Student Attitudes," *The Bison*, November 19, 1959; David Finley, "Finley's Findings," *The Bison*, March 10, 1960; "ACC Announces New Racial Policy," *The Bison*, May 17, 1962; Pat Caraway, "Tyrant to America Inside Borders Wearing the Disguise of Ignorance," *The Bison*, October 4, 1962; [Jimmy Arnold], "Now Is the Time To Stand," *The Bison*, September 26, 1963; and Eagles, *The Price of Defiance*.

40. Leon Locke, "The Congregational Attitude Toward Race Relationships"; J. W. Treat, "What Does the Bible Teach About Race Relationships?"; and J. Roy Willingham Jr., "What Should the Christian's Attitude Be Toward Race Relations," all sermons preached in February 1955 at Abilene Christian College Bible Lectures in Abilene, TX, Center for Restoration Studies, Abilene Christian University, Abilene.

41. Carl Spain, "Modern Challenges to Christian Morals," in *Christian Faith in the Modern World*.

42. Robert D. Hunter to President Morris, April 21, 1960; Mrs. Paul McClung to Otis Garner, March 30, 1961; and Bethel Smith to Charlie Marler, October 3, 1960, John C. Stevens Papers, box 222, folder Integration, Special Collections, Brown Library, Abilene Christian University, Abilene, TX. The donor's name was Robert E. Kelly.

43. LeMoine Lewis, "Notes on the Race Problem" (undated speech given at Abilene Christian College), MS34, box 17, file drawer VIII, Special Collections, Brown Library, Abilene Christian University, Abilene, TX; and LeMoine G. Lewis to Garvin Beauchamp, January 20, 1961, LeMoine Lewis Papers, Unprocessed, Special Collections, Brown Library, Abilene Christian University, Abilene, TX; and "Recommendation to the Board of Trustees," May 29, 1961, John C. Stevens Papers, box 5, Special Collections, Brown Library, Abilene Christian University, Abilene, TX.

44. All qualified applicants were finally accepted to the freshman and sophomore classes in the fall of 1964. Administrators indicated that this additional delay was due to a desire to protect SWCC, which was struggling to draw students. See Hughes, *Reviving the Ancient Faith*, 290–91, and "Recommendation to the Board of Trustees," May 23, 1964, John C. Stevens Papers, box 6, Special Collections, Brown Library, Abilene Christian University, Abilene, TX.

45. "Negro Enters Grad School," *The Optimist*, February 9, 1962; "Jr. and Sr. Classes to Be Integrated," *The Optimist*, May 11, 1962; "Students Probed on Integration," *The Optimist*, May 18, 1962; "Black Is Right," *The Optimist*, November 25, 1961; "What's the Matter With Mississippi?" *The Optimist*, October 5, 1962; and Eagles, *The Price of Defiance*.

46. [Arnold], "Now Is the Time"; Clifton L. Ganus Jr., "The Harding Legacy," in *Against the Grain*, ed. Burks, 58; Shelly, interview with author; Crawford, *Shattering the Illusion*, 97–100. By comparison, the first undergraduates enrolled at the University of Arkansas in 1954. Seventh-day Adventists were similarly pragmatic when they formally desegregated in 1965. See London, *Seventh-day Adventists and the Civil Rights Movement*, 84–85.

47. Ganus, interview with author; Haymes, "Race & the Church of Christ"; and George S. Benson, "Christ & Current World Problems" (sermon preached on October 13, 1966), Benson files, Sermons: 1960–69, Special Collections, Brackett Library, Harding University, Searcy, AR.

48. Floyd, "Why I Could Not Be a Career Preacher," in *Voices of Concern*, ed. Myers, 165.

49. Ganus, interview with author; John L. McClellan to the President, September 30, 1957; John L. McClellan to E. H. Brown, October 1, 1958; and Glenn A. Green to Honorable John L. McClellan, March 21, 1959, John McClellan Papers, box 25-A, Speech –Pepperdine College folder, Special Collections, Riley-Hickingbotham Library, Ouachita Baptist University, Arkadelphia, AR.

50. Geo. S. Benson to Senator John L. McClellan, July 3, 1959; and M. Norvel Young to Senator John L. McClellan, June 30, 1959, John McClellan Papers, box 25-A, Speech—Pepperdine College folder, Special Collections, Riley-Hickingbotham Library, Ouachita Baptist University, Arkadelphia, AR; and Honorary Doctorates Granted folder, Special Collections, Brackett Library, Harding University, Searcy, AR.

51. Athens Clay Pullias to Joe L. Evins, July 1, 1955, box 860, folder 2; Athens Clay Pullias to Joe L. Evins, January 2, 1962, and Don H. Morris to Joe L. Evins, April 13, 1962, box 716, folder 1; Athens Clay Pullias to Joe L. Evins, n.d., and Eunice B. Bradley to Secretary Joe L. Evins, June 23, 1967, box 857, folder 6; Joe L. Evins to Athens Clay Pullias, May 2, 1952, box 701, folder 5; and Athens Clay Pullias to Honorable Joe L. Evins, July 22, 1963, box 369, folder 2, Joe L. Evins Papers, Special Collections, Tennessee Tech University, Cookeville; Rose, interview with author; and Evans, interview with author.

52. "Letter to the Editor," *The Optimist*, December 13, 1946; Floyd, "Why I Could Not Be a Career Preacher," in *Voices of Concern*, ed. Myers, 165; Carl Spain, "Modern Challenges to Christian Morals," 217; "Harding College: When Is It Time?" James Bales Papers, Unprocessed, Special Collections, University of Arkansas Libraries, Fayetteville; and Shelly, interview with author.

53. Abilene Christian University, "ACU's History," www.acu.edu/aboutacu/history.html (accessed April 13, 2007); "The following information concerns Negro students . . . for the Fall, 1965," John C. Stevens Papers, box 6, Special Collections, Brown Library, Abilene Christian University, Abilene, TX.

54. Ganus, interview with author; and "We can do it," *The Bison*, February 6, 1964.

55. [Phil Sturm], "Racial Demonstrations Causing Shift In Pro-Integration Opinion," *The Bison*, October 31, 1963.

56. Don Johnson, "Voter Literacy Test Used in Alabama Often Varies According to Applicant," *The Bison*, February 18, 1965; Butch Foster to the Editor and Jim Worsham to the Editor, *The Bison*, March 4, 1965; and [Ken Starr], "Role of Dissenter Often Vital In U.S. Historical Development," *The Bison*, November 3, 1965. The biblical quotation is from Matthew 7:1 (KJV).

57. Butch Foster to the Editor, *The Bison*, March 4, 1965; and Jim Wilson, "Racial Prejudice Infects Church," *The Bison*, March 2, 1966.

58. [Don Johnson], "Comments of Students in Chapel Should Shame White Society," *The Bison*, March 8, 1967.

59. [Lynn McCauley], "Last Friday's Chapel Program Proved Harding Not Afraid of Hurting Image"; [Doug McBride], "Student Speakers Provide Interest"; and "Anthony, Wright Talk About Issues," *The Bison*, March 15, 1968.

60. Eugene Johnson, "Negro Student Urges Colorblindness"; Jerry Muir, "The Fourmongers"; and Doug McBride, "Laughter at Assassination of King Exemplifies Indifferent Attitude—An Attitude Harmful to America," *The Bison*, April 12, 1968.

61. Lynn McCauley, "A Christian Reaction," and Jean Flippin, "This Matter of Equality," *The Bison*, April 12, 1968; and Tyson, "Not Forgotten," 101. Also see "Commemoration: The King Holiday and Street Naming," in Kirk, ed., *Martin Luther King Jr. and the Civil Rights Movement*, 217–44, and Chappell, *Waking from the Dream*.

62. "The Constitution of the Ethnic Studies Forum of Abilene Christian College," Garvin V. Beauchamp to John C. Stevens, January 30, 1970, and Letter from John C. Stevens, January 21, 1970, John C. Stevens Papers, box 222; "A Study of Patterns of Institutional Response to Blacks in Higher Education," John C. Stevens Papers, box 215; and John C. Stevens to Robert D. Hunter, September 29, 1970, John C. Stevens Papers, box 221, Special Collections, Brown Library, Abilene Christian University, Abilene, TX.

63. Mrs. Billy Carlile to Mr. Stevens, September 11, 1972; John C. Stevens to Mrs. Billy Carlile, September 13, 1972; and John C. Stevens to Mrs. Billy Carlile, September 21, 1972, box 21, Special Collections, Brown Library, Abilene Christian University, Abilene, TX.

64. John C. Stevens to Charley Mayr, April 16, 1974, John C. Stevens Papers, box 28; Vernon Boyd to John Stevens, April 9, 1973, and John C. Stevens to Dr. Chris Chetsanga, April 20, 1973, John C. Stevens Papers, box 24, Special Collections, Brown Library, Abilene Christian University, Abilene, TX; and Royce Money to the ACU Family, November 16, 1999, Vertical File Leaders, Money, Royce, Center for Restoration Studies, Abilene Christian University, Abilene, TX.

65. Ganus, interview with author; Hicks, *"Sometimes in the Wrong but Never in Doubt"*; Moreton, *To Serve God and Wal-Mart*; Barclay Key, "'Out-Democratin' the Democrats,'" in *Painting Dixie Red*, ed. Feldman, 38–54.

4. Hear the Word of the Lord

1. Tyson, *Blood Done Sign My Name*, 247–48, 251.

2. Klarman, "How *Brown* Changed Race Relations."

3. Cameron, *The Origin and Development of the Negro Race*, 6–7; Haynes, *Noah's Curse*; Noll, *The Civil War as a Theological Crisis*; and Genesis 9:25b (KJV).

4. Cameron, *The Origin and Development of the Negro Race*; and Deuteronomy 7:2b-4 (KJV).

5. Cameron, *The Origin and Development of the Negro Race*.

6. Ibid.

7. Burns, "Why Desegregation Will Fail" (sermon preached on March 24, 1957, at West Seventh Street Church of Christ in Columbia, TN); Carroll Van West, "Clinton Desegregation Crisis,"

in *The Tennessee Encyclopedia of History and Culture*, tennesseeencyclopedia.net/entry.php?rec=279 (accessed July 19, 2013); Chappell, *A Stone of Hope*, 109, 251, 264; and Hughes, *Reviving the Ancient Faith*, 62.

8. Burns, "Why Desegregation Will Fail" (sermon preached on March 24, 1957, at West Seventh Street Church of Christ in Columbia, TN).

9. Ibid. Biblical quotations from the New King James Version.

10. Burns, "Why Desegregation Will Fail" (sermon preached on March 24, 1957, at West Seventh Street Church of Christ in Columbia, TN); and Ikard, *No More Social Lynchings*.

11. For example, see Leon C. Burns, "Opportunities Presented to the Church by Religious Conditions in the World," in *Harding College Bible Lectures, 1959*, 21–25.

12. Guthrie Dean, "The Christian Attitude Toward Integration" (sermon preached on September 22, 1957, over radio station KWCB in Searcy, AR), James Bales Papers, Unprocessed, Special Collections, University of Arkansas Libraries, Fayetteville.

13. Cameron, *The Origin and Development of the Negro Race*; and Dean, "The Christian Attitude Toward Integration," sermon, 1957, James Bales Papers, Unprocessed, Special Collections, University of Arkansas Libraries, Fayetteville.

14. Dean, "The Christian Attitude Toward Integration," sermon, 1957, James Bales Papers, Unprocessed, Special Collections, University of Arkansas Libraries, Fayetteville; and Charles Marsh, "The Civil Rights Movement as Theological Drama," in *The Role of Ideas in the Civil Rights South*, ed. Ownby, 19–38.

15. Marshall Keeble, interview with Julian Ernest Choate, undated cassette recording; and Houston Ezell, interview with Julian Ernest Choate, undated cassette recording, Special Collections, Beaman Library, David Lipscomb University, Nashville.

16. Keeble, interview with Julian Ernest Choate, undated cassette recording, Special Collections, Beaman Library, David Lipscomb University, Nashville.

17. Gray, *Bus Ride to Justice*, 144, 224–25.

18. O. B. Porterfield, [untitled] (sermon preached on March 24, 1965, at television station WKAB in Montgomery), Alabama Department of Archives and History, Montgomery; letter from Fred Gray to Barclay Key, February 9, 2006; and Renata Adler, "Letter from Selma," *The New Yorker*, April 10, 1965.

19. Porterfield, untitled sermon, March 24, 1965, Alabama Department of Archives and History, Montgomery.

20. Ibid.

21. Ibid.; and Newman, *Divine Agitators*.

22. Porterfield, untitled sermon, March 24, 1965, Alabama Department of Archives and History, Montgomery. Matthew 23:5 states, "But all their works they do for to be seen of men: they make broad their phylacteries, and enlarge the borders of their garments," while 1 Peter 4:16 says, "Yet if any man suffer as a Christian, let him not be ashamed; but let him glorify God on this behalf" (KJV).

23. Bales, *The Martin Luther King Story*; Douglas, "Power, Its Locus and Function in Defining Social Commentary in the Church of Christ," 273; and George S. Benson, "Christ & Current World Problems, sermon, October 13, 1966, Benson files, Sermons: 1960–69, Special Collections, Brackett Library, Harding University, Searcy, AR. Numerous pieces of correspondence between Goodpasture and Keeble are archived in the B. C. Goodpasture Papers, Disciples of Christ Historical Society, Nashville.

24. In this regard black Churches of Christ were comparable to black Pentecostals. See Stephens, *The Fire Spreads*, 241.

25. Rose, interview with author; Gray, interview with author; and Gray, *Bus Ride to Justice*, 256–57.

26. Gray, *Bus Ride to Justice*, 8–20.

27. Ibid., 22–24, 32–33, 39–40, 47–49; and Thornton, *Dividing Lines*, 53–55, 600–601n83.

28. Gray, *Bus Ride to Justice*, 36–37, 50–51, 68–73, 94–95; and Thornton, *Dividing Lines*, 53–96, 597–598n71. Thornton notes that Gray's autobiography is incorrect in asserting that Parks was charged with disorderly conduct. Gray's role in these events is also recounted in King, *Stride Toward Freedom*.

29. Gray, *Bus Ride to Justice*, 257; Joy L. McMillon, "Alabama: bar president named," *Christian Chronicle* 42, no. 8 (August 1985): 1. Final quotation is from interview with Gray conducted and transcribed by Jeffrey Bendix for *Case Magazine*, www.case.edu/pubs/cwrumag/fa112004/features/gray_full.html (accessed April 14, 2007).

30. Gray, *Bus Ride to Justice*, 238–53, 256, 310; and Gray, interview with author.

31. Rose, interview with author.

32. Ibid.; "Billie Sol Estes, Texas Con Man Whose Fall Shook Up Washington, Dies at 88," *New York Times*, May 14, 2013, www.nytimes.com/2013/05/15/us/billie-sol-estes-texas-con-man-dies-at-88.html (accessed July 16, 2013); and "Billie Sol Estes was a generous man, Abilene Nephew and Daughter Say," *Abilene Reporter-News*, May 14, 2013, www.reporternews.com/news/2013/may/14/billie-sol-estes-was-a-generous-man-abilene-and/ (accessed July 29, 2013).

33. Rose, interview with author.

34. Rose, *Beyond the Thicket*, 38–40.

35. Rose, interview with author; and Rose, *Beyond the Thicket*, 4–12, 27, 84–87.

36. Franklin D. R. Florence to Dr. John D. Young, January 17, 1961, Franklin Florence Papers, box 1, folder 10, Special Collections, Rush Rhees Library, University of Rochester.

37. Gus Nichols to Franklin D. R. Florence Sr., December 13, 1958, Franklin Florence Papers, box 2, folder 24; 1963 Reynolds Street Church of Christ Program, Franklin Florence Papers, box 1, folder 1; and Ira North to Franklin D. R. Florence Sr., January 26, 1960, Franklin Florence Papers, box 2, folder 19; and sermons by Batsell Barrett Baxter, B. C. Goodpasture, Ira North, and J. P. Sanders, box 1, folders 31 and 32, Special Collections, Rush Rhees Library, University of Rochester.

38. Franklin D. R. Florence to Dr. John D. Young, January 17, 1961; W. V. Maddox to Franklin D. Florence, January 20, 1961; F. D. R. Florence to W. V. Maddox, March 8, 1961; F. D. R. Florence to James W. Nichols, March 13, 1961; and Pat Boone to Franklin Florence, May 17, 1961, Franklin Florence Papers, box 1, folder 20, Special Collections, Rush Rhees Library, University of Rochester; and Hughes, *Reviving the Ancient Faith*, 305.

39. 1960 Reynolds Street Church of Christ program and "Activities during 1962," Franklin Florence Papers, box 1, folder 1; and Franklin Florence, "This Critical Hour" (sermon preached on May 28, 1961, at the baccalaureate service for NCI in Nashville), Franklin Florence Papers, box 1, folder 30, Special Collections, Rush Rhees Library, University of Rochester.

40. Wadhwani, "Kodak, FIGHT, and the Definition of Civil Rights in Rochester, New York," 59–75; and Hughes, *Reviving the Ancient Faith*, 304–5.

41. Wadhwani, "Kodak, FIGHT, and the Definition of Civil Rights in Rochester, New York," 74–75.

42. Ibid., 65, 70. Information regarding the split within Florence's church appears in the collection description for the Franklin Florence Papers, www.lib.rochester.edu/index.cfm?page=882 (accessed July 16, 2013).

43. Boyd, *Undying Dedication*, 64–67.

44. Gray, interview with author; and Rose, interview with author.

5. Judgment Days

1. Eric Foner, *Give Me Liberty! An American History*, 3rd ed. (New York: W. W. Norton Co., 2011), 1073; and Google Books Ngram Viewer, "national conversation on race," books.google .com/ngrams/graph?content=national+conversation+on+race&year_start=1800&year_end =2000&corpus=15&smoothing=3 (accessed July 1, 2013).

2. *More Than Conquerors*, 9, 33, 89; "Report on Race Relations Workshop," addendum to *Christian Chronicle*, May 10, 1968, 3; and David Jones Jr., interview with author.

3. "Report on Race Relations Workshop," addendum to *Christian Chronicle*, May 10, 1968, 3.

4. Ibid., 2–4; and Jones, interview with author.

5. "Report on Race Relations Workshop," addendum to *Christian Chronicle*, May 10, 1968, 4.

6. Ibid., 6–8.

7. Ibid., 8–10; Joseph, *Waiting 'Til the Midnight Hour*, 140–43; and Goudsouzian, *Down to the Crossroads*, 143–44.

8. "Report on Race Relations Workshop," addendum to *Christian Chronicle*, May 10, 1968, 17, 20–24; and Maraniss, *Strong Inside*.

9. "Report on Race Relations Workshop," addendum to *Christian Chronicle*, May 10, 1968, 10; and Jones, interview with author.

10. For reactions to King's death in other denominations, see Alvis, *Religion & Race*, 125–26; Collins, *When the Church Bell Rang Racist*, ix–x; Newman, *Getting Right With God*, 32, 83–84, 110, 126, 146, 186; Murray, *Methodists and the Crucible of Race, 1930–1975*, 202–3; and London, *Seventh-day Adventists and the Civil Rights Movement*, 148. Also see Crawford, *Shattering the Illusion*, 72.

11. Tucker, interview with author.

12. Robinson, *Show Us How You Do It*, 137; Rose, *Beyond the Thicket*, 37–38, 56; and Rose, interview with author. Historian Randall Stephens found similar sentiments among some black Pentecostals. See Stephens, *The Fire Spreads*, 266–67.

13. Lyndon Johnson, "Address to the Nation Upon Proclaiming a Day of Mourning" (speech delivered April 5, 1968), www.pbs.org/wgbh/americanexperience/features/primary-resources/lbj -mourning/ (accessed July 3, 2013); and Robert Meyers, "Can We Understand? (A sermon delivered on Sunday after a murder)," [April 7, 1968], John Allen Chalk Papers, box Race Relations, folder 92RR-Ch, Special Collections, Harding University Graduate School of Religion, Memphis.

14. Cled Wimbish, "On the Death of Martin Luther King, Jr.," [April 7, 1968]; John Allen Chalk, "The Continuing Message of Martin Luther King, Jr.," [around April 1968], John Allen Chalk Papers, box Race Relations, folder 92RR-COC-CJ-MLK, Special Collections, Harding University Graduate School of Religion, Memphis; and Shelly, interview with author. Biblical quotation from Hebrews 11:4 (KJV).

15. Dwain Evans, "Dr. Martin Luther King, Jr.," *Milestones* 6, no. 15 (April 11, 1968): 4, John

Allen Chalk Papers, box Race Relations, folder 92Ra-Ch, Special Collections, Harding University Graduate School of Religion, Memphis.

16. "Brother Keeble Passes," *Gospel Advocate* 110, no. 18 (May 2, 1968): 274.

17. "He Preached the Word!" bulletin of South Williamsport (PA) Church of Christ 5, no. 19 (May 10, 1968), John Allen Chalk Papers, box Race Relations, folder 92RR-COC-MK, Special Collections, Harding University Graduate School of Religion, Memphis.

18. Reuel Lemmons, "Marshall Keeble," *Firm Foundation*, May 14, 1968, 306; Reuel Lemmons to John Allen Chalk, May 16, 1968, John Allen Chalk Papers, box 1968 D–Z Correspondence, folder L; Jennings Davis Jr. to Reuel Lemmons, May 20, 1968; and Reuel Lemmons to Jennings Davis Jr., May 23, 1968, John Allen Chalk Papers, box Race Relations, folder 92RR-COC-MK, Special Collections, Harding University Graduate School of Religion, Memphis.

19. Norman R. Adamson to Reuel Lemmons, May 29, 1968; and Roosevelt Wells to Reuel Lemmons, June 7, 1968, John Allen Chalk Papers, box Race Relations, folder 92RR-COC-MK, Special Collections, Harding University Graduate School of Religion, Memphis.

20. Karl W. Pettus, "The Memorial to Marshall Keeble," *Gospel Advocate* 90, no. 29 (July 18, 1968): 449; and John Allen Chalk to Brother Goodpasture, undated, John Allen Chalk Papers, box Race Relations, folder 92RR-COC-MK, Special Collections, Harding University Graduate School of Religion, Memphis.

21. Noble Patterson, "Dr. Martin Luther King . . . And Some of Our Brethren," *Christian Journal*, July 1968, 2; *West End News* [weekly bulletin of Birmingham's West End Church of Christ] 20, no. 36 (September 6, 1968): 3–4; and Ernest Clevenger Jr. to John Allen Chalk, September 12, 1968, John Allen Chalk Papers, box 1968 A–C Correspondence, folder C, Special Collections, Harding University Graduate School of Religion, Memphis. Also see Noble Patterson, "'We Shall Overcome,'" *Christian Journal*, October 1968, 2.

22. "Open Forum" advertisement, John Allen Chalk Papers, box Race Relations, folder 92RR-COC-DO, Special Collections, Harding University Graduate School of Religion, Memphis; and "The Campbellites Are Coming," *Time*, February 15, 1963, 97–98.

23. "Open Forum" advertisement, John Allen Chalk Papers, box Race Relations, folder 92RR-COC-DO, Special Collections, Harding University Graduate School of Religion, Memphis.

24. Ibid. The specific text quoted in the latter sermon was Ephesians 2:11–22. Verses 14–18 state, "For he is our peace, who made both one, and brake down the middle wall of partition, having abolished in the flesh the enmity, even the law of commandments contained in ordinances; that he might create in himself of the two one new man, so making peace; and might reconcile them both in one body unto God through the cross, having slain the enmity thereby: and he came and preached peace to you that were far off, and peace to them that were nigh: for through him we both have our access in one Spirit unto the Father" (ASV).

25. Dwain Evans, "A Christian's View on Open Housing," transcript in John Allen Chalk Papers, box Race Relations, folder 92RR-COC-DO, Special Collections, Harding University Graduate School of Religion, Memphis.

26. Ibid.

27. Ibid.

28. Ivory James, "The Negro Church—The White Church—Why?" transcript in John Allen Chalk Papers, box Race Relations, folder 92RR-COC-DO, Special Collections, Harding University Graduate School of Religion, Memphis.

29. Ibid.

30. G. P. Holt, "Is Interracial Marriage Sinful?" transcript in John Allen Chalk Papers, box Race Relations, folder 92RR-COC-DO, Special Collections, Harding University Graduate School of Religion, Memphis.

31. John Allen Chalk, "The Other Wall," transcript in John Allen Chalk Papers, box Race Relations, folder 92RR-COC-DO, Special Collections, Harding University Graduate School of Religion, Memphis.

32. Zebedee Bishop, "Where Do We Go from Here?" transcript in John Allen Chalk Papers, box Race Relations, folder 92RR-COC-DO, Special Collections, Harding University Graduate School of Religion, Memphis.

33. Ibid.

34. Jimmy Allen, Eugene Lawton, and R. C. Wells to Brother Stevens, May 16, 1968, John C. Stevens Papers, box 215, folder Race Relations Meeting, Special Collections, Brown Library, Abilene Christian University, Abilene, TX.

35. An incomplete list of all attendees can be found in "Statement of Acknowledgment of Racial Prejudice and Proposals for Improving Race Relations in Churches of Christ," John Allen Chalk Papers, box Race Relations, folder 92RR-COC-AC, Special Collections, Harding University Graduate School of Religion, Memphis. Also see the photograph in *Christian Echo* 63, no. 9 (September 1968): 7, or *Mission* 2, no. 3 (September 1968): 89. The latter includes a caption listing the names of those pictured.

36. Ona Belknap to John Allen Chalk, June 28, 1968, John Allen Chalk Papers, box 1968 A–C Correspondence, folder B, Special Collections, Harding University Graduate School of Religion, Memphis.

37. Andrew J. Hairston, "Spiritual Equality in Christ," James Bales Papers, Unprocessed, Special Collections, University of Arkansas Libraries, Fayetteville.

38. Ibid.

39. Ibid. Hairston's final remark referred to another Pauline epistle, 1 Corinthians 13:1, which states, "If I speak with the tongues of men and of angels, but have not love, I am become sounding brass, or a clanging cymbal" (ASV).

40. The statement and its signatories can be found in "Conference on Race Relations," *Mission* 2, no. 3 (September 1968): 88–90. Also see Bob Hurt, "40 Protestant Pastors Ask Better Race Ties," *Atlanta Constitution,* undated newspaper clipping, Clifton L. Ganus Jr. Papers, Unprocessed, Administration Building, Harding University, Searcy, AR.

41. "Conference on Race Relations," *Mission* 2, no. 3 (September 1968): 88–90.

42. Dwain Evans, "The Meeting in Atlanta," *Milestones,* undated clipping, John Allen Chalk Papers, box Race Relations, folder 92RR-COC-AM, Special Collections, Harding University Graduate School of Religion, Memphis.

43. John C. Stevens to President Don H. Morris et al., July 1, 1968; and "JCS Impressions Growing Out of the Atlanta Meeting in Improving Race Relations," John C. Stevens Papers, box 215, folder Race Relations Meeting, Special Collections, Brown Library, Abilene Christian University, Abilene, TX.

44. John C. Stevens to Dwain Evans, July 2, 1968; and Dwain Evans to Dr. John C. Stevens, July 9, 1968, John C. Stevens Papers, box 215, folder Race Relations Meeting, Special Collections, Brown Library, Abilene Christian University, Abilene, TX; and Andrew J. Hairston to "Brother,"

July 8, 1968, Clifton L. Ganus Jr. Papers, Unprocessed, Administration Building, Harding University, Searcy, AR.

45. W. L. Totty, "A New Creed Appears," *Informer* (bulletin of Garfield Heights Church of Christ, Indianapolis), undated, John Allen Chalk Papers, box Race Relations, folder 92RR-COC-AM; and Shelby C. Smith to Brother Chalk, November 7, 1968, John Allen Chalk Papers, box 1968 D–Z Correspondence, folder S, Special Collections, Harding University Graduate School of Religion, Memphis.

46. Clipping of Foster L. Ramsey, "And Now There Are Ecumenical Councils!" August 9, 1968, John Allen Chalk Papers, box 1968 Herald of Truth Correspondence, folder 92RR-COC-AM, Special Collections, Harding University Graduate School of Religion, Memphis.

47. Bob Anderson, "To Whom It May Concern" [undated]; Jennings Davis Jr. to Bob Anderson, October 16, 1968; and Dwain Evans to Bob Anderson, October 23, 1968, John Allen Chalk Papers, box 1968 Herald of Truth Correspondence, folder 92RR-COC-AM, Special Collections, Harding University Graduate School of Religion, Memphis.

48. Clipping of "The Atlanta Conference (1)," *The Getwell Reminder* 9, no. 44 (September 12, 1968), John Allen Chalk Papers, box 1968 Herald of Truth Correspondence, folder 92RR-COC-AM; and John Allen Chalk to Don and Regina Stevens, November 18, 1968, John Allen Chalk Papers, box 1968 D–Z Correspondence, folder S, Special Collections, Harding University Graduate School of Religion, Memphis.

49. Herald of Truth, "Our History," www.heraldoftruth.org/about/ (accessed July 8, 2010); and "Questions and Answers Concerning Herald of Truth," undated document, Herald of Truth Papers, ser. 2, box 16, folder Disapprove, Special Collections, Brown Library, Abilene Christian University, Abilene, TX. The average contribution for a single church in 1967 was approximately $305, while individuals gave an average of $39.

50. "Three American Revolutions," undated document, Herald of Truth Papers, ser. 2, box 15; and Dr. A. E. Thompson to Sirs, undated letter typed on advertisement, Herald of Truth, ser. 2, box 15, folder Approve M–Z, Special Collections, Brown Library, Abilene Christian University, Abilene, TX.

51. W. R. Davis to The Elders, Highland Church of Christ, August 8, 1968; and Jack Evans to The Elders, Highland Church of Christ, August 2, 1968, Herald of Truth Papers, ser. 2, box 16, folder Approve A–L, Special Collections, Brown Library, Abilene Christian University, Abilene, TX. At least twenty-seven black listeners wrote letters, and all approved the sermons.

52. John Allen Chalk, "Is Jehovah God a Racist?" (sermon broadcast on July 14, 1968), Herald of Truth Papers, box 35, folder Radio Scripts, 859–75, Radio Sermon No. 859; and John Allen Chalk, "Three American Revolutions" (sermon broadcast on June 2, 1968), Herald of Truth Papers, box 34, folder Radio Scripts, 851–58, Radio Sermon No. 853, Special Collections, Brown Library, Abilene Christian University, Abilene, TX.

53. John Allen Chalk, "Hatred Is Only Skin Deep" (sermon broadcast on July 7, 1968), Herald of Truth Papers, box 34, folder Radio Scripts, 851–58, Radio Sermon No. 858, Special Collections, Brown Library, Abilene Christian University, Abilene, TX.

54. John Allen Chalk, "Hatred Is Only Skin Deep" (sermon broadcast on July 7, 1968), Herald of Truth Papers, box 34, folder Radio Scripts, 851–58, Radio Sermon No. 858; John Allen Chalk, "Some of My Best Friends" (sermon broadcast on July 21, 1968), Herald of Truth Papers, box 35, folder Radio Scripts, 859–75, Radio Sermon No. 860; and John Allen Chalk, "Are You a Respecter of Persons?" (sermon broadcast on July 28, 1968), Herald of Truth Papers, box 35, folder Radio

Scripts, 859–75, Radio Sermon No. 861, Special Collections, Brown Library, Abilene Christian University, Abilene, TX.

55. I disagree with some of the classifications. For example, at least one "neutral" letter expressed wholehearted agreement with the sermons on race, while a few others seemed to express skepticism, if not disapproval, but were not placed in the "disapproval" folder. For the most part, however, the letters seem to have been filed correctly, so I have followed the statistics compiled by the *Herald of Truth*, except for correcting what appear to be a few minor mathematical errors.

56. "Herald of Truth Radio Sermons Report—The Three American Revolutions Series," December 4, 1968, Herald of Truth Papers, ser. 2, box 15; James D. Glasse to Mr. John Allen Chalk, July 10, 1968; and Thomas B. Warren to John Allen, July 11, 1968, Herald of Truth Papers, ser. 2, box 16, folder Approve M–Z, Special Collections, Brown Library, Abilene Christian University, Abilene, TX.

57. For examples, see Sokol, *There Goes My Everything*; Palmer, *Living as Equals*; and Harwell, "Wednesdays in Mississippi."

58. Miss Grace Dove to John Allen Chalk, July 18, 1968; Ronald H. Jones to John Allen Shaw, July 11, 1968; and enclosure with Jim Henry to Mr. Chalk, July 23, 1968, Herald of Truth Papers, ser. 2, box 16, folder Approve A–L; Paul D. Phillips to John Allen Chalk, July 26, 1968; and Mrs. Harold Sandiford to John Allen Chalk, postmarked July 22, 1968, Herald of Truth Papers, ser. 2, box 16, folder Approve M–Z, Special Collections, Brown Library, Abilene Christian University, Abilene, TX.

59. Eugene Lawton to A. L. Haddox, July 6, 1968; and Jim Henry to Mr. Chalk, July 23, 1968, Herald of Truth Papers, ser. 2, box 16, folder Approve A–L, Special Collections, Brown Library, Abilene Christian University, Abilene, TX.

60. Patricia Griffin to Brethren, undated letter, Herald of Truth Papers, ser. 2, box 16, folder Approve A–L, Special Collections, Brown Library, Abilene Christian University, Abilene, TX.

61. Ibid.; and John Allen Chalk to Mrs. Patricia Griffin, September 13, 1968, John Allen Chalk Papers, box 1968 D–Z Correspondence, folder G, Special Collections, Harding University Graduate School of Religion, Memphis.

62. Ray Dutton to Bro. Chalk, July 10, 1968, Herald of Truth Papers, ser. 2, box 16, folder Approve A–L. Special Collections, Brown Library, Abilene Christian University, Abilene, TX.

63. John Allen Chalk to Mr. Ray Dutton, July 25, 1968, Herald of Truth Papers, ser. 2, box 16, folder Approve A–L, Special Collections, Brown Library, Abilene Christian University, Abilene, TX.

64. Romano, *Race Mixing*, 185–215.

65. Evelyn E. Edes to Mr. Chalk, July 18, 1968, Herald of Truth Papers, ser. 2, box 16, folder Approve A–L, Special Collections, Brown Library, Abilene Christian University, Abilene, TX.

66. John Allen Chalk to Ora Traughber, August 12, 1968. John Allen Chalk Papers, box 1968 D–Z Correspondence, folder T. Special Collections, Harding University Graduate School of Religion, Memphis.

67. Brad Brumley to John Allen Chalk, November 22, 1968; and John Allen Chalk to Brad Brumley, December 2, 1968, John Allen Chalk Papers, box 1968 A–C Correspondence, folder B, Special Collections, Harding University Graduate School of Religion, Memphis. Also see Beecham, *The Difference*. Beecham described his experiences as a black man who encountered several obstacles when he chose to attend a white Church of Christ in New Jersey and fell in love with a young woman there.

68. Harvey, *Freedom's Coming*, 229–34; Chappell, *A Stone of Hope*, 105–30; Mrs. A. B. Baxley to Mr. John Allen Chalk, July 19, 1968; and Eldon McIntosh to Sir, July 21, 1968, Herald of Truth Papers, ser. 2, box 16, folder Disapprove; and Mrs. James Ash to Mr. John Allen Chalk, July 7, 1968, Herald of Truth Papers, ser. 2, box 16, folder Approve A–L, Special Collections, Brown Library, Abilene Christian University, Abilene, TX. For more on segregationist fears of interracial romance, see Dailey, "Sex, Segregation, and the Sacred after *Brown*," 119–44.

69. L. C. Rice et al. to The Elders, Highland Church of Christ, July 31, 1968; W. R. Craig to Mr. Frank Cawyer, July 12, 1968; and Jimmy W. Garner to W. F. Cawyer, July 18, 1968, Herald of Truth Papers, ser. 2, box 16, folder Disapprove, Special Collections, Brown Library, Abilene Christian University, Abilene, TX.

70. John Allen Chalk, "Hatred Is Only Skin Deep" (sermon broadcast on July 7, 1968), Herald of Truth Papers, box 34, folder Radio Scripts, 851–58, Radio Sermon No. 858, Special Collections, Brown Library, Abilene Christian University, Abilene, TX.

71. Richard Hall to Bro. Chalk, undated letter, Herald of Truth Papers, ser. 2, box 16, folder Approve A–L; and John Allen Chalk, "Three American Revolutions" (sermon broadcast on June 2, 1968), Herald of Truth Papers, box 34, folder Radio Scripts, 851–58, Radio Sermon No. 853, Special Collections, Brown Library, Abilene Christian University, Abilene, TX.

72. Jim Henry to Mr. Chalk, July 23, 1968, Herald of Truth Papers, ser. 2, box 16, folder Approve A–L; William Schettle to Rev. John Allen Chalk, June 2, 1968; and L. P. Walker to John Allen Scott, July 28, 1968, Herald of Truth Papers, ser. 2, box 16, folder Approve M–Z. Special Collections, Brown Library, Abilene Christian University, Abilene, TX.

6. Exorcising Demons

1. Newman, *Getting Right with God*, 191–96; and Murray, *Methodists and the Crucible of Race, 1930–1975*, 200–231.

2. R. N. Hogan, "The Contribution an Integrated Congregation Can Make to the Community," *Christian Echo* 69 (April 1971): 2, 6; and John Waddey, "A Plea to My Black Brethren," *Christian Echo* 67 (November–December 1969): 3.

3. Eugene Green, "The Trouble with Skin," *Christian Echo* 63 (July 1968): 5; and Hogan, "The Contribution an Integrated Congregation Can Make to the Community," *Christian Echo* 69 (April 1971): 2.

4. C. E. Gaines, "Christianity in Action," *Christian Echo* 60 (August 1965): 1.

5. Ibid.; Letter from Bessie Elam, *Christian Echo* 60 (June 1965): 9; and Dick Bartholomee to John Allen Chalk, July 13, 1968, John Allen Chalk Papers, box 1968 A–C Correspondence, folder B, Special Collections, Harding University Graduate School of Religion, Memphis. In the 2003 compilation of *Churches of Christ in the United States*, ed. Lynn, the South Side church in Tucson was listed as an African American church.

6. "Races Unite in Church Merger," *Christian Echo* 64 (January 1969): 10.

7. John Allen Chalk to Ivory James, September 13, 1968, John Allen Chalk Papers, box 1968 D–Z Correspondence, folder J, Special Collections, Harding University Graduate School of Religion, Memphis; McMullen, interview with author; Brown, interview with author; Holsendolph, interview with author; "History of the West End Congregation," www.thewestender.com/about wend.htm (accessed August 12, 2014); and Kruse, *White Flight*.

8. Batsell Barrett Baxter to John Allen Chalk, October 22, 1968, John Allen Chalk Papers, box 1968 A–C, folder B, Special Collections, Harding University Graduate School of Religion, Memphis; and Letter from John C. Whitley, *Christian Echo* 68 (April 1970): 10.

9. Fred Gray, "What a Personal Workshop Can Do for Your Congregation," *Christian Echo* 61 (March 1966): 1; Norrell, *Reaping the Whirlwind*, 131–33, 210; Gray, *Bus Ride to Justice*, 211–12, 259–60, 286, 293–94; Gray, *The Tuskegee Syphilis Study*, 84; and Gray, interview with author.

10. "Greetings to the Brotherhood," *Christian Echo* 61 (June 1966): 7.

11. Letter from Clanton, Ala., *Christian Echo* 70 (July 1972): 9.

12. John Allen Chalk to C. H. Agnew, November 29, 1968, John Allen Chalk Papers, box 1968 Herald of Truth Correspondence, folder A; Eugene Lawton to M. A. Shelton & Elders, Union Avenue Church of Christ, February 25, 1969, John Allen Chalk Papers, box Race Relations, folder 92RR-CC; and Charles Shelton to John Allen Chalk, April 14, 1969, John Allen Chalk Papers, box Race Relations, folder 92RR-CC, Special Collections, Harding University Graduate School of Religion, Memphis.

13. M. A. Shelton to John Allen Chalk, December 18, 1968; and John Allen Chalk to M. A. Shelton, December 30, 1968, John Allen Chalk Papers, box 1968 D–Z Correspondence, folder S, Special Collections, Harding University Graduate School of Religion, Memphis.

14. R. L. Ramsey to Jack Evans, May 27, 1970, John Allen Chalk Papers, box Race Relations, folder 92RR-COC, Special Collections, Harding University Graduate School of Religion, Memphis.

15. Jack Evans to R. L. Ramsey, June 2, 1970, John Allen Chalk Papers, box Race Relations, folder 92RR-COC, Special Collections, Harding University Graduate School of Religion, Memphis.

16. Harold Bowie to Elders and Deacons, Highland Street Church of Christ, June 10, 1970, John Allen Chalk Papers, box Race Relations, folder 92RR-COC, Special Collections, Harding University Graduate School of Religion, Memphis.

17. Ibid. Details about Bowie's personal life are available from his obituary, www.memorialparkfuneralandcemetery.com/obituaries/Dr-Harold-Bowie/#!/Obituary (accessed July 8, 2015).

18. H. E. Steele to John Allen Chalk, February 7, 1971, John Allen Chalk Papers, box 1971 Correspondence, folder G, Special Collections, Harding University Graduate School of Religion, Memphis.

19. John Allen Chalk to H. E. Steele, February 18, 1971, John Allen Chalk Papers, box 1971 Correspondence, folder G, Special Collections, Harding University Graduate School of Religion, Memphis.

20. David Jones Jr. to The Elders, Highland Church of Christ [Abilene, TX], July 31, 1968; and Jesse Johnson to The Elders, Highland Church of Christ [Abilene, TX], August 4, 1968, John Allen Chalk Papers, box Race Relations, folder 92RR-COC-HCC, Special Collections, Harding University Graduate School of Religion, Memphis.

21. Z. P. Stokes to John Allen Chalk, April 16, 1968; Henry Stokes to John Allen Chalk, April 12, 1968; and John Allen Chalk to Z. P. Stokes, April 19, 1968, John Allen Chalk Papers, box 1968 Herald of Truth Correspondence, folder S, Special Collections, Harding University Graduate School of Religion, Memphis. On the Nation of Islam, see Turner, *Islam in the African-American Experience*.

22. John Allen Chalk to Henry Stokes, April 24, 1968; Henry Stokes to John Allen Chalk, April 27, 1968; John Allen Chalk to Henry Stokes, May 21, 1968; and John Allen Chalk to Z. P. Stokes, June 17, 1968, John Allen Chalk Papers, box 1968 Herald of Truth Correspondence, folder S, Special Collections, Harding University Graduate School of Religion, Memphis.

23. R. N. Hogan, "Debate with a Black Muslim Minister," *Christian Echo* 69 (October 1971): 2, 4.

24. Charles 20X, "Wait-for-Heaven line of Christians smashed by debate of Muslim minister," *Muhammad Speaks,* September 3, 1971; and R. N. Hogan, "The Black Muslim Cult," *Christian Echo* 69 (November–December 1971): 8, 11.

25. R. N. Hogan, "The Black Muslim Cult," *Christian Echo* 70 (February 1972): 2.

26. Lucy Mae Harris, "Because My Skin is Black," *Christian Echo* 60 (July 1965): 8.

27. *More than Conquerors,* 76–77; and BlackPast.org, "Asante, Molefi Kete/Arthur Lee Smith Jr. (1942–)," www.blackpast.org/aah/asante-molefi-kete-arthur-lee-smith-jr-1942 (accessed July 10, 2015).

28. Bill Goodpasture to John Allen Chalk, September 23, 1968, John Allen Chalk Papers, box 1968 D–Z Correspondence, folder G; and Humphrey Foutz to Prentice Meador, October 7, 1968, John Allen Chalk Papers, box Race Relations, folder 92RR-COC-HOT, Special Collections, Harding University Graduate School of Religion, Memphis.

29. Stanton, *Faith and Works*; Faulkner, *Mumblings,* 374–76; and Carter, *The Politics of Rage.*

30. Carter, *The Politics of Rage,* 93, 96; and Stanton, *Faith and Works,* 144–45.

31. Stanton, *Faith and Works,* 105, 149–50, 153; and Carter, *The Politics of Rage,* 300.

32. Stanton, *Faith and Works,* 97; and "About Faulkner," www.faulkner.edu/about-faulkner/ (accessed July 10, 2015).

33. BlackPast.org, "Groove Phi Groove Social Fellowship (1962–)," www.blackpast.org/aah /groove-phi-groove-social-fellowship-1962 (accessed July 8, 2015); "SA Holds Non-Typical Conference; Campus Leaders Hear Negro Panel," *Bison,* Special Edition, March 18, 1969; and Bales, *The Martin Luther King Story.*

34. "Conference on Improving Race Relations in the Churches of Christ," Clifton Ganus Jr. Papers, Unprocessed, Office of Clifton Ganus Jr., Administration Building, Harding University, Searcy, AR. "Harding College Faculty Meeting Minutes," Faculty Meetings Minutes, 1968–69 folder; "Report of Financial Aid Awarded to Negro Students Fall Semester 1968," Race Relations folder, Special Collections, Brackett Library, Harding University, Searcy, AR. Ganus, interview with author.

35. Gowen, interview with author; and Gowen, untitled editorial, *Bison,* January 17, 1969.

36. "To Those Concerned," "Human Relations Seminar at OCC Draws Seventeen Harding Students," and Kay Gowen, untitled editorials, *Bison,* February 14 and 21, 1969; and Ganus, interview with author.

37. *Bison,* Special Edition, March 18, 1969.

38. David Crouch, "Love thy neighbor as thy self" [*sic*], *Bison,* Special Edition, March 18, 1969.

39. Donna Holmquist and Jerry Flowers, "Bison Poll Draws Variety of Comments," *Bison,* Special Edition, March 18, 1969.

40. "Committee Report on Suggestions for Improvement of Race Relations," Race Relations folder, Special Collections, Brackett Library, Harding University, Searcy, AR.

41. Clifton L. Ganus Jr., "Race Relations at Harding" (speech given at Harding College on March 20, 1969), Race Relations folder, Special Collections, Brackett Library, Harding University, Searcy, AR.

42. Ibid.; and Ginger Shiras, "Blacks Get Up, Leave as Harding Head Explains Race Situation, Calls for 'Closer Walk With God,'" *Arkansas Gazette,* March 21, 1969.

43. Wayne Jordan, "NEP Pamphlets Are Burned In Harding Negroes' Protest," *Arkansas Ga-*

zette, April 17, 1969; Jordan, "Students Using Techniques of Communists, Forum Told," *Arkansas Gazette*, April 18, 1969; Kay Gowen, untitled editorial, *Bison*, April 18, 1969; Ganus, interview with author; Edwin Hendrix to Dr. Ganus, March 20, 1969; and Alice Jo Stokes to Bro. Ganus, March 23, 1969, Clifton Ganus Jr. Papers, Unprocessed, Office of Clifton Ganus Jr., Administration Building, Harding University, Searcy, AR.

44. Dochuk, *From Bible Belt to Sunbelt*, 293–94, 323.

45. Crawford, *Shattering the Illusion*, 131–37; Dochuk, *From Bible Belt to Sunbelt*, 83; and John E. Acuff to Brothers, January 11, 1971, John Allen Chalk Papers, box Race Relations, folder 92RR-COC, Special Collections, Harding University Graduate School of Religion, Memphis.

46. Williams, *God's Own Party*; Moreton, *To Serve God and Wal-Mart*, 163; G. P. Holt, "Tension Between the Black and White Church," *Christian Echo* [64]: 4; and Crawford, *Shattering the Illusion*, 143–77, where this separation is further explicated.

Conclusion: Repentance, Reconciliation, and Resistance

1. "Vicksburg Churches Merge," *Magnolia Messenger* 27, no. 2 (April–May 2005): 4.

2. This particular turn of phrase is frequently used because it alludes to a Pauline text that states, "For as often as you eat this bread and drink this cup, you proclaim the Lord's death till He comes. Therefore whoever eats this bread or drinks this cup of the Lord in an unworthy manner will be guilty of the body and blood of the Lord. But let a man examine himself, and so let him eat of the bread and drink of the cup" (I Corinthians 11:26–28, NKJV).

3. "Vicksburg Churches Merge," *Magnolia Messenger* 27, no. 2 (April–May 2005): 4.

4. Burks, ed., *Against the Grain*, 41, 58.

5. Michelle Morris, "'The Right Thing to Do,'" *ACU Today*, Spring 2000.

6. Kim Chaudoin, "History-making civil rights attorney Fred Gray to receive honorary doctorate," May 29, 2012, www.lipscomb.edu/news/history-making-civil-rights-attorney-fred-gray -receive-honorary-doctorate; "Lipscomb to recognize former MLK attorney Fred D. Gray by naming Institute for Law, Justice & Society in his honor," November 2, 2016, www.lipscomb.edu/news /lipscomb-recognize-former-mlk-attorney-fred-d-gray-naming-institute-law-justice-society-his; and "First Fred D. Gray Scholarships for law, justice and society recipients announced," September 29, 2017, www.lipscomb.edu/news/first-fred-d-gray-scholarships-law-justice-and-society-recipients-announced (accessed February 26, 2019).

7. Shelly, interview by author.

Bibliography

PRIMARY SOURCES

Archives

Alabama Department of Archives and History, Montgomery

Abilene Christian University, Abilene, TX
  Representative Omar Burleson Papers.
  Herald of Truth Papers.
  Lemoine Lewis Papers.
  Don Morris Papers.
  John C. Stevens Papers.

Center for Restoration Studies, Abilene Christian University, Abilene, TX
  Reuel Lemmons Papers.
  James L. Lovell Papers.
  E. W. McMillan Papers.
  Race Issues Collection.

David Lipscomb University, Nashville
  Batsell Barrett Baxter Papers.
  A. M. Burton Papers.
  Herald of Truth Collection.
  Marshall Keeble Collection.
  Nashville Christian Institute Papers.

Disciples of Christ Historical Society, Nashville
  B. C. Goodpasture Papers.

Harding University, Searcy, AR
    James Bales Papers.
    George Benson Papers.
    Clifton Ganus Jr. Papers.
    University Archives.

Harding University Graduate School of Religion, Memphis
    John Allen Chalk Papers.

Ouachita Baptist University, Arkadelphia, AR
    Senator John L. McClellan Papers.

Tennessee Tech University, Cookeville
    Representative Joe L. Evins Papers.

University of Arkansas, Fayetteville
    Center Street Church of Christ Records, 1897–1986.
    James Bales Papers.

University of Rochester, Rochester, NY
    Franklin Florence Papers.

Periodicals

Babbler.
Bible Banner.
Bison.
California Christian.
Christian Chronicle.
Christian Echo.
Christian Journal.
Firm Foundation.
Gospel Advocate.
Mission.
Optimist.
Singapore-Far East Newsletter.
Skyrocket.
Time.
Truth.
20th Century Christian.

Interviews (conducted by author unless otherwise noted)

Adamson, Norman. April 27, 2007. Nashville, AR.
Anderson, Joel. April 26, 2007. Little Rock, AR.
Brown, Wesley. July 18, 2006. Atlanta.
Chalk, John Allen. July 25, 2006. Fort Worth, TX.
Evans, Jack, Sr. June 22, 2005. Terrell, TX.
Ganus, Clifton, Jr. May 10, 2005. Searcy, AR.
Gardner, E. Claude. June 26, 2005. Henderson, TN.
Garrett, Leroy. June 16, 2005. Jacksonville, FL.
Gowen, Kay. May 10, 2005. Searcy, AR.
Gray, Fred. May 17, 2005. Tuskegee, AL.
Haymes, Don. June 1, 2006. Temple Terrace, FL.
Holsendolph, Ernest. July 19, 2006. Stone Mountain, GA.
Jarrett, Gary. June 16, 2005. Jacksonville, FL.
Jones, David, Jr. November 8, 2008. Nashville, TN.
Keeble, Marshall. Conducted by J. E. Choate, about 1967. Nashville, TN.
McMullen, Evans. July 21, 2006. Valdosta, GA.
Morrison, Woodie. July 26, 2006. Mineral Wells, TX.
Rollinson, Harold. June 16, 2005. Jacksonville, FL.
Rose, Floyd. June 8, 2005. Valdosta, GA.
Shelly, Rubel. June 28, 2005. Nashville, TN.
Tucker, John Mark. July 27, 2006. Abilene, TX.

Books and Articles

Bales, James D. *The Martin Luther King Story.* Tulsa, OK: Christian Crusade Publications, 1967.
Banowsky, William S. *The Mirror of a Movement: Churches of Christ as Seen Through the Abilene Christian College Lectureship.* Dallas: Christian Publishing Co., 1965.
Beecham, Charles W. *The Difference.* New York: Carlton Press, 1971.
Burks, David B., ed. *Against the Grain: The Mission of Harding University.* Searcy, AR: Harding University, 1998.
Cameron, W. Alan. *The Origin and Development of the Negro Race.* St. Petersburg, FL: Westbrook Printing, 1954.
Campbell, Will. *Race and the Renewal of the Church.* Philadelphia: Westminster Press, 1962.
Cassius, S. R. *The Third Birth of a Nation.* Rev. ed. Cincinnati: F. L. Rowe, 1925.
Choate, J. E. *Roll Jordan Roll: A Biography of Marshall Keeble.* Nashville: Gospel Advocate Co., 1968.

Christian Faith in the Modern World: The Abilene Christian College Annual Bible Lectures,
    1960. Abilene, TX: Abilene Christian College Students Exchange, 1960.
Clevenger, Ernest, Jr. *Comprehensive Topical and Textual Lesson Commentary Index to*
    Elam's Notes Annual Lesson Commentary Teacher's Annual Lesson Commentary. 3rd
    ed. Birmingham, AL: Parchment Press, 1973.
Elam, E. A., and H. Leo Boles, eds. *Elam's Notes on Bible School Lessons: 1929.* Nashville:
    Gospel Advocate Co., 1929.
Faulkner, Jimmy. *Mumblings: about people, places and politics.* Winona, MS: J. C. Choate
    Publications, 2004.
Gardner, Don, ed. *Victorious Living Today.* Nashville: Christian Family Books, 1966.
Gender and Ministry: Freed-Hardeman University Preachers' and Church Workers' Forum
    1990. Huntsville, AL: Publishing Designs, 1990.
Goodpasture, B. C. *Biography and Sermons of Marshall Keeble, Evangelist.* Nashville: Gos-
    pel Advocate Co., 1931. Rpt. 1964.
Gray, Fred. *Bus Ride to Justice: Changing the System by the System: The Life and Works of*
    Fred Gray. Montgomery, AL: Black Belt Press, 1995.
———. *The Tuskegee Syphilis Study: The Real Story and Beyond.* Montgomery, AL: New-
    South Books, 1998.
Harding College Bible Lectures, 1959. Austin, TX: Firm Foundation Publishing House, 1960.
Harding College Bible Lectures, 1961. Austin, TX: Firm Foundation Publishing House, 1962.
Hinds, John T. *Annual Lesson Commentary on Improved Uniform Series of International Bible*
    Lessons: 1932. Nashville: Gospel Advocate Co., 1932.
Holt, Thelma, ed. *Life and Times of G. P. Bowser.* Nashville: Associated Publishing Co., 1964.
King, Martin Luther, Jr. *Stride Toward Freedom: The Montgomery Story.* New York: Harper,
    1958.
Meyers, Robert, ed. *Voices of Concern: Critical Studies in Church of Christism.* St. Louis,
    MO: Mission Messenger, 1966.
Moody, Anne. *Coming of Age in Mississippi.* New York: Laurel, 1968.
More Than Conquerors: History & Growth of the Schrader Lane Church of Christ, Nashville,
    Tennessee. Franklin, TN: Providence House Publications, 2000.
Muncy, Eloise, and John Williams. *Making History: Ray Muncy in His Time.* Orange, CA:
    New Leaf Books, 2002.
Olbricht, Thomas H. *Hearing God's Voice: My Life with Scripture in the Churches of Christ.*
    Abilene, TX: Abilene Christian University Press, 1996.
Philbrick, Herbert A., and James D. Bales. *Communism and Race in America.* Searcy, AR:
    Bales Bookstore, 1965.
Redekop, John Harold. *The American Far Right: A Case Study of Billy James Hargis and*
    Christian Crusade. Grand Rapids, MI: William B. Eerdmans Publishing Co., 1968.
Rose, Floyd E. *An Idea Whose Time Has Come.* Columbus, GA: Brentwood Christian Press,
    2002.
———. *Beyond the Thicket.* Columbus, GA: Brentwood Christian Press, 2003.

Teacher's Annual Lesson Commentary on Uniform Bible Lessons for the Churches of Christ: 1949. Nashville: Gospel Advocate Co., 1949.
Teacher's Annual Lesson Commentary on Uniform Bible Lessons for the Churches of Christ: 1951. Nashville: Gospel Advocate Co., 1951.
Tuggle, Annie C. *Another World Wonder.* Introduction by Carroll Pitts Jr. N.p., 1973.
Whitesides, R. L. *Annual Commentary on Improved Uniform Series of International Bible Lessons: 1944.* Nashville: Gospel Advocate Co., 1944.
Zanden, James W. Vander. "The Ideology of White Supremacy." *Journal of the History of Ideas* 20, no. 3 (June–September 1959): 385–402.

SECONDARY SOURCES

Books

Allen, C. Leonard. *Distant Voices: Discovering a Forgotten Past for a Changing Church.* Abilene, TX: Abilene Christian University Press, 1993.
Allen, C. Leonard, and Richard T. Hughes. *Discovering Our Roots: The Ancestry of Churches of Christ.* Abilene, TX: Abilene Christian University, 1988.
———. *Illusions of Innocence: Protestant Primitivism in America, 1630–1875.* Chicago: University of Chicago Press, 1988.
Alvis, Joel A., Jr. *Religion & Race: Southern Presbyterians, 1946–1983.* Tuscaloosa: University of Alabama Press, 1994.
Anderson, R. Bentley. *Black, White, and Catholic: New Orleans Interracialism, 1947–1956.* Nashville: Vanderbilt University Press, 2005.
Ayers, Edward L. *The Promise of the New South: Life After Reconstruction.* New York: Oxford University Press, 1992.
Badger, Tony, Walter Edgar, and Jan Nordby Gretlund, eds. *Southern Landscapes.* Tübingen, Germany: Stauffenburg-Verlag, 1996.
Balmer, Randall. *Mine Eyes Have Seen the Glory: A Journey into the Evangelical Subculture in America.* New York: Oxford University Press, 2014.
Barnes, Kenneth C. *Journey of Hope: The Back-to-Africa Movement in Arkansas in the Late 1800s.* Chapel Hill: University of North Carolina Press, 2004.
Bartley, Numan V. *The Rise of Massive Resistance: Race and Politics in the South during the 1950s.* Baton Rouge: Louisiana State University Press, 1969.
Bass, S. Jonathan. *Blessed Are the Peacemakers: Martin Luther King, Jr., Eight White Religious Leaders, and the "Letter from Birmingham Jail."* Baton Rouge: Louisiana State University Press, 2001.
Blum, Edward J. *Reforging the White Republic: Race, Religion, and American Nationalism, 1865–1898.* Baton Rouge: Louisiana State University Press, 2005.
Boles, John B., and Evelyn Thomas Nolen, eds. *Interpreting Southern History: Historio-*

graphical Essays in Honor of Sanford W. Higginbotham. Baton Rouge: Louisiana State University Press, 1987.

Bowers, Calvin H. *Realizing the California Dream: the Story of Black Churches of Christ in Los Angeles.* Los Angeles: Calvin Bowers, 2001.

Boyd, R. Vernon. *Undying Dedication: The Story of G. P. Bowser.* Nashville: Gospel Advocate Co., 1985.

Branch, Taylor. *Parting the Waters: America in the King Years, 1954–63.* New York: Simon & Schuster, 1988.

———. *Pillar of Fire: America in the King Years, 1963–65.* New York: Simon & Schuster, 1998.

———. *At Canaan's Edge: America in the King Years, 1965–68.* New York: Simon & Schuster, 2006.

Cannon, Katie Geneva. *Katie's Canon: Womanism and the Soul of the Black Community.* New York: Continuum, 1995.

Carter, Dan T. *The Politics of Rage: George Wallace, the Origins of the New Conservativism, and the Transformation of American Politics.* 2nd ed. Baton Rouge: Louisiana State University Press, 2000.

Casey, Michael W. *Saddlebags, City Streets, and Cyberspace: A History of Preaching in the Churches of Christ.* Abilene, TX: Abilene Christian University Press, 1995.

Cauthen, Kenneth. *I Don't Care What the Bible Says: An Interpretation of the South.* Macon, GA: Mercer University Press, 2003.

Chafe, William H. *Civilities and Civil Rights: Greensboro, North Carolina, and the Black Struggle for Freedom.* New York: Oxford University Press, 1980.

Chalmers, David M. *Hooded Americanism: The History of the Ku Klux Klan.* 3rd ed. Durham, NC: Duke University Press, 1981.

Chappell, David L. *Inside Agitators: White Southerners in the Civil Rights Movement.* Baltimore: Johns Hopkins University Press, 1994.

———. *A Stone of Hope: Prophetic Religion and the Death of Jim Crow.* Chapel Hill: University of North Carolina Press, 2004.

———. *Waking from the Dream: The Struggle for Civil Rights in the Shadow of Martin Luther King, Jr.* New York: Random House, 2014.

Clark, E. Culpepper. *The Schoolhouse Door: Segregation's Last Stand at the University of Alabama.* New York: Oxford University Press, 1993.

Collins, Donald E. *When the Church Bell Rang Racist: The Methodist Church and the Civil Rights Movement in Alabama.* Macon, GA: Mercer University Press, 1998.

Crawford, Wes. *Shattering the Illusion: How African American Churches of Christ Moved from Segregation to Independence.* Abilene, TX: Abilene Christian University Press, 2013.

Crespino, Joseph. *In Search of Another Country: Mississippi and the Conservative Counterrevolution.* Princeton, NJ: Princeton University Press, 2007.

Cunningham, W. J. *Agony at Galloway: One Church's Struggle with Social Change.* Jackson: University Press of Mississippi, 1980.

Cutler, Donald R., ed. *The Religious Situation: 1969.* Boston: Beacon Press, 1969.

Daniel, Pete. *Lost Revolutions: The South in the 1950s.* Chapel Hill: University of North Carolina Press, 2000.

Davis, Jack. *Race Against Time: Culture and Separation in Natchez since 1930.* Baton Rouge: Louisiana State University Press, 2001.

Dittmer, John. *Local People: The Struggle for Civil Rights in Mississippi.* Urbana: University of Illinois Press, 1994.

Dochuk, Darren. *From Bible Belt to Sun Belt: Plain-Folk Religion, Grassroots Politics, and the Rise of Evangelical Conservatism.* New York: W. W. Norton, 2011.

Douglas, Kelly Brown. *The Black Christ.* Maryknoll, NY: Orbis Books, 1994. Rpt., 2006.

Eagles, Charles W. *Outside Agitator: Jon Daniels and the Civil Rights Movement in Alabama.* 1993. Rpt., Tuscaloosa: University of Alabama Press, 2000.

———. *The Price of Defiance: James Meredith and the Integration of Ole Miss.* Chapel Hill: University of North Carolina Press, 2009.

Emerson, Michael O., and Christian Smith. *Divided by Faith: Evangelical Religion and the Problem of Racism in America.* New York: Oxford University Press, 2000.

Eskew, Glenn T. *But for Birmingham: The Local and National Movements in the Civil Rights Struggle.* Chapel Hill: University of North Carolina Press, 1997.

Fairclough, Adam. *Better Day Coming: Blacks and Equality, 1890–2000.* New York: Viking, 2001.

Felder, Cain Hope, ed. *Stony the Road We Trod: African American Biblical Interpretation.* Minneapolis: Fortress Press, 1991.

Feldman, Glenn, ed. *Reading Southern History: Essays on Interpreters and Interpretations.* Tuscaloosa: University of Alabama Press, 2001.

———, ed. *Painting Dixie Red: When, Where, Why, and How the South Became Republican.* Gainesville: University Press of Florida, 2011.

Ferguson, Everett. *The Church of Christ: A Biblical Ecclesiology for Today.* Grand Rapids: William B. Eerdmans Publishing Co., 1996.

Ferguson, Robert Hunt. *Remaking the Rural South: Interracialism, Christian Socialism, and Cooperative Farming in Jim Crow Mississippi.* Athens: University of Georgia Press, 2018.

Flynt, Wayne. *Alabama Baptists: Southern Baptists in the Heart of Dixie.* Tuscaloosa: University of Alabama Press, 1998.

Foster, Douglas A., Paul M. Blowers, Anthony L. Dunnavant, and D. Newell Williams, eds. *The Encyclopedia of the Stone-Campbell Movement: Christian Church (Disciples of Christ), Christian Churches/Churches of Christ, Churches of Christ.* Grand Rapids, MI: William B. Eerdmans Publishing Co., 2004.

Frazier, E. Franklin. *The Negro Church in America.* New York: Schocken Books, 1964.

Frederickson, Kari. *The Dixiecrat Revolt and the End of the Solid South, 1932–1968.* Chapel Hill: University of North Carolina Press, 2001.

Friedland, Michael B. *Lift Up Your Voice Like a Trumpet: White Clergy and the Civil Rights Movements, 1954–1973.* Chapel Hill: University of North Carolina Press, 1998.

Garrett, Leroy. *The Stone-Campbell Movement: The Story of the American Restoration Movement.* Rev. ed. Joplin: College Press, 1994.

Garrow, David J. *Bearing the Cross: Martin Luther King, Jr., and the Southern Christian Leadership Conference.* New York: Random House, 1986.

Giggie, John M. *After Redemption: Jim Crow and the Transformation of African American Religion in the Delta, 1875–1915.* New York: Oxford University Press, 2008.

Gilmore, Glenda Elizabeth. *Gender & Jim Crow: Women and the Politics of White Supremacy in North Carolina, 1896–1920.* Chapel Hill: University of North Carolina Press, 1996.

———. *Defying Dixie: The Radical Roots of Civil Rights, 1919–1950.* New York: W. W. Norton, 2008.

Goudsouzian, Aram. *Down to the Crossroads: Civil Rights, Black Power, and the Meredith March Against Fear.* New York: Farrar, Straus and Giroux, 2014.

Grant, Robert M., with David Tracy. *A Short History of the Interpretation of the Bible.* 2nd ed. Minneapolis: Fortress Press, 1984.

Greenberg, Cheryl Lynn, ed. *A Circle of Trust: Remembering SNCC.* New Brunswick, NJ: Rutgers University Press, 1998.

Greene, Alison Collis. *No Depression in Heaven: The Great Depression, the New Deal, and the Transformation of Religion in the Delta.* New York: Oxford University Press, 2016.

Gregory, James N. *Southern Diaspora: How the Great Migrations of Black and Whites Southerners Transformed America.* Chapel Hill: University of North Carolina Press, 2005.

Hackett, David G. *Religion and American Culture: A Reader.* 2nd ed. New York: Routledge, 2003.

Hahn, Steven. *A Nation Under Our Feet: Black Political Struggles in the Rural South from Slavery to the Great Migration.* Cambridge, MA: Harvard University Press, 2003.

Harding, Vincent. *There Is a River: The Black Struggle for Freedom in America.* San Diego, CA: Harcourt Brace, 1981.

Harrell, David Edwin, Jr. *Quest for a Christian America, 1800–1865.* Vol. 1, *A Social History of the Disciples of Christ.* 1966. Rpt. Tuscaloosa: University of Alabama Press, 2003.

———. *White Sects and Black Men in the Recent South.* Nashville: Vanderbilt University Press, 1971.

———. *The Social Sources of Division in the Disciples of Christ, 1865–1900.* Vol. 2: *A Social History of the Disciples of Christ.* 1973. Rpt. Tuscaloosa: University of Alabama Press, 2003.

———. *The Churches of Christ in the 20th Century: Homer Hailey's Personal Journey of Faith.* Tuscaloosa: University of Alabama Press, 2000.

Harris, J. William. *Deep Souths: Delta, Piedmont, and Sea Island Society in the Age of Segregation.* Baltimore: Johns Hopkins University Press, 2001.

Harvey, Paul. *Redeeming the South: Religious Cultures and Racial Identities among Southern Baptists, 1865–1925*. Chapel Hill: University of North Carolina Press, 1997.

———. *Freedom's Coming: Religious Culture and the Shaping of the South from the Civil War through the Civil Rights Era*. Chapel Hill: University of North Carolina Press, 2005.

Hatch, Nathan O. *The Democratization of American Christianity*. New Haven, CT: Yale University Press, 1989.

Hayes, John. *Hard, Hard Religion: Interracial Faith in the Poor South*. Chapel Hill: University of North Carolina Press, 2017.

Haynes, Stephen R. *Noah's Curse: The Biblical Justification of American Slavery*. New York: Oxford University Press, 2002.

Heyrman, Christine Leigh. *Southern Cross: The Beginnings of the Bible Belt*. New York: Alfred A. Knopf, 1997.

Hicks, L. Edward. *"Sometimes in the Wrong but Never in Doubt": George S. Benson and the Education of the New Religious Right*. Knoxville: University of Tennessee Press, 1994.

Hill, Samuel S., Jr. *Southern Churches in Crisis*. New York: Holt, Rinehart and Winston, 1967.

———. *One Name but Several Faces: Variety in Popular Christian Denominations in Southern History*. Athens: University of Georgia Press, 1996.

———. *Southern Churches in Crisis Revisited*. Tuscaloosa: University of Alabama Press, 1999.

Holloway, Gary, and John York. *Unfinished Reconciliation: Justice, Racism, and Churches of Christ*. Abilene, TX: Abilene Christian University Press, 2003.

Honey, Michael K. *Going Down Jericho Road: The Memphis Strike, Martin Luther King's Last Campaign*. New York: W. W. Norton, 2007.

Hooper, Robert E. *A Distinct People: A History of Churches of Christ in the 20th Century*. West Monroe, LA: Howard Publishing Co., 1993.

Houck, Davis W., and David E. Dixon, eds. *Rhetoric, Religion, and the Civil Rights Movement, 1954–1965*. Waco, TX: Baylor University Press, 2006.

Houston, Benjamin. *The Nashville Way: Racial Etiquette and the Struggle for Social Justice in a Southern City*. Athens: University of Georgia Press, 2012.

Hughes, Richard T. *Reviving the Ancient Faith: The Story of Churches of Christ in America*. Grand Rapids, MI: William B. Eerdmans Publishing Co., 1996.

Hughes, Richard T., and R. L. Roberts. *The Churches of Christ*. Westport: Greenwood Press, 2001.

Hurt, R. Douglas, ed. *African-American Life in the Rural South, 1900–1950*. Columbia: University of Missouri Press, 2003.

Ikard, Robert W. *No More Social Lynchings*. Franklin, TN: Hillsboro Press, 1997.

Jacoway, Elizabeth. *Turn Away Thy Son: Little Rock, the Crisis That Shocked the Nation*. New York: Free Press, 2007.

Johnson, Paul E., ed. *African-American Christianity: Essays in History*. Berkeley: University of California Press, 1994.

Johnson, Paul E., and Sean Wilentz. *The Kingdom of Matthias: A Story of Sex and Salvation in 19th-Century America*. New York: Oxford University Press, 1994.

Joseph, Peniel E. *Waiting 'Til the Midnight Hour: A Narrative History of Black Power in America*. New York: Henry Holt, 2006.

Kidd, Colin. *The Forging of Races: Race and Scripture in the Protestant Atlantic World, 1600–2000*. Cambridge, UK: Cambridge University Press, 2006.

Kirk, John A. *Redefining the Color Line: Black Activism in Little Rock, Arkansas, 1940–1970*. Gainesville: University Press of Florida, 2002.

———, ed. *Martin Luther King Jr. and the Civil Rights Movement: Controversies and Debates*. New York: Palgrave Macmillan, 2007.

———, ed. *Race and Ethnicity in Arkansas*. Fayetteville: University of Arkansas Press, 2014.

Kruse, Kevin. *White Flight: Atlanta and the Making of Modern Conservatism*. Princeton, NJ: Princeton University Press, 2005.

Kruse, Kevin, and Stephen Tuck, eds. *Fog of War: The Second World War and the Civil Rights Movement*. New York: Oxford University Press, 2012.

Kyvig, David E. *Daily Life in the United States, 1920–1940: How Americans Lived through the "Roaring Twenties" and the Great Depression*. Chicago: Ivan R. Dee, 2002. Rev. ed., 2004.

Lambert, Frank. *The Battle of Ole Miss: Civil Rights v. States' Rights*. New York: Oxford University Press, 2010.

Lewis, Warren, and Hans Rollman, eds. *Restoring the First-century Church in the Twenty-first Century: Essays on the Stone-Campbell Restoration Movement in Honor of Don Haymes*. Eugene, OR: Wipf and Stock Publishers, 2005.

Lincoln, C. Eric. *The Black Muslims in America*. Boston: Beacon Press, 1961.

———. *The Black Church since Frazier*. New York: Schocken Books, 1974.

London, Samuel G., Jr. *Seventh-day Adventists and the Civil Rights Movement*. Oxford: University Press of Mississippi, 2009.

Lynn, Mac, ed. *Churches of Christ in the United States*. Nashville: 21st Century Christian, 2003.

MacLean, Nancy. *Behind the Mask of Chivalry: The Making of the Second Ku Klux Klan*. New York: Oxford University Press, 1994.

Manis, Andrew M. *Southern Civil Religions in Conflict: Black and White Baptists and Civil Rights, 1947–1957*. Athens: University of Georgia Press, 1987.

———. *Southern Civil Religions in Conflict: Civil Rights and the Culture Wars*. Macon, GA: Mercer University Press, 2002.

Maraniss, Andrew. *Strong Inside: Perry Wallace and the Collision of Race and Sports in the South*. Nashville: Vanderbilt University Press, 2014.

Marsden, George. *Fundamentalism and American Culture: The Shaping of Twentieth-Century Evangelicalism, 1870–1925*. New York: Oxford University Press, 1980. Rpt., 1982.

Marsh, Charles. *God's Long Summer: Stories of Faith and Civil Rights*. Princeton, NJ: Princeton University Press, 1997.

———. *The Last Days: A Son's Story of Sin and Segregation at the Dawn of a New South*. New York: Basic Books, 2001.

Martin, William. *A Prophet with Honor: The Billy Graham Story*. New York: William and Morrow, 1991.

Mathisen, Robert R. *Critical Issues in American Religious History*. 2nd rev. ed. Waco, TX: Baylor University Press, 2006.

Maxwell, Angie. *The Indicted South: Public Criticism, Southern Inferiority, and the Politics of Whiteness*. Chapel Hill: University of North Carolina Press, 2014.

McAdam, Doug. *Freedom Summer*. New York: Oxford University Press, 1988.

McBride, James. *The Color of Water: A Black Man's Tribute to His White Mother*. New York: Riverhead Books, 1996.

McKenzie, Steven L. *All God's Children: A Biblical Critique of Racism*. Louisville, KY: Westminster John Knox Press, 1997.

McMillen, Neil R. *The Citizens' Council: Organized Resistance to the Second Reconstruction, 1954–1964*. Urbana: University of Illinois Press, 1971.

McMillen, Sally G. *To Raise Up the South: Sunday Schools in Black and White Churches, 1865–1915*. Baton Rouge: Louisiana State University Press, 2002.

Miller, Keith D. *Voice of Deliverance: The Language of Martin Luther King, Jr., and Its Sources*. Athens: University of Georgia Press, 1992. Rpt., 1998.

Miller, Steven P. *Billy Graham and the Rise of the Republican South*. Philadelphia: University of Pennsylvania Press, 2009.

Montgomery, William Edward. *Under Their Own Vine and Fig Tree: The African-American Church in the South, 1865–1900*. Baton Rouge: Louisiana State University Press, 1992.

Moreton, Bethany. *To Serve God and Wal-Mart: The Making of Christian Free Enterprise*. Cambridge, MA: Harvard University Press, 2009.

Murray, Peter C. *Methodists and the Crucible of Race, 1930–1975*. Columbia: University of Missouri Press, 2004.

Newman, Mark. *Getting Right With God: Southern Baptists and Desegregation, 1945–1995*. Tuscaloosa: University of Alabama Press, 2001.

———. *Divine Agitators: The Delta Ministry and Civil Rights in Mississippi*. Athens: University of Georgia Press, 2004.

Noll, Mark A., ed. *Religion & American Politics: From the Colonial Period to the 1980s*. New York: Oxford University Press, 1990.

———. *A History of Christianity in the United States and Canada*. Grand Rapids, MI: William B. Eerdmans Publishing Co., 1992.

———. *The Civil War as a Theological Crisis*. Chapel Hill: University of North Carolina Press, 2006.

Norrell, Robert J. *Reaping the Whirlwind: The Civil Rights Movement in Tuskegee*. New York: Alfred A. Knopf, 1985.

Ownby, Ted. *Subduing Satan: Religion, Recreation, and Manhood in the Rural South, 1865–1920.* Chapel Hill: University of North Carolina Press, 1990.

———, ed. *The Role of Ideas in the Civil Rights South.* Oxford: University Press of Mississippi, 2002.

Palmer, Phyllis. *Living as Equals: How Three White Communities Struggled to Make Interracial Connections During the Civil Rights Era.* Nashville: Vanderbilt University Press, 2008.

Patterson, Noble, and Terry J. Gardner, eds. *Foy E. Wallace, Jr.: Soldier of the Cross.* Fort Worth, TX: Wallace Memorial Fund, 1999.

Robinson, Edward. *To Save My Race from Abuse: The Life of Samuel Robert Cassius.* Tuscaloosa: University of Alabama Press, 2007.

———. *The Fight Is On in Texas: A History of African American Churches of Christ in the Lone Star State, 1865–2000.* Abilene, TX: Abilene Christian University Press, 2008.

———, ed. *A Godsend to His People: The Essential Writings and Speeches of Marshall Keeble.* Knoxville: University of Tennessee Press, 2008.

———. *Show Us How You Do It: Marshall Keeble and the Rise of Black Churches of Christ in the United States, 1914–1968.* Tuscaloosa: University of Alabama Press, 2008.

———, ed. *To Lift Up My Race: The Essential Writings of Samuel Robert Cassius.* Knoxville: University of Tennessee Press, 2008.

———. *I Was Under a Heavy Burden: The Life of Annie C. Tuggle.* Abilene, TX: Abilene Christian University Press, 2011.

Romano, Renee C. *Race Mixing: Black-White Marriage in Postwar America.* Cambridge, MA: Harvard University Press, 2003.

Sensbach, Jon F. *Rebecca's Revival: Creating Black Christianity in the Atlantic World.* Cambridge, MA: Harvard University Press, 2005.

Shattuck, Gardiner H., Jr. *Episcopalians and Race: Civil War to Civil Rights.* Lexington: University Press of Kentucky, 2000.

Sokol, Jason. *There Goes My Everything: White Southerners in the Age of Civil Rights, 1945–1975.* New York: Alfred A. Knopf, 2006.

Stanton, Elvin. *Faith and Works: The Business, Politics, and Philanthropy of Alabama's Jimmy Faulkner.* Montgomery, AL: NewSouth Books, 2002.

Stephens, Randall J. *The Fire Spreads: Holiness and Pentecostalism in the American South.* Cambridge, MA: Harvard University Press, 2008.

Stern, Mark. *Calculating Visions: Kennedy, Johnson, and Civil Rights.* New Brunswick, NJ: Rutgers University Press, 1992.

Stokes, Melvyn. *D. W. Griffith's The Birth of a Nation: A History of "The Most Controversial Motion Picture of All Time."* New York: Oxford University Press, 2007.

Sugrue, Thomas J. *Sweet Land of Liberty: The Forgotten Struggle for Civil Rights in the North.* New York: Random House, 2008.

Sullivan, Clayton. *Called to Preach, Condemned to Survive: The Education of Clayton Sullivan.* Macon, GA: Mercer University Press, 1985.

Sullivan, Patricia. *Days of Hope: Race and Democracy in the New Deal Era.* Chapel Hill: University of North Carolina Press, 1996.

Sutton, Matthew Avery. *Aimee Semple McPherson and the Resurrection of Christian America.* Cambridge, MA: Harvard University Press, 2007.

Thornton, J. Mills, III. *Dividing Lines: Municipal Politics and the Struggle for Civil Rights in Montgomery, Birmingham, and Selma.* Tuscaloosa: University of Alabama Press, 2002.

Turner, Richard Brent. *Islam in the African-American Experience.* 2nd ed. Bloomington: University of Indiana Press, 2003.

Tyson, Timothy B. *Blood Done Sign My Name: A True Story.* New York: Crown Publishers, 2004.

Wacker, Grant. *Heaven Below: Early Pentecostals and American Culture.* Cambridge, MA: Harvard University Press, 2001.

Ward, Brian. *Radio and the Struggle for Civil Rights in the South.* Gainesville: University Press of Florida, 2004.

Ward, Jason Morgan. *Defending White Democracy: The Making of a Segregationist Movement & the Remaking of Racial Politics, 1936–1965.* Chapel Hill: University of North Carolina Press, 2011.

Webb, Clive. *Fight Against Fear: Southern Jews and Black Civil Rights.* Athens: University of Georgia Press, 2001.

Weisenfeld, Judith, and Richard Newman, eds. *This Far by Faith: Readings in African-American Women's Religious Biography.* New York: Routledge, 1996.

Wilkerson, Isabel. *The Warmth of Other Sons: The Epic Story of America's Great Migration.* New York: Random House, 2010.

Williams, Daniel K. *God's Own Party: The Making of the Christian Right.* New York: Oxford University Press, 2010.

Williams, Juan, and Quinton Dixie. *This Far by Faith: Stories from the African American Religious Experience.* New York: HarperCollins, 2003.

Williamson, Joel. *A Rage for Order: Black-White Relations in the American South since Emancipation.* New York: Oxford University Press, 1986.

Willis, Alan Scot. *All According to God's Plan: Southern Baptist Missions and Race, 1945–1970.* Lexington: University of Kentucky Press, 2004.

Wilson, Charles Reagan. *Baptized in Blood: The Religion of the Lost Cause, 1865–1920.* Athens: University of Georgia Press, 1980.

——, ed. *Religion in the South.* Jackson: University Press of Mississippi, 1985.

——. *Judgment & Grace in Dixie: Southern Faiths from Faulkner to Elvis.* Athens: University of Georgia Press, 1995.

Woods, Jeff. *Black Struggle Red Scare: Segregation and Anti-Communism in the South, 1948–1968.* Baton Rouge: Louisiana State University Press, 2004.

Woodson, William. *Standing for Their Faith: A History of Churches of Christ in Tennessee, 1900–1950.* Henderson, TN: J&W Publications, 1979.

Woodward, C. Vann. *The Strange Career of Jim Crow.* 3d ed. New York: Oxford University Press, 1974.

Wynn, Neil. *The Afro-American and the Second World War.* New York: Holmes and Meirer, 1976.

Articles

Anderson, R. Bentley. "Black, White, and Catholic: Southern Jesuits Confront the Race Question, 1952." *Catholic Historical Review* 91 (July 2005): 484–505.

Badger, Tony. "Southerners Who Refused to Sign the Southern Manifesto." *Historical Journal* 42 (1999): 517–34.

Best, Wallace. "'The Right Achieved and the Wrong Way Conquered': J. H. Jackson, Martin Luther King, Jr., and the Conflict over Civil Rights." *Religion and American Culture* 16 (Summer 2006): 195–226.

Casey, Michael W. "The Origins of the Hermeneutics of the Churches of Christ, Part One: The Reformed Tradition." *Restoration Quarterly* 31 (1989): 75–91.

———. "The Origins of the Hermeneutics of the Churches of Christ, Part Two: The Philosophical Background." *Restoration Quarterly* 31 (1989): 193–206.

———. "Pacifism and Non-Violence: The Prophetic Voice in the African American Churches of Christ." *Discipliana* 59 (Summer 1999): 35–49.

———. "From Religious Outsiders to Insiders: The Rise and Fall of Pacifism in the Churches of Christ." *Journal of Church and State* 44 (Summer 2002): 455–75.

———. "'Come Let Us Reason Together': The Heritage of the Churches of Christ as a Source for Rhetorical Invention." *Rhetoric & Public Affairs* 7 (2004): 487–98.

Chappell, David L. "Religious Ideas of the Segregationists." *Journal of American Studies* 32 (1998): 237–62.

———. "A Stone of Hope: Prophetic Faith, Liberalism, and the Death of Jim Crow." *Journal of the Historical Society* 3 (Spring 2003): 129–62.

Cohen, Robert. "'Two, Four, Six, Eight, We Don't Want to Integrate': White Student Attitudes Toward the University of Georgia's Desegregation." *Georgia Historical Quarterly* 80 (Fall 1996): 616–45.

Dailey, Jane. "Sex, Segregation, and the Sacred after *Brown.*" *Journal of American History* 91 (June 2004): 119–44.

Eagles, Charles W. "Toward New Histories of the Civil Rights Era." *Journal of Southern History* 66 (November 2000): 815–48.

———. "The Closing of Mississippi Society: Will Campbell, *The $64,000 Question,* and Religious Emphasis Week at the University of Mississippi." *Journal of Southern History* 67 (May 2001): 331–72.

Fisher, Holly. "Oakwood College Students' Quest for Social Justice before and during the Civil Rights Era." *Journal of African American History* 88 (Spring 2003): 110–25.

Harrell, David Edwin, Jr. "The Sectional Origins of the Churches of Christ." *Journal of Southern History* 30 (August 1964): 261–77.

Harwell, Debbie Z. "Wednesdays in Mississippi: Uniting Women across Regional and Racial Lines, Summer 1964." *Journal of Southern History* 76, no. 3 (August 2010): 617–54.

Haymes, Don. "Race & the Church of Christ." *Restoration Movement: Issues & Themes,* www.mun.ca/rels/restmov/texts/race/haymes12.html (accessed April 13, 2007).

Holifield, E. Brooks. "Theology as Entertainment: Oral Debate in American Religion." *Church History* 67 (September 1998): 499–520.

Horowitz, David Alan. "White Southerners' Alienation and Civil Rights: The Response to Corporate Liberalism, 1956–1965." *Journal of Southern History* 54 (May 1988): 173–200.

Key, Barclay. "On the Periphery of the Civil Rights Movement: Race and Religion at Harding College," *Arkansas Historical Quarterly* 68 (Autumn 2009): 283–311.

Killingsworth, Blake. "'Here I Am, Stuck in the Middle with You': *The Baptist Standard,* Texas Baptist Leadership, and School Desegregation, 1954–1956." *Baptist History and Heritage* 41 (Spring 2006): 78–92.

Klarman, Michael J. "How *Brown* Changed Race Relations: The Backlash Thesis." *Journal of American History* 81 (June 1994): 81–118.

McDermott, Jim. "A Quiet Change of Course: The Integration of Spring Hill College." *America* 196 (April 9, 2007): 10–16.

———. "A Professor, a President and the Klan." *America* 196 (April 16, 2007): 15–17.

Miller, Steven P. "From Politics to Reconciliation: Katallagete, Biblicism, and Southern Liberalism." *Journal of Southern Religion* 7 (2004). jsr.fsu.edu/Volume7/Millerarticle .htm (accessed February 7, 2019).

Mouw, Ted, and Barbara Entwisle. "Residential Segregation and Interracial Friendship in Schools." *American Journal of Sociology* 112 (September 2006): 394–441.

Robinson, Edward. "'The Two Old Heroes': Samuel W. Womack, Alexander Campbell and the Origins of the Black Churches of Christ in the United States." *Discipliana* 65 (Spring 2005): 3–20.

Sitkoff, Harvard. "Racial Militancy and Interracial Violence in the Second World War." *Journal of American History* 58 (1971): 663–83.

Tyson, Timothy B. "Not Forgotten: Martin Luther King and the Southern Dream of Freedom." *Southern Cultures* 11 (Winter 2005): 96–107.

Wadhwani, R. D. G. "Kodak, FIGHT, and the Definition of Civil Rights in Rochester, New York: 1966–1967." *The Historian* 60 (Fall 1997): 59–76.

Wilson, Charles Reagan. "Religion and the US South." *Southern Spaces* (March 16, 2004). southernspaces.org/2004/overview-religion-and-us-south (accessed February 7, 2019).

Theses and Dissertations

Asante, Molefi Kete [Arthur Lee Smith]. "A Rhetorical Analysis of the Speaking of Marshall Keeble." MA thesis, Pepperdine College, 1965.

Barton, John Marion. "The Preaching on Herald of Truth Radio, 1952–1969." PhD diss., Pennsylvania State University, 1975.

Casey, Michael W. "The Development of Necessary Inference in the Hermeneutics of the Disciples of Christ/Churches of Christ." PhD diss., University of Pittsburgh, 1986.

Douglas, Robert Christy. "Power, Its Locus and Function in Defining Social Commentary in the Church of Christ, Illustrated by a Case Study of Black Civil Rights." PhD diss., University of Southern California, 1980.

Evans, Jack. "The History of Southwestern Christian College, Terrell, Texas." MA thesis, Texas Western College, 1963.

Hardin, John C. "B. C. Goodpasture and the *Gospel Advocate:* The 'Standard Bearer' for Churches of Christ, 1939–1977." PhD diss., Auburn University, 2007.

Hayes, Franklin Delano. "An Administrative History of Harding University, 1924–1987." MA thesis, University of Arkansas, 1989.

Money, Royce. "Church-State Relations in the Churches of Christ Since 1945: A Study in Religion and Politics." PhD diss., Baylor University, 1975.

Nichols, James Don. "A History of Harding College, 1924–1984." EdD diss., University of Arkansas, 1985.

Phillips, Myers. "A Historical Study of the Attitude of the Churches of Christ Toward Other Denominations." PhD diss., Baylor University, 1983.

Pitts, Carroll, Jr. "A Critical Study of Civil Rights Practices, Attitudes, and Responsibilities in Churches of Christ." MA thesis, Pepperdine College, 1969.

Rhoads, Forrest Neil. "A Study of the Sources of Marshall Keeble's Effectiveness as a Preacher." PhD diss., Southern Illinois University, 1970.

Royse, Nyal D. "A Study of the Environment of Harding College as Perceived by Its Students and Faculty and as Anticipated by Entering Students." EdD diss., Memphis State University, 1969.

Verkler, Billy Duan. "An Application of Cognitive Dissonance Theory to Reference Group Behavior: A Study of Racial Attitudes of Church Members in Searcy, Arkansas." PhD diss., Mississippi State University, 1970.

Index

www.ingramcontent.com/pod-product-compliance
Lightning Source LLC
Chambersburg PA
CBHW030301100426
42812CB00002B/528